BRITAIN'S
BEST BIKE RIDE

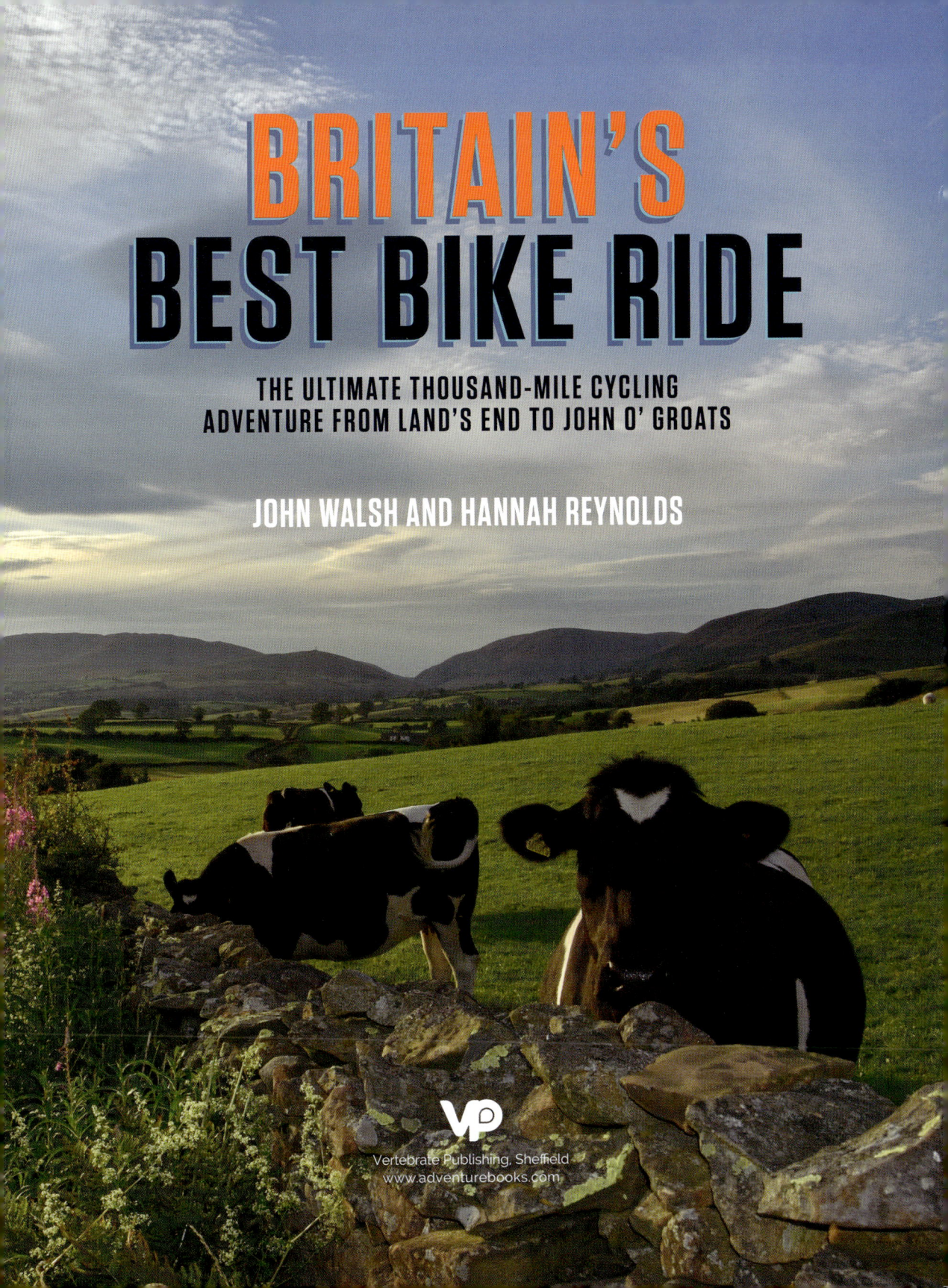

BRITAIN'S
BEST BIKE RIDE

THE ULTIMATE THOUSAND-MILE CYCLING ADVENTURE FROM LAND'S END TO JOHN O' GROATS

JOHN WALSH AND HANNAH REYNOLDS

Vertebrate Publishing, Sheffield
www.adventurebooks.com

BRITAIN'S
BEST BIKE RIDE

**THE ULTIMATE THOUSAND-MILE CYCLING
ADVENTURE FROM LAND'S END TO JOHN O' GROATS**

JOHN WALSH AND HANNAH REYNOLDS

First published in 2022 by Vertebrate Publishing.

 Vertebrate Publishing, Omega Court, 352 Cemetery Road, Sheffield S11 8FT, United Kingdom.
www.adventurebooks.com

A CIP catalogue record for this book is available from the British Library.

ISBN 978-1-83981-113-5 (Paperback)
ISBN 978-1-83981-114-2 (Ebook)

Front cover illustration by Neil Stevens, www.crayonfire.co.uk
Photography by John Walsh and Hannah Reynolds unless otherwise credited.

Mapping contains data from OS © Crown copyright and database right (2022)
and © OpenStreetMap contributors, Openstreetmap.org/copyright
Relief shading produced from data derived from U.S. Geological Survey, National Geospatial Program.
Cartography by Richard Ross, Active Maps Ltd. – www.activemaps.co.uk

Edited by Helen Parry, design and production by Rosie Edwards, www.adventurebooks.com

Printed and bound in Europe by Latitude Press.

Vertebrate Publishing is committed to printing on paper from sustainable sources.

CONTENTS

OVERVIEW

Map vi
The stages vii
The route ix
The regions x
The journey xii
Best stages for xiv
British hospitality xviii
The Classic: 2-week itinerary xx
The Explorer: 3-week itinerary xxii
The Challenge: 10-day itinerary xxiv

THE RIDE

The beginning – Land's End xxvii
Cornwall & Devon xxx
Somerset 32
Wales 46
Herefordshire & Shropshire 62
Cheshire & Lancashire 82
Cumbria 108
The halfway point – Sedbergh 117
Scottish Borders & Lowlands 130
Scottish Highlands 158
The end – John o' Groats 203

INFORMATION

Packing and preparation 206
Essentials 207
Acknowledgements 209
Photography 209
What's next? 209

Download the
Britain's Best Bike Ride
GPX files from
www.lejog1000.cc/tracks
hello@lejog1000.cc

THE STAGES

Stage	From	To	Miles	Km	Metres ascent	Rating	Page
CORNWALL & DEVON							
1	Land's End	Perranporth	44	71	900	Moderate	3
2	Perranporth	Wadebridge	23	37	570	Moderate	9
3	Wadebridge	Launceston	32	52	600	Moderate	15
4	Launceston	Chulmleigh	34	55	800	Moderate	21
5	Chulmleigh	Dulverton	24	38	690	Challenging	27
SOMERSET							
6	Dulverton	Glastonbury	51	81	750	Moderate	35
7	Glastonbury	Chew Stoke	27	44	510	Moderate	41
WALES							
8	Chew Stoke	Tintern Abbey	33	54	550	Moderate	49
9	Tintern Abbey	Ross-on-Wye	21	34	500	Moderate	57
HEREFORDSHIRE & SHROPSHIRE							
10	Ross-on-Wye	Ludlow	37	60	570	Moderate	65
11	Ludlow	Ironbridge	27	43	430	Moderate	71
12	Ironbridge	Market Drayton	25	39	350	Moderate	77
CHESHIRE & LANCASHIRE							
13	Market Drayton	Knutsford	34	55	200	Gentle	85
14	Knutsford	Blackrod	28	45	250	Gentle	91
15	Blackrod	Mellor	20	32	490	Moderate	97
16	Mellor	High Bentham	31	50	910	Challenging	103
CUMBRIA							
17	High Bentham	Sedbergh	22	36	380	Moderate	111
18	Sedbergh	Langwathby	31	50	520	Moderate	119
19	Langwathby	Brampton	21	33	320	Moderate	125
SCOTTISH BORDERS & LOWLANDS							
20	Brampton	Langholm	25	41	540	Moderate	133
21	Langholm	Peebles	50	80	950	Moderate	139
22	Peebles	Queensferry	36	58	440	Moderate	145
23	Queensferry	Perth	42	68	680	Moderate	153
SCOTTISH HIGHLANDS							
24	Perth	Braemar	50	80	970	Challenging	161
25	Braemar	Grantown-on-Spey	46	73	1,110	Challenging	167
26	Grantown-on-Spey	Inverness	36	59	440	Moderate	173
27	Inverness	Bonar Bridge	45	73	570	Moderate	179
28	Bonar Bridge	Altnaharra	31	51	360	Moderate	185
29	Altnaharra	Bettyhill	24	39	170	Gentle	191
30	Bettyhill	John o' Groats	50	80	710	Moderate	197

THE ROUTE

From great historical landmarks to quirky, hidden local gems, grand vistas to intimate secluded valleys, rocky cliffs and sandy beaches, tranquil riverside routes to epic Scottish climbs, LEJOG1000 is the ultimate thousand-mile route, the greatest British bike ride. It is designed to create balance, offering the progress needed to make your way there combined with the intrigue and discovery offered by the meandering little lanes and byways in which the British landscape is rich.

There are numerous routes between Land's End and John o' Groats – you can make it as direct or meandering as you wish, depending on why you are doing it. The route used by most record-breaking attempts is the shortest and most direct; this frequently means busy roads and bypassing the places of most interest.

LEJOG1000 is not necessarily for those with a constant eye on the time – although to be the fastest rider on LEJOG1000 is a worthy accolade. It has been designed to be the most enjoyable ride and the ultimate thousand miles across Britain: to go through the places of interest, not bypass them, to offer up the best scenery and provide the opportunities to sample the local food, drink the local brews and immerse yourself in the culture and heritage which makes each place special. Equally, 1,000 miles on carefully hand-picked roads presents the ultimate challenge for any cyclist, and those completing LEJOG1000 can take pride in having accomplished a distinctive cycling goal.

From the start we want to show the best of each region. In Cornwall this means hugging the rocky cliffs of the north coast and discovering its stunning sandy beaches. We opt for crossing Exmoor, one of the smallest national parks in Britain, which adds extra climbing, but also wide-open space and free-roaming animals to contrast with the high enclosed hedgerows that can dominate the lanes of Cornwall and Devon. The Severn Bridge delivers you to Wales, without which you cannot call this a truly British ride. Following the meandering River Wye, with its dramatic limestone gorges edged with deep native woodlands, immerses you in this Area of Outstanding Natural Beauty.

Entering Herefordshire and Shropshire, where food and landscape are inextricably linked, the market towns are rich with local produce and Ludlow is a source of foodie delight. Ironbridge, the birthplace of the Industrial Revolution, marks the shift from sparsely populated agricultural land into a more urban landscape as the route makes its way into the North West.

Carefully picking its way through the former industrial heartlands of North West England, LEJOG1000 seeks out the most peaceful experience possible in this most densely populated portion of the journey. Old mill buildings, remnants of coal mining and occasional smoking chimneys remind you that dark satanic mills are as much part of the fabric and landscape of Britain as the wild, remote Scottish Highlands and picture-postcard views of South West England.

A distinct shift occurs upon climbing Waddington Fell: the urban landscape is left behind in favour of the open spaces of North Lancashire and a dip into the Yorkshire Dales. The journey continues through the fells of Cumbria to the picturesque LEJOG1000 halfway staging town of Sedbergh. The Anglo–Scottish border is crossed near to one of the best-preserved observation towers on Hadrian's Wall.

The rolling hills and dense forests of the Borders lead to the grand city of Edinburgh, passing directly under the shadow of the castle itself and onwards towards Perth and Scone Palace, where Scottish kings were crowned, before joining the 'snow roads' over Glenshee and The Lecht. This takes you through the heart of the Cairngorms, avoiding the busier alternative routes, to reach Inverness. From Inverness, LEJOG1000 heads into the interior and some of the most isolated and wild places of the Highlands, emerging on the north coast for the final stretch from Bettyhill to John o' Groats.

THE REGIONS

The LEJOG1000 route is the longest possible diagonal cross-section of mainland Britain from the furthest south-west point to the north-east. Following its narrow line takes you through an ever-changing landscape. In some places the changes are slow and subtle. Other changes happen more dramatically, crossing a bridge into a different country, or sweeping down from an escarpment into a flat lowland area.

British people can be fiercely protective of local identity, whether that is in the food, the accent or the history. It is not unusual to see the emblem of the white rose in Yorkshire or the red rose in Lancashire. However, boundaries are seldom as neat as local government offices would like them to be. County names and borders shift and change but the identity of how an individual feels may not. We have divided the route into eight regions based on where the majority of riding time is spent in each region. In the Somerset region you are briefly in Avon, you dabble with Yorkshire between Lancashire and Cumbria, but the name encapsulates where you will spend the majority of your riding time.

CORNWALL & DEVON

One of the most visited parts of the UK, Cornwall and Devon's rugged coastline and seductive sandy beaches are the vision of summer holidays, but it is much more than that. Steep-banked hedgerows topped with an explosion of wild flowers, delicious food and drink, freshly caught sea fish, orchards and fertile agricultural land give a feeling of rich bounty, but the remnants of tin and copper mining and decaying chimneys of wheal houses silhouetted against the skyline speak of a very different and not-so-distant history.

SOMERSET

Hills rise as mystical islands from the sea of mist coating the Somerset Levels. Legends of King Arthur, the sacred springs of Glastonbury and the intricate honey-coloured spires of Wells all create stages that have elements of the spiritual, as well as dramatic riding in the shape of Cheddar Gorge.

WALES

Crossing the Severn Bridge into Wales marks a clear transition of entering a new country – from the moment your wheels arrive back on land the signposts are dual-lingual. The small nation of Wales was one of Celtic Europe's most prominent political and cultural centres and still proudly retains cultures that are markedly different from England's. Admire the castle at Chepstow/Cas-Gwent and follow the River Wye past Tintern Abbey and Symonds Yat Rock before recrossing the border.

HEREFORDSHIRE & SHROPSHIRE

Continuing along the Wye and through the Marches, close to the frontier with Wales, this largely unspoilt, agricultural region is punctuated with ancient market towns. The heritage of these bustling trading posts can be seen in the still thriving farmers' markets and popular food festivals. A historical shift from agriculture to industry occurs as you cross the famous bridge at Ironbridge, a world first in engineering and known as the birthplace of the Industrial Revolution.

CUMBRIA

With the Pennines to the east and Lake District mountains to the west, this is a region with space to breathe. Wide open skies, stone walls and trickling streams abound. The flat and lush Eden Valley contrasts with the steep slopes of the green open fellsides nibbled short by native-breed sheep, and the drama and the challenge of the riding is turned up a notch.

SCOTTISH BORDERS & LOWLANDS

Entering the wild and contested borderlands brings a completely new scale of panoramic scenery as well as distinctively different Scottish foods and culture. It is a place of turbulent history, the occasional genteel town and imposing grand castles. The Borders serve up perfect roads for cyclists with friendly climbs and little traffic. After vibrant Edinburgh, spectacular bridges span the Firth of Forth at Queensferry and transport you northwards to Tayside strawberry country.

CHESHIRE & LANCASHIRE

With Roman remains, half-timbered buildings and the elaborate mansions of Premier League footballers – Cheshire has its fair share of history, affluence and industry. Impressive feats of Victorian architecture from the canal system to reservoirs and pumping stations, grand mansions and elaborate parkland occasionally punctuate rows of terraced housing and fill this more urban part of the route with interest.

SCOTTISH HIGHLANDS

Vast, wild and remote, the Highlands offer light, scenery and space like nowhere else in mainland Britain. With mountain passes and glens, roaring rivers and deep forests, the landscape is stimulating and challenging. Distant grand castles contrast with tiny crofts, villages are few and far between and a warm welcome awaits those who make the effort to visit the far north.

THE JOURNEY

John o' Groats is an aspiration, as much as a destination. No one wants to simply 'go' to John o' Groats; they want to run there, drive their classic car, walk, crawl on their hands and knees, push a hospital bed or, of course, cycle there. You don't just go to John o' Groats from home, you go there from Land's End. So, more than any other place on Earth, John o' Groats is really far more about the journey than the destination.

LEJOG, as Land's End to John o' Groats is popularly called, is often picked as a fundraising ride. It's easy to explain, has a clear start and end, and is hard enough to persuade people to part with their cash. It also doesn't sound too much like fun. For 'bucket list' types it fits alongside running a marathon, or an Ironman, in the tick-sheet of their sporting life, but is there anything to recommend it just for itself? For no other reason than it's a pleasant bike ride? Yes, we think there is.

Ernest Hemingway famously said of cycling: 'it is by riding a bicycle that you learn the contours of a country best, since you have to sweat up the hills and coast down them'. Riding from the most southwesterly point to the most northeasterly does not just give you geographical knowledge, invaluable though that is, it gives you an intimate and most importantly slow-paced understanding of the differences and nuances of every area you pass through.

For those of us who live in Britain it is easy to overlook what is on our own doorstep, seeking out more far-flung destinations when we wish to travel. However, the landscapes of Britain, from the vast to the intimate, offer unique experiences all of their own. Celia Fiennes (1662–1741) was a pioneer of travel and wrote a memoir of her journeys, published posthumously. Her ethos of travel for its own sake still stands as she urged that others: 'spend some of their time in journeys to visit their native land, and to be curious to inform themselves and make observations of the pleasant prospects, good buildings, different produces and manufactures of each place'.

Wherever you call home, LEJOG1000 will offer change and difference. Despite being a small island, mainland Britain is far from homogenous. Each region has its own dish and dialect. The British Cheese Board states there are 700 different and unique cheeses made in the UK. From craft beers to gin distilleries to Highland whisky, there is plenty of *terroir* on our own soil.

Language changes from place to place – that narrow cut-through you take on your bike can be a ginnel, a snicket, an alley, a twitch or a passage, depending where you are and who you ask.

A pub, a school and a church – damnation, education

and salvation – are the foundation of the quintessential British village. While over 400 pubs closed as drinking establishments in 2021 alone and rural primary schools continue to be vulnerable to closure, many villages along LEJOG1000 are still lucky enough to feature all three. No ride through the British countryside would feel complete without spotting the pinnacle of a spire or a square tower punctuating the view.

For every closed pub there seems to be another community intent on reversing their village's fortunes. In several villages, such as St Mabyn in Cornwall, once the commercial shops were forced into closure the locals joined together to create their own.

You may find this journey challenges your personal perception of 'Britishness'; the vision of Britain many of us carry in our minds is shaped by where we live, where we grew up and the very selective cultural representation of Britain. Not every part of the journey is scenic and beautiful, but it is complete and honest. Britain is full of contrast and this linear journey highlights that. The idea of something being 'quintessentially British' is a myth. In a country as diverse as Britain, no one image can encapsulate everything. Enjoy your LEJOG1000 journey.

Hannah and John
www.lejog1000.cc
#LEJOG1000
hello@lejog1000.cc

BEST STAGES FOR ...

We've handpicked our favourite places along the route – we hope you enjoy them too. As you ride, you will discover many others that will form part of your unique memories of the trip, and become the story of your journey.

CHALLENGING CLIMBING

Land's End to Perranporth *p3*
The jagged Cornish coastline provides around 900 metres of climbing on the first stage of LEJOG1000.

Mellor to High Bentham *p103*
The highest point of the route in England topping out at 427 metres.

Perth to Braemar *p161*
At 665 metres above sea level, riding the Cairnwell Pass you are conquering the highest mountain pass in Britain with a dramatic descent down to Braemar.

Braemar to Grantown-on-Spey *p167*
The start of The Lecht climb at a gradient of 17 per cent is the toughest section of tarmac of the whole journey.

STUNNING VIEWS

Tintern Abbey to Ross-on-Wye *p57*
Symonds Yat is a classic viewpoint overlooking the meandering River Wye.

Peebles to Queensferry *p145*
Marvel at the grandeur of the series of three bridges crossing the Firth of Forth.

Inverness to Bonar Bridge *p179*
The Struie Viewpoint is worth interrupting a descent for – it offers a classic view over the Kyle of Sutherland.

Bonar Bridge to Altnaharra *p185*
The lonely yet welcoming Crask Inn sits in the shadows of towering Ben Kilbreck.

FOODIE HEAVEN

Land's End to Perranporth *p3*
Warrens Bakery in St Just was the first commercial bakery to sell traditional Cornish pasties in 1860.

Glastonbury to Chew Stoke *p41*
The Original Cheddar Cheese Company shop offers a great choice of cheese samples.

Ross-on-Wye to Ludlow *p65*
Ludlow Food Festival is one of the country's original foodie celebrations – it started long before such festivals became fashionable.

Perth to Braemar *p161*
The fertile banks of the River Tay mean great roadside stalls selling strawberries and raspberries near Blairgowrie.

GETTING OFF THE BEATEN TRACK

Chulmleigh to Dulverton *p27*
Exmoor is one of Britain's smallest national parks, but offers great ridgeline riding.

High Bentham to Sedbergh *p111*
Barbondale is a hidden valley perfect for cycling with a babbling brook and bracken-clad slopes.

Langwathby to Brampton *p125*
The Eden Valley abounds with quiet rural farming communities a world away from the nearby, tourist-heavy Lake District.

Langholm to Peebles *p139*
Four gentle climbs in the tranquil and often overlooked Scottish Borders.

CASTLES AND RUINS

Dulverton to Glastonbury *p35*
Sunrise and sunset are the best times to climb to Glastonbury Tor for great vistas over the Somerset Levels.

Chew Stoke to Tintern Abbey *p49*
While not as busy as it was in its heyday of tourism, Tintern Abbey has remained an iconic site for visitors.

WILD SWIMMING

Land's End to Perranporth *p3*
Three miles of golden sands stretch along the coastline from St Ives to Gwithian Beach.

Dulverton to Glastonbury *p35*
Wimbleball Lake hosts triathlons and is a good opportunity for a dip.

Tintern Abbey to Ross-on-Wye *p57*
Paddlers and painters head to the bucolic banks of the River Wye.

Altnaharra to Bettyhill *p191*
Farr Bay promises invigorating sea temperatures and golden sands.

Brampton to Langholm *p133*

Hadrian's Wall is the most well-known and the best-preserved frontier of the Roman Empire.

Peebles to Queensferry *p145*

Avoid the entrance fee and be enchanted by the view from the esplanade near Edinburgh Castle.

DRINKING BRITAIN

Perranporth to Wadebridge *p9*

Take a detour along the Camel Valley Trail for wine by the glass on the sun terrace overlooking the vineyards at Camel Valley.

Launceston to Chulmleigh *p21*

Sam's Cider offers one of a handful of opportunities to taste the fruits of English orchards.

High Bentham to Sedbergh *p111*

Kirkby Lonsdale Brewery, with its interior a nod to all things cycling and great ales, is worth a short detour.

Bettyhill to John o' Groats *p197*

Head to John o' Groats Brewery for a celebratory pint overlooking the Pentland Firth.

BRITISH HOSPITALITY

What makes good hospitality? British hospitality is not the same all over; for a start we are talking about three different countries. Hospitality varies between town and country, between areas busy with tourists and working towns, and how unusual it is to see a cyclist at the door. In our experience of travelling as cyclists, the most memorable stays are where we have been given a warm welcome and felt a genuine connection. One of the warmest welcomes we experienced anywhere was at the Crask Inn, which is in one of the most inaccessible and remote places on the route.

As cycling and cycle touring have grown in popularity it is becoming easier to find places that understand the little extra touches that make travelling cyclists feel well looked after. Places with good bike storage, basic tools and clothes-washing facilities make a difference to your experience of life on the road. Nothing is more dispiriting than the angry frown on the face of a landlady when you arrive freezing cold and dripping wet.

Bed and breakfasts in private family homes used to be much more commonplace, but increasingly self-catering options are taking over. One-night stays – an essential for anyone doing a route like this – can be hard to come by, which limits options in some of the busiest tourist areas. Inns are one of the few places left to reliably offer one-night stays.

Hospitality is not just where you stay, but where you eat and drink. While village pubs are being lost all the time, there are still enough really good ones around to keep the culture of this British institution alive. It's not the quality of the beer that defines a great pub but that difficult-to-manufacture asset: its atmosphere.

George Orwell in his essay *The Moon Under Water*, published in the *Evening Standard* in February 1946, described the pub that we all wish we lived near, where there is a good fire burning, it is always quiet enough to talk and 'the barmaids know most of their customers by name, and take a personal interest in everyone'.

While *The Moon Under Water* turned out to be fantasy, his wish list hasn't dated: 'And if anyone knows of a pub that has draught stout, open fires, cheap meals, a garden, motherly barmaids and no radio, I should be glad to hear of it.' There are a few on this route that can satisfy that description.

While the number of traditional pubs is declining, craft beer bars, micro-pubs and independent breweries are increasing in number and are often the places where the culture of the pub is strongest.

Another British tradition is the desire to appreciate a view without doing too much exercise. In the eyes of many visitors, they are searching for the holy grail of a destination which offers 'a view, a brew and a loo'. This means that often where there is a scenic spot, you'll also find a cafe, car park and public toilet.

One of the joys of cycle touring is contrast: the warmth of the fire after being cold, a full belly after riding on empty, stretching out the legs after hours of pedalling. We want our journey to be wild, but we crave the comfort of civilisation at the end of the day and to savour the work of artisan cooks, brewers, bakers and chefs.

THE CLASSIC: 2-WEEK ITINERARY

Fourteen days adds up to just the right amount of time to cover the miles at a pace that doesn't feel like you are racing against the clock but still allows you to pack your LEJOG1000 journey into two weeks of holiday.

There will be some long days in the saddle, but all have been kept under 90 miles with three days at around the 50-mile mark to allow that little bit extra rest, recuperation and refreshment time.

DAY	FROM	TO	MILES	KM	METRES ASCENT	STAGES
1	Land's End	Wadebridge	67	108	1,470	1, 2
2	Wadebridge	Chulmleigh	66	107	1,400	3, 4
3	Chulmleigh	Glastonbury	75	119	1,440	5, 6
4	Glastonbury	Ross-on-Wye	81	132	1,560	7, 8, 9
5	Ross-on-Wye	Market Drayton	89	142	1,350	10, 11, 12
6	Market Drayton	Mellor	82	132	940	13, 14, 15
7	Mellor	Sedbergh	53	86	1,290	16, 17
8	Sedbergh	Langholm	77	124	1,380	18, 19, 20
9	Langholm	Peebles	50	80	950	21
10	Peebles	Perth	78	126	1,120	22, 23
11	Perth	Braemar	50	80	970	24
12	Braemar	Inverness	82	132	1,550	25, 26
13	Inverness	Altnaharra	76	124	930	27, 28
14	Altnaharra	John o' Groats	74	119	880	29, 30

THE EXPLORER: 3-WEEK ITINERARY

Designed to allow plenty of time for getting to know the places you pedal through, this itinerary allows you to look around, savour your environment, properly relax and absorb the experience.

Four days are over 70 miles which are scheduled close to the rest day and on the last two stages when the end is in sight. Shorter rides provide you with the freedom to stop whenever the fancy takes you, and fully embrace the carefree life of the open road.

DAY	FROM	TO	MILES	KM	METRES ASCENT	STAGES
1	Land's End	Perranporth	44	71	900	1
2	Perranporth	Launceston	55	89	1,170	2, 3
3	Launceston	Dulverton	58	93	1,490	4, 5
4	Dulverton	Glastonbury	51	81	750	6
5	Glastonbury	Tintern Abbey	60	98	1,060	7, 8
6	Tintern Abbey	Ludlow	58	94	1,070	9, 10
7	Ludlow	Market Drayton	52	82	780	11, 12
8	Market Drayton	Blackrod	62	100	450	13, 14
9	Blackrod	Sedbergh	73	118	1,780	15, 16, 17
10	Rest day	–	–	–	–	–
11	Sedbergh	Brampton	52	83	840	18, 19
12	Brampton	Peebles	75	121	1,490	20, 21
13	Peebles	Queensferry	36	58	440	22
14	Queensferry	Perth	42	68	680	23
15	Perth	Braemar	50	80	970	24
16	Braemar	Grantown-on-Spey	46	73	1,110	25
17	Grantown-on-Spey	Inverness	36	59	440	26
18	Inverness	Altnaharra	76	124	930	27, 28
19	Altnaharra	John o' Groats	74	119	880	29, 30

THE CHALLENGE: 10-DAY ITINERARY

Ten days to cover LEJOG1000 is a tough but achievable challenge. A high level of fitness and preparation is needed before taking it on. Long days in the saddle will see the landscape change rapidly as you pedal your way from one region to the next.

The three longest days which are the wrong side of 110 miles are generally balanced out by sub-100-mile days. Overnight stops which offer accommodation where you can eat, drink and sleep in the same establishment have been carefully chosen to help any tired legs.

DAY	FROM	TO	MILES	KM	METRES ASCENT	STAGES
1	Land's End	Launceston	99	160	2,070	1, 2, 3
2	Launceston	Glastonbury	109	174	2,240	4, 5, 6
3	Glastonbury	Ludlow	118	192	2,130	7, 8, 9, 10
4	Ludlow	Knutsford	86	137	980	11, 12, 13
5	Knutsford	Sedbergh	101	163	2,030	14, 15, 16, 17
6	Sedbergh	Peebles	127	204	2,330	18, 19, 20, 21
7	Peebles	Perth	78	126	1,120	22, 23
8	Perth	Grantown-on-Spey	96	153	2,080	24, 25
9	Grantown-on-Spey	Altnaharra	112	183	1,370	26, 27, 28
10	Altnaharra	John o' Groats	74	119	880	29, 30

THE BEGINNING | LAND'S END

Penwith, Land's End peninsula, is surrounded on three sides by the Atlantic Ocean. It is a place of abundance. Warm waters filled with fish and sea life, thick seams of tin and a mild climate have been drawing humans there for thousands of years. Here at the end of the land you can find beauty, myth and luminous ocean light.

More than 500,000 people visit Land's End every year, partly for the novelty of being at the end of the land, England's most south-western point, and partly because of the stunning natural beauty. While it is undeniably a tourist attraction, with a well-beaten track to its door, if you visit late in the evening, when the crowds have departed, you can appreciate a different side to the place. Turn your back on the gift shops and channel your gaze to the vast horizon ahead. On the very tip of the peninsula, gazing out across the Atlantic Ocean, there is a certain magic to Land's End, if you take the time to seek it.

Beyond the cliff's edge the ocean conceals the mythical lost kingdom of Lyonesse, its bells still ringing beneath the waves. Stone caves and hidden tongues of pure golden sand are dotted around the end of the peninsula. The water, warmed by the Gulf Stream, is home to a vast array of sea creatures – an occasional dolphin or porpoise might be seen breaking the surface, or the dark shadow of a harmless basking shark seen beneath the waves.

It is a place that artists and photographers have long sought out. Light abounds, glinting and reflecting from the water that borders you on three sides. Land's End's west-facing cliffs mean you can get spectacular, long-lasting sunsets. The setting sun hangs on the horizon, pools of golden light flood the cliffs and glint on the waves, as it takes an age to finally dip out of sight.

While most people arrive at Land's End eager to get going on their journey, it does have plenty to offer the visitor willing to linger. Nearby beaches, such as Sennen Cove, the UK's most westerly surf spot, are delightful, and are lively without the artifice of Land's End itself. Just along the cliffs from Land's End is Nanjizal, a secluded beach with a distinctive arch, rock pools and sea caves, where the pounding waves reverberate in its vast echo chamber. Escape here for a more natural experience of this rocky peninsula.

Despite the natural beauty and rich history of Penwith, tourism puts a gloss on an area that faces problems with economic deprivation, an absence of year-round work and locals who are priced out of the housing market by holiday home ownership. It might not be visible to those who visit to relax and explore, but the crumbling mines which look evocative and romantic in holiday snaps speak of employment that has not been fully replaced.

A SINGLE PEDAL STROKE

Standing in Land's End with the full thousand-mile journey stretching out ahead of you, a mix of emotions might be felt: trepidation, an eagerness to get going, uncertainty, impatience and excitement. Don't rush this moment, it sets the scene for the days of riding to come. Get your picture with the sign, draw a breath, put your foot to the pedal and begin.

GETTING TO THE START

Many people choose to be dropped off by friends or relatives at the start, but Penzance railway station is just 10 miles from Land's End with direct trains arriving from a wide range of places. A taxi or a pedal from Penzance are your options. If you are arriving from further afield you may choose to fly to Cornwall Airport Newquay or opt to courier your bike from home to your Land's End hotel.

TRAIN

Penzance is the end of the train line. Great Western Railway and CrossCountry serve the station. You can take your bike for free, but you may need to reserve a place in advance.
www.gwr.com
www.crosscountrytrains.co.uk

PLANE

Cornwall Airport Newquay is around 50 miles from Land's End. Served by a range of airlines, you can fly direct to Newquay from a number of destinations across the UK and Europe. Check with individual airlines for their rules on bike transportation and packaging.
www.cornwallairportnewquay.com

BIKE TRANSPORT

PENZANCE TAXI

They can help get you and your bike the short hop from Penzance to Land's End if you don't want to pedal and prefer to save your legs for the official start.
T 01736 366 366
www.penzancetaxis.co.uk

SHERPR BIKE BOXES

Order one of Sherpr's custom boxes to deliver your bike to your accommodation in Land's End, leaving you to travel with ease. Unpack your bike and they will arrange a collection of the box.
www.sherprbikebox.com

SLEEP

THE LAND'S END HOTEL & LUXURY STAYS
Great views out to the Isles of Scilly from atop towering granite cliffs. Only 100 metres from the start line of your epic journey.
Land's End, TR19 7AA
T 01736 871 844
www.landsendhotel.co.uk

LAND'S END HOSTEL
A combination of private rooms, bunk rooms and bed and breakfast options, a short distance from the start line.
Mill Barn, Trevescan, TR19 7AQ
T 07585 625 774
www.landsendholidays.co.uk

LAND'S END CAMPING & GLAMPING
This site is situated next to the Land's End Hostel and boasts a new shower and toilet block as well as a communal campfire.
Trevescan Farm, Trevescan, TR19 7AQ
T 07376 535 882
www.landsendcamp.co.uk

EAT

FIRST & LAST INN
A watering hole for smugglers since the seventeenth century, you are nowadays likely to find a mix of locals and tourists in the beer garden or huddling by the log fires depending on what weather the Atlantic winds are bringing ashore.
Sennen, TR19 7AD
T 01736 871 680
www.firstandlastinn.co.uk

SUPPLIES

Sennen and Land's End Post Office incorporates a small general store – this is situated a short distance into your LEJOG1000 journey for any last-minute supplies. If you can wait, you will find more choice in St Just, the first sizable settlement on route.

BIKE

CARN BIKES
Appointment-only mechanic near Land's End. They can also arrange for your bike to be couriered to the start of your journey using Sendbike.
T 07838 637 678
http://carn.bike

CORNWALL & DEVON

1

STAGE

44 miles / 71km
900 metres ascent

LAND'S END TO PERRANPORTH

Cornwall – the county with the longest coastline. Stunning beaches and coves provide a scenic start to the journey, with ghostly remains of wheal houses silhouetted against the sky harking back to the times of tin mining. Instead of turning inland from Land's End like many routes, LEJOG1000 hugs the rugged coastline to fully appreciate the wild, exposed cliffs and stunning sandy beaches.

If you had some vague notion that the 'tough' riding wouldn't start until Scotland, stage 1 will quickly disabuse you of this naivety! The repeated short, sharp spikes of Cornish hills tot up to around 900 metres of climbing. The first stage is one of the toughest of the trip and can come as a bit of a shock, not least because your legs, while fresh, might not be accustomed to daily cycling just yet. The views are stunning and the joy of starting a cycle tour (and perhaps a Cornish pasty) will sustain you through the ride. Setting off from Land's End will be one of the most memorable moments of the trip. Ambitious record breakers and genteel cycle tourists alike all take a moment for a picture under the iconic signpost to gaze out to sea and ponder the journey ahead.

LAND'S END TO ST IVES

Beginning in the furthest corner of the South West of mainland Britain, the whole thousand-mile route is still ahead of you; you will be hoping that those southwesterly winds stay behind you, providing a helping hand up the country. Starting out along a quiet stretch of the A30 you pass the First & Last Inn; although it's most likely too early for a pint it is still worth a snap before you head on your way. Shortly after the inn you take a left turn towards St Just. Your first significant and steep climb finishes just as you arrive at the junction with the A road on the edge of St Just where you turn left. Only 6 miles past Land's End, St Just is the most westerly town in mainland Britain,

and your first opportunity to stock up on pasties is at the bakery in the Market Square.

Leaving St Just you are treated to a descent down to a small river. At a five-way junction after the river bridge our route opts for the wonderfully named No Go By Hill, the former main road. The new road (the B3306 that we rejoin later) was installed in the mid-1800s in response to the ever-expanding industrial importance of the valley. Milling was well established here in the eighteenth century when the valley was full of stamping and corn mills, leats, ponds and sluices, running all the way down to the shoreline. Riding the old road allows you to see some of the farming cottages that predate this industry.

Turn right at the T-junction to rejoin the B3306. It is a roller coaster of a road to St Ives with short and often sharp climbs interspersed with equally short descents; it continues like this until mile 17, when you reach the top of Rosewall Hill by the small National Trust car park. Should you fancy a stroll, walking up the hill will reward you with panoramic views of the North Cornwall coastline, across the Penwith Hills and St Ives. Nearby there are old Cornish tin mine workings and visible Neolithic and Iron Age groundworks remain. From the car park a glorious 2 miles of descent leads you into the narrow streets of St Ives. Follow the main road round to the right then the blue of St Ives Bay comes into view below on your left, the cliffside road lined with a sprinkling of palm trees.

ST IVES TO PORTREATH

St Ives is a bustling town with a historic connection to the arts. With the Tate St Ives and many galleries, museums and gardens, St Ives may be somewhere you mark down as a place to return to as it will take more than a coffee stop to do it justice. The road follows the curve of the bay; 3 miles of golden sands stretch along the coastline with St Ives at one end, the busy port town of Hayle at the mouth of the River Hayle in the middle and Gwithian Beach to the east. This area is popular with sandcastle-building families and surfers alike; on a day with good swell it is worth pausing for a moment to watch the bobbing bodies on boards out in the bay.

Reach the end of the bay and turn very briefly inland after the village of Gwithian. The headland to the left is owned by the National Trust; beyond that standing on its own rocky island is the 26-metre octagonal Godrevy Lighthouse, immortalised by Virginia Woolf in *To The Lighthouse*, but you'll need to walk along the footpath from the car park to see it clearly. Further along, at the top of the cliffs you will see signs for a car park and cafe. Hell's Mouth is every bit as dramatic as it sounds; take a moment to cautiously lean over the sheer cliffs and gaze into the roaring sea below.

With an almost endless horizon, where the wild landscape reaches across to sea and sky, this section to Portreath can feel windy and exposed. As you pass near Carvannel Farm, Porth-cadjack Cove lies to your northern side. The rocky cove is flanked on one side by Samphire Island. Rock samphire was harvested from rocks and eaten after being pickled. It usually grows in the most inaccessible of places. As many people have met with an untimely end while gathering samphire, it's probably best to miss this ingredient out of your meal plans on this trip.

PORTREATH TO PERRANPORTH

Descending into Portreath you are welcomed into another sandy bay, popular with surfers and families. The road offers you a good view so you can stay in the saddle and continue your journey, turning your back to the sea and beginning to climb inland again. Take the minor road to the left, signed *Porthtowan*. As you reach the bottom of the descent after Porthtowan, the road rises up before you again and an ancient, rusted fingerpost points you straight on towards *St Agnes* and *Perranporth*. Just after the crest of the hill, immediately following a lay-by and opposite The Victory Inn, take the left turn, which takes you downhill a little, then not unexpectedly back uphill again.

Turn right at a four-way junction towards St Agnes. The pretty terraced miners' cottages lead down to the sea to your left, steeply stacked against each other, to reach the harbour wall. The thriving village shops are still at the centre of a true community and the quintessentially Cornish, picture-postcard beach

is hemmed in by cliffs and well worth a visit. Follow the signs for *Perranporth* through St Agnes, around the one-way system and out the other side.

From here the navigation is easy. Follow the B3285 all the way, finally dropping down into Perranporth just after its diminutive airfield to finish this stage at the end of Beach Road. In sight of the sands, it is a perfect place to end your day or grab a quick lunch before heading onwards.

SLEEP

SEINERS ARMS
Attractive, modern bed and breakfast with its own bar and restaurant, just a few steps from the sandy beach.
Beach Road, Perranporth, TR6 0JL
T 01872 573 118
www.seiners.co.uk

YHA PERRANPORTH
Hostel with bunk rooms, private rooms and a very limited amount of weather-dependent camping.
Droskyn Point, Perranporth, TR6 0GS
T 03453 719 755
www.yha.org.uk/hostel/yha-perranporth

TOLLGATE FARM
Family-run site with camping, eco-cabins and fabulous views across the sand dunes and sea.
Budnick Hill, Perranporth, TR6 0AD
T 01872 572 130
www.tollgatefarm.co.uk

EAT

SUMMERHOUSE
Stunning views across the sands with a beautiful terrace to catch the last rays with a drink in hand, this is a fantastic place to end your first day in the saddle.
The Dunes, 38 Ponsmere Road, Perranporth, TR6 0FJ
T 01872 228 222
www.thesummerhouse.co.uk

SUPPLIES

Perranporth has a small supermarket (**Co-op Food**) and a community-run country market in the Memorial Hall on Friday mornings where you can buy fresh home-grown fruit and vegetables, cakes, jams, eggs, honey and crafts.

BIKE

HAYLE CYCLES
The first opportunity to get your bike checked out on the journey. Closed Wednesdays and Sundays.
36 Penpol Terrace, Hayle, TR27 4BQ
T 01736 753 825
www.haylecycles.com

STAGE 1 LAND'S END TO PERRANPORTH *44 / 1000 MILES* MODERATE

193 m
3 m
0 miles
10
20
30
40

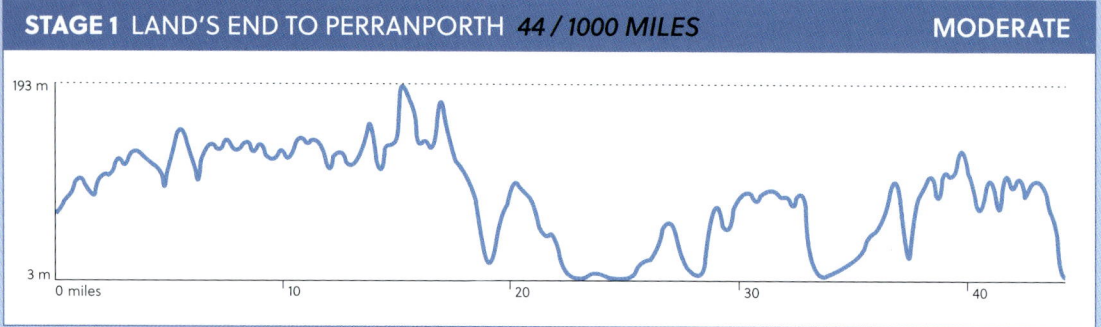

Atlantic Ocean
St Ives
St Ives Bay
Carbis Bay
Phillack
Hayl
Trendrine
Zennor
B3306
A3074
Halsetown
Treen
Kerrowe
B3311
Porthmeor
Rosemergy
Morvah
Trevowhan
Higher Boscaswell
Bojewyan
Pendeen
Trewellard
Carnyorth
B3318
Botallack
Truthwall
St Just
Nancherrow
A3071
Newbridge
Heamoor
A30
Crowlas
St Erth
B3302
Bosavern
Kelynack
Penzance
Marazion
Goldsithney
A394
B3306
Newlyn
A30
Mount's Bay
Whitesand Bay
Sennen Cove
Mayon
Sennen
LAND'S END
S
B3315
B3283
St Buryan
Mousehole

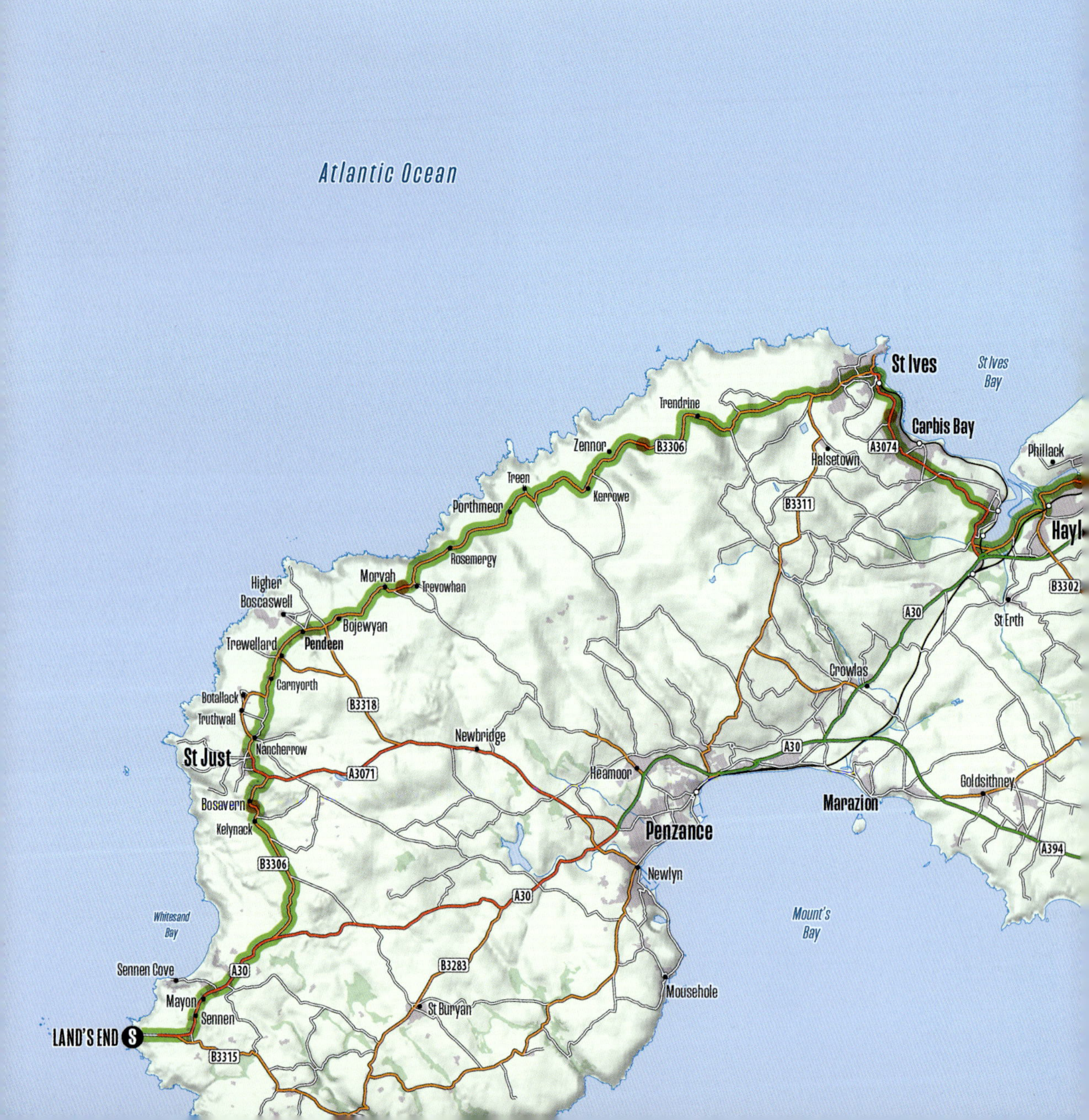

STAGE 2

2

23 miles / 37km
570 metres ascent

PERRANPORTH TO WADEBRIDGE

Lanes lined with steep-sided banked hedgerows topped with glorious wild flower displays guide you to lesser-visited inland Cornwall, revealing tales of indestructible saints and smugglers' haunts. Leaving the coast offers a far-reaching view to Bodmin Moor before plunging down to the ancient market town of Wadebridge, a crucial crossing point of the River Camel for centuries.

Exploring more deeply the scenes and stories that make Cornwall a perennial fascination, this stage begins by climbing away from the coast; the road's undulations mimic the rising and falling of the waves that surfers seek at nearby Newquay. Before leaving the sea views behind, there is just time to spot Penhale's impressive sand dunes and learn more of the history of Cornwall hidden beneath. The route wiggles its way to Wadebridge avoiding the arterial roads that flood the beaches and attractions with tourists. The upward undulations culminate in the highest point of your journey so far on a wind-farm-covered hill. Take a moment to feel the breeze on your back before descending to cross the River Camel at Wadebridge. Take a detour to Camel Valley wines and discover the sparkling wine that made growers in Champagne feel nervous.

PERRANPORTH TO ST NEWLYN EAST

Leave Perranporth in the direction of Newquay, keeping left at the mini-roundabout at the end of the main street. The road starts to climb with an old tin mine chimney and a caravan park to your right, a nod to Cornwall's past and present as tourism has most definitely superseded tin mining. The climb tops out at about 80 metres with the main road bending sharply to the right. Instead, turn left, signed *Trebellan 2*, down an initially very narrow lane which widens affording views in

the breaks in the high-banked hedgerows across to the dunes of Penhale Sands and the sea beyond.

Penhale is the largest and most diverse sand dune system in Cornwall. Part buried beneath the dunes is St Piran's Oratory; dating from the sixth century, it is one of the oldest and most important Christian sites in the UK and claims to be the oldest Christian church in the country.

Legend goes that Piran was a sixth-century Irish monk. Rulers, jealous of his power, threw him off a high cliff in Ireland with a millstone tied to his neck. His enemies were disappointed as instead of drowning the saint floated on his millstone across the sea to Cornwall. Many claim Piran gave his name to Perranporth, the location where his surprisingly buoyant boat came ashore.

St Piran became the saint of tin miners after discovering how to smelt tin. The Cornish flag of St Piran flutters in many gardens; its distinctive white cross on a black background symbolises the light of God in a dark world but also the white tin metal against the black rock. St Piran is celebrated on 5 March with a similar passion and vigour as a St Patrick's night out in Ireland with much merriment and singing in the hostelries – fitting for a hard-living holy man.

Leaving St Piran's sand dunes behind the road descends sharply and steeply; at the bottom turn left up a narrow, steep chute of a lane which is signed *Smugglers Den*. After the hamlet of Trebellan turn right on to a wider

road signed to *Newlyn East*. It is just over 2 miles to St Newlyn East; take care at a staggered crossroads over a main road heading right then immediately left.

ST NEWLYN EAST TO ST COLUMB MAJOR

The village of St Newlyn East suffered a disaster in 1846 when the East Wheal Rose Mine was flooded during a heavy thunderstorm, killing 39 local miners. A pit dug in memoriam is still used for village celebrations. Fork left in the village, signed *Lappa Valley Railway*. A short steep descent after the village plunges down to a small stream and across the steam railway. A line once used to transport ore now transports holidaying day trippers on steam trains.

Shortly after crossing the railway turn right at a T-junction following the sign for *St Columb*. At a staggered crossroads head straight over the lane then drop downhill in a tunnel of trees before climbing between yet more high hedgerows. After passing under a railway arch head straight over the main road signed *St Columb Major*.

The road and the railway are key arteries pumping a steady flow of summer tourists in and out of the nearby surf resort of Newquay. The closest sensation to waves on this ride is the pitching and rolling of the undulating Cornish landscape, the latest little up and down delivering you to the edge of St Columb Major. Turn left down a dead-end lane with a blue pedestrian sign to St Columb Major, as this allows an easier crossing of one of the busy roads to Newquay. Head straight across on to Trekenning Road which leads you into the large village of St Columb Major.

As well as providing a healthy range of independent shops, St Columb is also home to 'hurling the silver ball', a tradition with pagan origins which takes place on Shrove Tuesday. Once popular throughout Cornwall, it is thought that St Columb is one of only two places where the games still take place (St Ives – which you rode through in stage 1 – being the other). Each year local shopkeepers board up their windows to protect them from the cricket-ball-sized ball made of applewood and coated in silver. Also known as 'Cornish hurling', a scrum forms by mid-afternoon between 'countrymen' and 'townsmen'; following a 'throw up' in the Market Square, teams pass the silver ball until they reach their respective goals at opposite parish boundaries.

Roads remain open so if you happen to be cycling through on Shrove Tuesday watch out, although the scrum is paused if a non-playing member of the public handles the ball as it is thought to bring health and fertility. Once the winner is established the ball is returned to the Market Square before it visits every pub in town, the ball is dipped in a pint and shared around the winning team.

ST COLUMB MAJOR TO WADEBRIDGE

Turn right then immediately left in the centre of the village passing The Silver Ball pub and follow the

narrow one-way system. The road climbs a little out of town underneath a busy A road. Shortly after riding underneath the main road turn right and go through Tregamere; this is followed by a short steep downhill over a narrow bridge. Turn right at the T-junction on to the B3274 (ignoring the signpost for *Wadebridge* which points to the left). After passing Lower Tremayne Farm turn left down an unmarked lane.

In the hamlet of Rosenannon turn left, then the road begins to climb up the southern side of St Breock Downs. High hedgerows briefly give way to open moorland with cattle grazing. A liberal sprinkling of wind turbines off to your left dominates the skyline as the road reaches just under 200 metres and your highest point of the journey so far. On a clear day the expanse of Bodmin Moor can be seen brooding on the very distant horizon.

The ensuing descent lasts almost all the way to Wadebridge, the narrow lane engulfed with high hedgerows sprouting for the heavens from deep earth mounds where the road is dug in. Take it easy, as it is not a lane you want to meet the local bin wagon on, and you need to be ready to stop and search for the security of the nearest gateway.

The River Camel splits Wadebridge in two; the town grew as a key crossing point of the river. The stage ends as the road reaches the bridge over the river in the centre of town. One of North Cornwall's main market towns, Wadebridge is also the gateway to the popular Camel Trail. If you are in no hurry head north to the coast along the old railway line cycle path for the finest fish and chips by the sea in Padstow or south inland for a wine tasting at Camel Valley Vineyard.

CAMEL VALLEY VINEYARD
Climate change is not bad for every business. English wine is booming not just in quantity but in quality. Back in 2010 shock waves were sent round champagne houses as Camel Valley's Pinot Noir Rosé Brut was crowned the world's best sparkling rosé at the International Wine Challenge. The climate of the South West is slightly cooler than Champagne; grapes grow more slowly and spend longer on the vine, giving them slightly different flavours, along with acidity and freshness.

Part of the early pioneers of the English wine scene, owners Bob and Annie Lindo initially farmed sheep and cattle but later planted vines on the sun-drenched south-facing slopes of the Camel Valley and have been producing wine since 1989.

Pedal approximately 4 miles inland along the Camel Valley Trail for wine by the glass on the sun terrace overlooking the vineyards. For tours it is best to book.
Nanstallon, Bodmin, PL30 5LG
T 01208 77959
www.camelvalley.com

SLEEP

ST ENODOC HOTEL

If you want to breathe the fresh sea air, pedal 5 miles off route to the sought-after seaside village of Rock overlooking the Camel Estuary and treat yourself to a night in this stylish boutique hotel. There is an outdoor pool and an option of a massage to relieve any early trip tension.
Rock, PL27 6LA
T 01208 863 394
www.enodoc-hotel.co.uk

LITTLE BODIEVE HOLIDAY PARK

Not exactly a wild camping experience, but there are places to pitch your tent and a heated pool and a slide. About 1 mile north of the centre of Wadebridge.
Bodieve Road, Wadebridge, PL27 6EG
T 01208 815 547
www.littlebodieve.co.uk

MOLESWORTH ARMS HOTEL

Known by locals as 'the moley', this townhouse hotel has been serving the locals of Wadebridge and travellers since the sixteenth century. Offers traditional pub food, or head to The Boatyard which specialises in steak and seafood.
Molesworth Street, Wadebridge, PL27 7DP
T 01208 812 055
www.moleswortharms.co.uk

EAT

THE STEPPING STONE

Hidden on a side street but worth seeking out for fresh Cornish ingredients and a warm welcome.
Polmorla Road, Wadebridge, PL27 7ND
T 01208 816 377
www.thesteppingstonewadebridge.co.uk

SUPPLIES

A bakery and a **Co-op Food** supermarket sit on the corner just before the bridge over the River Camel in Wadebridge.

BIKE

THE WADEBRIDGE BIKE SHOP

Spares and a range of cycling kit and shades, handy if the Cornish sun is out.
9 Polmorla Walk, Wadebridge, PL27 7NS
T 01208 815 262
www.wadebridgebikeshop.co.uk

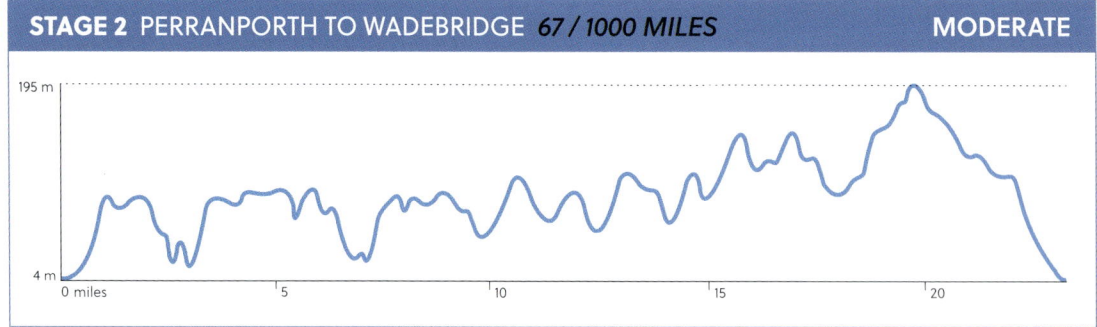

STAGE 2 PERRANPORTH TO WADEBRIDGE *67 / 1000 MILES*   MODERATE

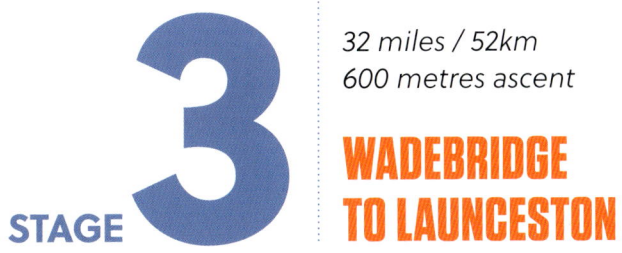

STAGE **3**

32 miles / 52km
600 metres ascent

WADEBRIDGE TO LAUNCESTON

Visiting the former capital of Cornwall, this stage features the bleak heather-covered granite uplands of Bodmin Moor, home to the legend of King Arthur and the mysterious Beast of Bodmin Moor. From typical high Cornish hedgerows to sunken roads, windswept airfields and the atmospheric moor, it is a stage with something new around every corner.

Varied riding means this is a stage that will keep you on your toes, and the texture of the surface beneath your wheels tells a story all of its own. Old main roads through once bustling villages where grass verges and expanding hedgerows try to reclaim the tarmac speak of bypasses, out-of-town shopping and modern living. Ancient stone bridges, cobbled fords and meandering tracks tell of the slow passage of carthorses and drovers across the moorland edges. Twentieth-century travel is represented in the perfect smoothness and arrow-straight construction of a World War II airstrip. Even the old mainline London to Padstow railway, now a narrow-gauge steam railway and visitor attraction, has a tale to tell of the changing methods of travel in this part of Cornwall.

WADEBRIDGE TO WENFORDBRIDGE

Cross the bridge over the River Camel and turn right following the sign for *Bodmin*. Keeping the river on your right, continue to a T-junction and turn right on to the A389, turning left when you see the small lane signed to *St Mabyn*. Unlike many Cornish lanes, the lower banking here allows far-reaching views across the river valley.

St Mabyn is a pretty, sleepy village at the top of a hill with its old cottages cosily gathered around a green. In a classic story of large bypass roads and supermarkets, the number of shops in St Mabyn dwindled until the final shop and post office was scheduled for closure in 2018. At this point the community rallied and St Mabyn's

community shop and post office is now a thriving hub for locals and visitors.

Following what was once the main road from Wadebridge, the tarmac quickly narrows and deteriorates to a rural lane. The road gently descends through undulating farmland where the high hedges overflow with greenery before climbing up to St Tudy, again on top of a small hill. St Tudy's most famous resident was Captain William Bligh, who was set adrift by his crew during the mutiny on the *Bounty*.

Leaving St Tudy, the route continues to climb until you reach a crossroads; continue travelling straight on. Turn left around 800 metres after the crossroads following the sign for *St Breward*. A descent takes you to Wenfordbridge and a crossing of the River Camel, close to the start of the Camel Trail where you will also find a fabulous cycle cafe.

WENFORDBRIDGE TO DAVIDSTOW AIRFIELD

Fork left around 800 metres after Wenfordbridge. From here until just after Davidstow Airfield we follow Sustrans National Route 3. Navigation is aided here by following the large bikes painted on the tarmac, but they are easy to miss if covered in mud. It is roughly 1 mile from Wenfordbridge to the next village of St Breward, but you will need to be ready for a couple of short, steep sections. Turn right between a small green and some houses. As you leave St Breward, the road narrows down to a single strip of tarmac between the short,

rough grass verges. Here you enter Bodmin Moor –
a place of so many stories, superstitions and unusual
happenings that the name alone sends a shiver down
the spine.

Just inside the edge of Bodmin Moor lies King
Arthur's Hall. You need to know where to look and it
requires some walking from the main road. This stone
enclosure made of 56 standing stones facing inwards
like chairs around a table, dates back to Neolithic times.
The Arthurian connection is much more recent, being
found in a document from the 1950s. Whatever its
history, it is a strangely eerie place to visit, hidden as it is
in the depths of the moor.

The edge of the moor changes its character
depending on the weather. On a sunny day it is
picturesque and inviting, the gently grazing animals
making it feel tranquil. In thick fog, howling winds or
torrential rain the spirit of the moor seems much less
benign. Any loss of cattle in this area is quickly blamed
on the Beast of Bodmin Moor. The Beast, whatever it is,
is still occasionally spotted.

When you reach a T-junction turn right then cross
two streams in quick succession. Another open stretch
of moor follows where if you let your imagination play
the gnarled windswept shapes of low-growing trees and
gorse bushes can take on sinister forms in the mist.

On a single-track lane the route turns left at a large
traffic triangle in the open moorland. As you approach

this junction you can see two of Cornwall's best-known
landmarks, Rough Tor and Brown Willy, rising out of
the moor to your right. Rough Tor rises to a height
of 400 metres and is the second-highest point in
Cornwall. Brown Willy, about a mile to the south-east,
is the highest at 420 metres. Shortly after the triangle
junction turn right, still following Sustrans National
Route 3. The narrow lane continues passing a disused
chimney, which is testament to the tin industry. A cattle
grid announces the return of hedgerows and stone walls.

Enclosures of conifer forests create dark regular
patches on the landscape, contrasting with the
perpetually flowering bright yellow gorse. There is a
local saying that when gorse is out of flower, love is out
of fashion. As the road sweeps to the left you are given
the exciting choice of a weak bridge or a shallow ford.

As you pass Crowdy Reservoir on your right keep an
eye out for the black-headed gulls who nest and breed
there in spring or in the autumn for the murmurations
of starlings filling the sky above with wondrous shapes.
A sharp right-hand turn takes you on to Davidstow
Airfield and a long straight opens up in front of you.

DAVIDSTOW AIRFIELD TO LAUNCESTON

Exposed and completely straight, Davidstow Airfield
runway is a demoralising place to cycle on a windy day.
RAF Davidstow Moor was in use from 1942 until 1945;
when it closed the three-runway airfield hosted three

Formula 1 races in the 1950s. The nearby creamery makes Davidstow and Cathedral City cheeses.

At the end of the straight airstrip the payback arrives for the height you have been steadily gaining for the last 10 miles. While it is definitely not 'downhill all the way' you can comfortably relax and freewheel for a short while. Just over 7 miles after turning on to the airstrip, a sudden left takes you down a sunken lane towards Trewen. Leaning trees lower their green canopies over the road so that it feels cool here even on a hot day. The change in gradient as you climb almost to the church in Trewen may have you using un-godlike language.

When you reach a T-junction with the A395, *Launceston* appears on the signs. Take a right then immediately left towards *Egloskerry*. In places along here the road is not much wider than a footpath, with grass slowly making its advance to narrow it even further. The last few miles are a series of small ups and downs that break your pedalling rhythm.

On the edge of Launceston, a left takes you over the old railway line that now carries narrow-gauge steam trains between the town and the hamlet of Newmills along the glorious Kensey Valley. Cross the River Kensey on an old narrow cobbled packhorse bridge. The stage ends outside the White Horse Inn on a mini-roundabout in the north side of Launceston.

LAUNCESTON

Launceston was once the capital of Cornwall. Its castle holds a strong strategic position above the town and its fortified walls and three town gates protected the town. Only three gates were needed as to the east the steep incline leading up from the Kensey Valley was enough to prevent a surprise attack. At the time of building, it was the only walled town in Cornwall. To reach the centre of the old town and the castle from the stage end turn right to arrive at what was the Northgate.

SLEEP

THE EAGLE HOUSE HOTEL
Built in 1764 this stunning house has a restaurant, distillery and gin bar, as well as a choice of rooms and style to suit all budgets. This is a delightful place to spend an evening.
3 Castle Street, Launceston, PL15 8BA
T 01566 774 488
www.theeaglehousehotel.com

ROSE COTTAGE
Bed and breakfast in a central location with castle views. It offers secure bike lock-up, a hearty breakfast and a packed lunch to go if needed.
5 Lower Cleaverfield, Launceston, PL15 8ED
T 01566 779 292
www.rosecottagecornwall.co.uk

GOODMANSLEIGH
Farmhouse bed and breakfast located 1 mile outside of Launceston. Set on a working farm running alongside the River Tamar with views of Dartmoor and Launceston Castle.
Lower Goodmansleigh, Launceston, PL15 9QS
T 01566 776 354
www.goodmansleigh.co.uk

EAT

THE BELL INN
Launceston's oldest known pub and the perfect place for an evening meal or a post-ride pint. Local ales served on tap and a warm welcome.
1 Tower Street, Launceston, PL15 8BQ
T 01566 779 970
www.bellinnlaunceston.co.uk

SUPPLIES

Launceston has a wide range of supermarkets with a **Co-op Food** in the centre and other larger shops on the periphery. There is a traditional bakery on the High Street.

BIKE

LAUNCESTON CYCLES
Helpful bike shop on a business park just south of the town and the A30.
Douglas Business Park, Launceston, PL15 7FU
T 01566 776 102
www.launcestoncycles.co.uk

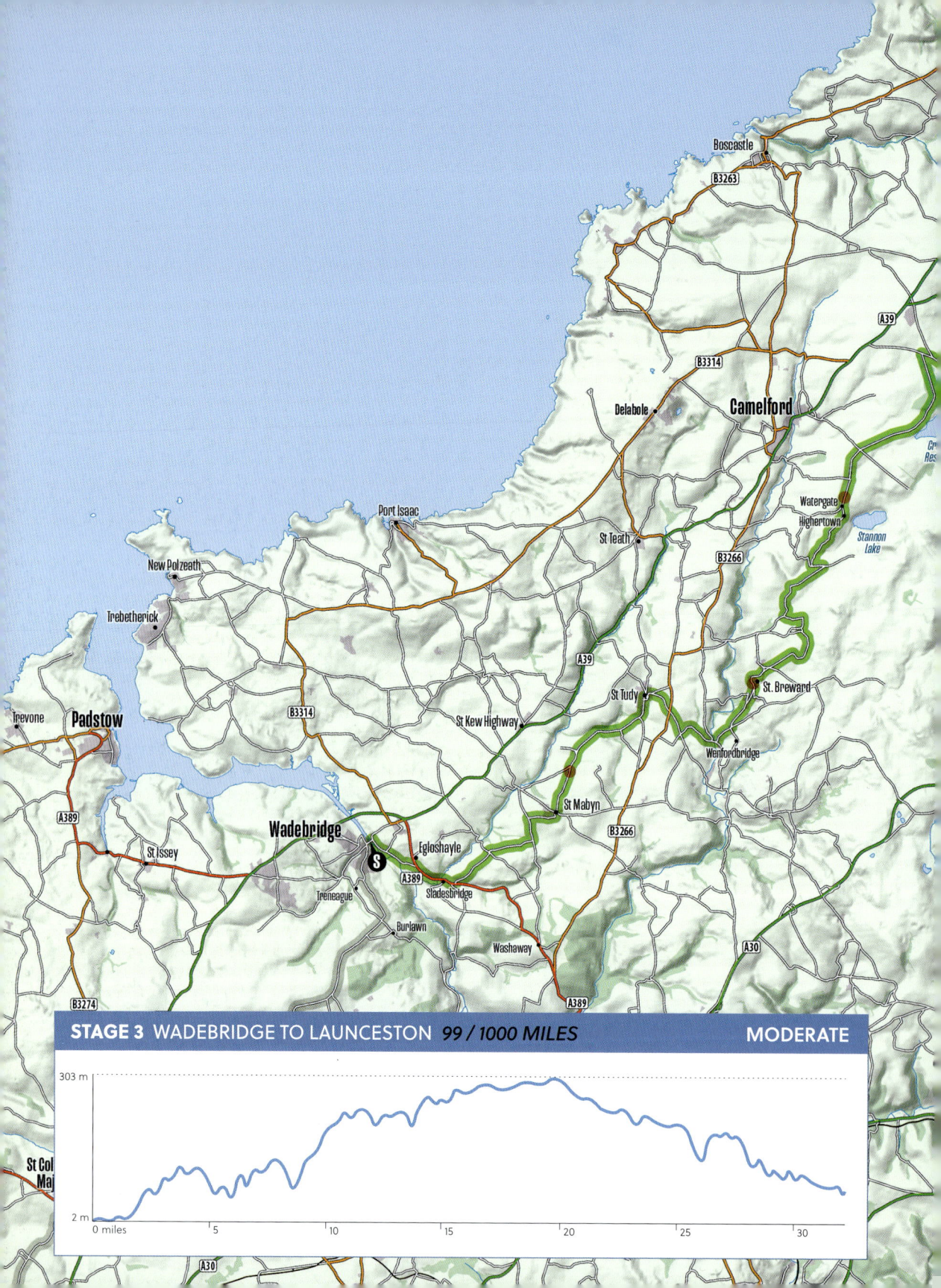

Boscastle
B3263

A39

B3314

Delabole
Camelford

Watergate
Highertown
Stannon
Lake

Port Isaac

St Teath

B3266

New Polzeath

Trebetherick

A39

St Tudy
St. Breward

Trevone
Padstow

B3314
St Kew Highway

Wenfordbridge

A389

St Mabyn

Wadebridge

Egloshayle
B3266

St Issey
Ⓢ
A389
Stadesbridge

Treneague

A30

Burlawn

Washaway

A389

B3274

St Col
Maj

A30

STAGE 3 WADEBRIDGE TO LAUNCESTON *99 / 1000 MILES*   MODERATE

303 m

2 m
0 miles   5   10   15   20   25   30

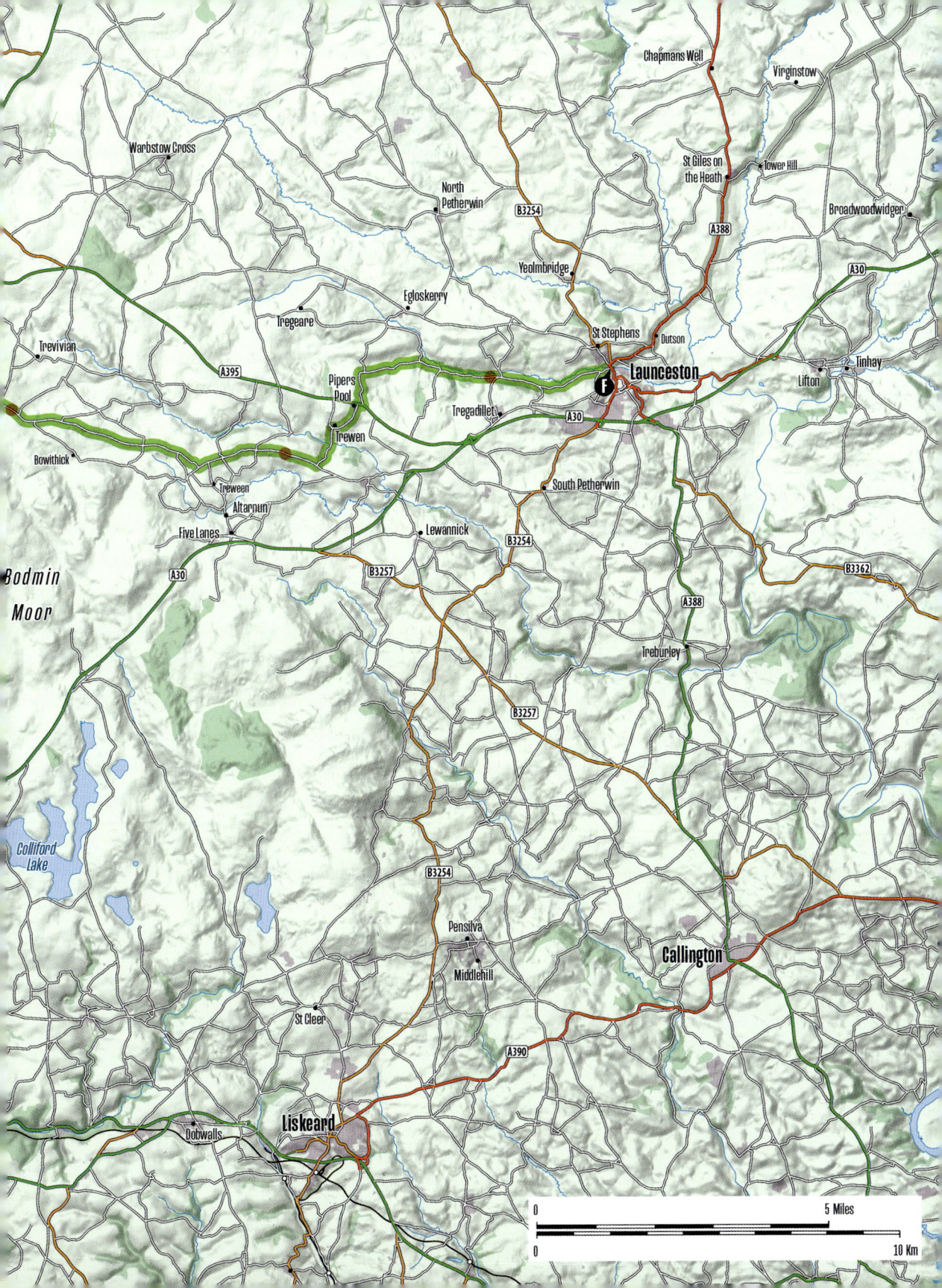

34 miles / 55km
800 metres ascent

STAGE **4**

LAUNCESTON TO CHULMLEIGH

A milestone moment in the journey as the route crosses the first county boundary between Cornwall and Devon. Cutting a line between the North Devon Coast and Dartmoor National Park to the south, the route travels beside fertile, red-soiled fields, through apple orchards and past grazing cows. This bucolic bike ride opens the door to Devon.

A continuously rolling ride within the folds of this soft landscape takes you down to little stream crossings and propels you up the other side in a continuous roller coaster. Blasting in and out of warm Devonshire sunshine on the tops and plunging into deep dark green shade along the valley bottoms creates distinct changes in your ride. The steeply undulating terrain is a signature of the South West and one that should not be underestimated. Only a few of the climbs are truly taxing on their own but, taken in succession, they can feel quite wearing. Thankfully there are plenty of places to pause and make the most of the scenery. Finishing the stage at a hilltop village, while a harsh end to a day, also tells something of the history of the town and the landscape that surrounds it.

LAUNCESTON TO METHERELL CROSS

As soon as you leave Launceston on the A388 towards Holsworthy you are faced with a half-mile climb – a gentle introduction to the longer climbs ahead. As you descend on the other side you will cross the River Tamar, the boundary between Cornwall and Devon. The route follows the new road, but just to the side you can spot the original medieval packhorse bridge, which in the latter half of the eighteenth century was part of the turnpike road from Launceston to Holsworthy for which travellers were charged tolls to use.

When you reach St Giles on the Heath it is time to leave the main travellers' route behind, turning right

past the Pint and Post, an old thatched pub with, as you might have expected, a postbox embedded in its front wall. The road becomes a gentle narrow lane, taking you across the River Carey, which marks the beginning of the ascent of Tower Hill. Inconsistent in its gradient, it can be hard to gauge how much further you have to go, but when you arrive at a T-junction with the A3079 at Metherell Cross you have reached the highest point of this stage.

METHERELL CROSS TO MONKOKEHAMPTON

A right turn on to the A3079, followed quickly by a left, and you are back on to a single-track lane. The height you gained affords you views across Dartmoor National Park to your right and the North Devon Coast to your left. Midway through the descent, at the white fingerpost sign marked 'Benny's Cross', turn right towards *Patchacott*. At the bottom there is a little stream crossing, meandering between Devon hedgerows filled with wild flowers. This section is a series of dips down to rivers and climbs back up. It can be tiring on the legs but somehow the tunnel of bright fresh foliage draws you on.

After the stream, go straight ahead at a crossroads. When you arrive at a T-junction turn left, signed *Northlew*. Passing through the village of Northlew and over the River Lew, continue straight ahead along this peaceful lane signed in the direction of *Hatherleigh*. Keep following signs to *Hatherleigh* until meeting the A3072 at a T-junction; turn right here. Go straight ahead

at a roundabout, and shortly afterwards fork right, following the sign for *Monkokehampton* and a blue Sustrans sign. A residential road of thatched cottages and more recent additions leads you out of town, becoming ever smaller and narrower as you once again climb.

A fingerpost sign and a well-placed picnic bench marks the top of the hill, providing just the right spot to enjoy the view. Descending takes you past another fingerpost, pointing the way to *Monkokehampton* and a crossing of the River Okement at the bottom of the hill.

MONKOKEHAMPTON TO CHULMLEIGH

When you arrive at a T-junction in Monkokehampton, opposite a long thatched cottage, turn left. A wedge-shaped house appears to have been fitted into the fork of the road; continue on the left-hand fork towards *Iddesleigh* and *Winkleigh*. Shortly after a stream crossing keep an eye out for a right-hand turn signposted

Winkleigh, where a challenging 15 per cent climb awaits you. The climb goes on more or less continuously for 3 miles, but the good news is that when you reach the top there is a cider farm where a cold apple juice or traditional cloudy cider will slake your thirst.

In the village of Winkleigh you will meet the A3124; cross straight over on to a small lane heading towards Eggesford. With almost a sense of inevitability the road drops down to a little stream before rising again this time up Bude Hill. From the top you can take in a panoramic view of the red soil and fertile farmland so typical of this area of Devon. There is little to mark where you pass through Wembworthy except some pretty cottages, a tin-roofed village hall and playpark. The Heywood fingerpost at the end of the village points you confidently in the direction of *Chulmleigh*.

At the stop sign turn left to cross over the River Taw, closely followed by a level crossing and a left-hand turn to join the A377 by Eggesford railway station. After just

under a mile on the main road an unsigned right-hand turn leads to a quieter, back-roads route into Chulmleigh village. Follow the *Chulmleigh* signs on the network of lanes which climb and then descend to cross the Little Dart River. The stage finishes with a cruel leg-burning power climb to emerge into the village next to the garden of The Old Rectory.

CHULMLEIGH

Chulmleigh, as your legs will tell you, is a small hilltop town; it has been populated since Saxon times and has a mix of homes from throughout its history including cob cottages and much grander town houses. It has all the necessities to make it a community – a school, a pub and a church. It also has a fantastic bakery; whether it is midway through your day or an overnight stopover it is definitely worth popping in for a pastry.

SLEEP
THE OLD COURT HOUSE
The Old Court House is a traditional thatched country inn dating from 1633. It is in the Good Beer Guide and offers tasty home-cooking, perfect for hungry cyclists, as well as bed and breakfast.
South Molton Street, Chulmleigh, EX18 7BW
T 01769 580 045

THE RED LION
Traditional pub offering bed and breakfast. Basic pub grub, good beer and a lively atmosphere.
East Street, Chulmleigh, EX18 7DD
T 01769 580 384
www.theredlionchulmleigh.co.uk

EAT
CHULMLEIGH TANDOORI
If you fancy a proper curry this is the place to head. Great food and friendly staff make this a popular restaurant with locals and visitors.
Cooper House, Fore Street, Chulmleigh, EX18 7BR
T 01769 580 797
www.chulmleightandoorirestaurant.co.uk

SUPPLIES
With **The Chulmleigh Bakery** and **The Old Dairy** (a general store and deli), you have the makings of a delicious picnic lunch in Chulmleigh. There is also a convenience store.

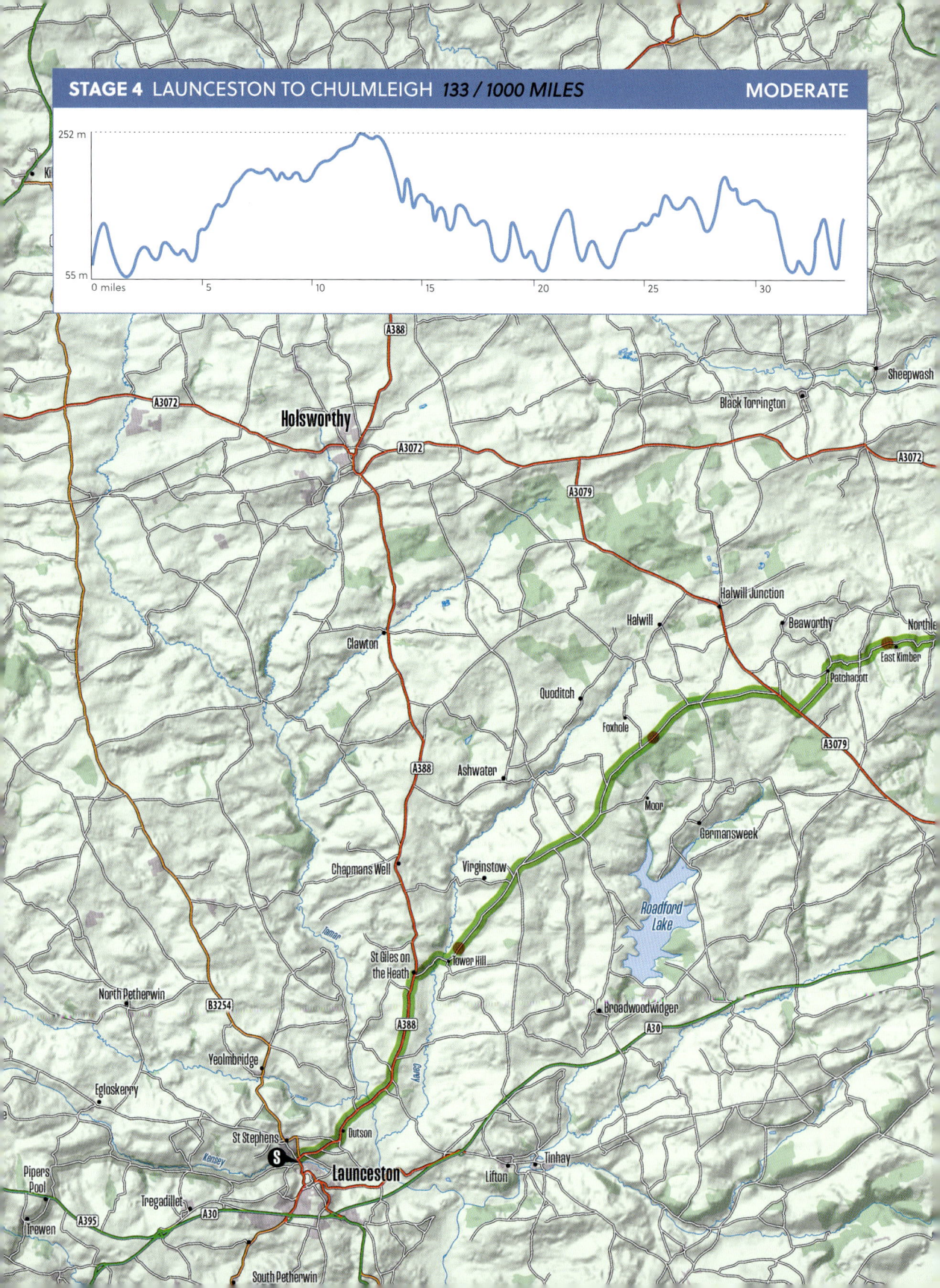

252 m

55 m

0 miles   5   10   15   20   25   30

Sheepwash

A3072

Holsworthy

A3072

Black Torrington

A3072

A3072

A3079

Halwill Junction

Halwill

Beaworthy

Northle

East Kimber

Clawton

Patchacott

Quoditch

A3079

Foxhole

A388

Ashwater

Moor

Germansweek

Chapmans Well

Virginstow

Roadford Lake

Tamar

St Giles on the Heath

Tower Hill

North Petherwin

Broadwoodwidger

B3254

A30

Yeolmbridge

Egloskerry

Kensey

Dutson

Tinhay

St Stephens

A388

Pipers Pool

S

Lifton

Launceston

Tregadillet

A30

Trewen

A395

South Petherwin

5

24 miles / 38km
690 metres ascent

CHULMLEIGH TO DULVERTON

From one independent small community town to another via Exmoor, one of Britain's least visited national parks, to arrive in Somerset, the third county of the journey so far. Wild ponies frolic and forage on the flat ridgelines of the expanse of Exmoor. Small characterful local communities thrive here in their thatched-roofed cottages with pretty gardens.

A stage for the climbers; it has the potential to feel like one of the hardest of the whole journey. Just because it is in the sunny, benign South West, don't underestimate its difficulty, mentally or physically. Your legs will certainly feel the strain of the steep ups and downs where height is lost and needs to be clawed back again almost immediately. While you never climb particularly high, the constant undulations, lack of easy descending and accumulated height gain across the whole ride will be felt by the end of the day. Each ascent is rewarded with a view and each steep descent plunges you into a new wooded ravine, a little world of its own. On a journey like LEJOG1000, every rider will have their preferred type of cycling and even those who prefer pan-flat riding will enjoy the exhilarating views from expansive moorland, while inwardly cursing each climb that takes them there.

CHULMLEIGH TO SOUTH MOLTON

Leave Chulmleigh on the narrow South Molton Street heading slightly uphill then with the community college ahead of you turn right, following the sign for *Kings Nympton*. You will not actually pass through Kings Nympton but carry straight on heading for its cousin, the village of George Nympton, which is 6 miles from Chulmleigh. The lanes are quiet but there is hard work for the legs and mind as you tackle three climbs and descents before George Nympton. The last descent is a mile long down to the genteel River Mole before

climbing again, this time more gradually, through the small village.

From George Nympton, the 2 miles to the thriving town of South Molton are less aggressively undulating and easier on the legs. On the edge of South Molton at a T-junction turn right on to the B3226, signposted *Town centre*. Arriving in the centre on the aptly named Broad Street, turn right and follow the one-way system. The road is lined with shops, and a pedestrianised island adorned with trees sits in the middle of the road; the road then narrows and takes you to the left of the Medical Hall which occupies an island site in the middle of the main street with its distinctive Greek-style columns and balcony. Medieval, Georgian and Elizabethan buildings can all be found in this busy little town.

South Molton grew as a centre for the wool trade but as the industry declined in the nineteenth century it found a new role as an important local service centre for the surrounding scattered villages and farms. The twice-weekly pannier market has the added bonus of being inside a classic market hall building so local traders can tout their wares whatever the weather. Pannier markets are commonplace in Devon; they take their name from the panniers once used to carry goods to market on the back of pack animals. The market may be a source of produce for your own panniers (or to slide into your sleek streamlined bikepacking kit) as energy is needed to attack the hills of Exmoor in the second half of this stage.

SOUTH MOLTON TO DULVERTON

Continue out of town descending slightly past pastel-coloured houses. One mile after the Medical Hall in the town centre and shortly before the crest of a small rise where the entrance to South Molton sign is for those arriving into town, turn left down an unsigned minor road. Around 800 metres after the unmarked turn the route passes over a busy A road via a modern bridge – the last glimpse of hurried life before heading for the hills. After a slight dip the route begins to climb over the next 5 miles, just below the summit of Round Hill on the southern fringes of Exmoor National Park. The climb starts in a gradual, benign way on tree-lined lanes with hedgerows parcelling up fields into tiny pockets. After around 3 miles of gradual climbing, turn right at Kensal crossroads, signposted Twitchen. The route then descends slightly and crosses Ball Bottom Bridge in a wooden glade, the lane sunken between earth mounds enclosing either side of the road, then rises up again to enter the hamlet of Twitchen.

Entering Twitchen, continue straight on past the little church, then turn right and then immediately left following the signs for Molland. The lane is very narrow; cross a cattle grid then the lane rises steeply around an alpine-esque switchback turn which in an understated Devon way is complete with the odd bit of moss and clips of grass that have made a home in a strip down the centre of the lane. A bright white crossroad marker protrudes from the bracken; turn left, following the sign for Withypool, and continue uphill. You are now riding through a classic open moorland landscape with birds wheeling up from the long grass as the whir of your wheels disturbs them from their nests. Just before the road descends to a crossroads you reach 362 metres, the highest point of the route so far.

The South of England is often perceived as a flat land of genteel gradients. This corner of the South West, as your legs will now be telling you, is definitely not. At the crossroads continue straight over, watching out for sheep and cows warming themselves on the tarmac. The wide-open views of Exmoor National Park are vast and the feeling of insignificance in the landscape yet exhilaration of having reached such heights is palpable as you glide along the relatively flat ridgeline for 5 carefree miles. Little height is lost through the open expanses of Mollard, West Anstey and East Anstey commons, areas linked to local more sheltered villages where the locals have the right to graze their animals.

Exmoor ponies roam free and it's unusual to ride this stage without seeing someone out on horseback. As the open common land nears an end the road starts to descend; despite the gradual gradient it is easy to pick up speed. Continue straight on towards Dulverton at the crossroads and at a fork in the road stay on the

principal road to the left. It is a long and steep descent which requires caution and regular brake feathering as the road plunges 150 metres in height in around a mile. The ancient woodland-lined lane feels narrow and enclosed in contrast to the open moorland. With your brakes emitting plenty of heat, cross over the River Barle at the bottom of the descent. Turn right when you reach the more major yet still narrow B3223 and follow the left bank of the river for 1 mile as it meanders downstream to Dulverton. The stage ends at the crossroads with Fore Street.

DULVERTON

As the steep slope into Dulverton suggests, it is situated at the bottom of a deep wooded valley stuffed with ancient oaks and singletrack trails through hidden combes. The town houses the headquarters of Exmoor National Park Authority and is used as a base by many for exploring the park. The River Barle babbles on the edge of town on its journey south and is an important habitat for salmon, brown trout and dippers, while the shady and moist woodlands fed by streams dashing down from the moorlands are ideal for lichens, butterflies and redstarts.

Dulverton sees it fair share of tourists, but it is also a no fuss country town with over 30 independent shops. Fishing tackle shops, gun sellers and farm supplies are equally as important to the vibrancy of the town as the classic South West gift shops and cafes selling cream teas.

EXMOOR NATIONAL PARK

One of England's smallest national parks, Exmoor could lay claim to being the most diverse, bottling all the variety of English countryside in an area little over 20 miles east to west and 12 miles north to south: dramatic sea cliffs to the north; ancient oak-choked river valleys and moorland stretching to the horizon; a skirting of rolling fields and towering hedgerows to the south. It nearly has a mountain – the highest point on Exmoor, Dunkery Beacon, just falls 91 metres short at 519 metres.

You may not have time to explore much of the park on your journey but if this stage has given you a taste for challenging climbs – the sort which are packed full of chevrons on an Ordnance Survey map – take a short yet preposterously punchy ride north of Dulverton to Tarr Steps. It is more of a paddle than a wild swimming paradise in most conditions, but the ancient stone clapper bridge is a great spot to hang out, release your cycling shoes and cool your toes in a moment of freedom for your ever-expanding feet. The eccentrically laid bridge is said to have been constructed by the devil for sunbathing. Adventurous cyclists have been known to ride across it, but if you want to make it to John o' Groats maybe save it for next time rather than risk a dunk into the River Barle.

SLEEP

MARSH BRIDGE COTTAGE

Traditional bed and breakfast located in a restored Victorian gamekeeper's cottage. Thanks to Dulverton's location on the edge of Exmoor National Park many providers can only accommodate guests who are staying for a minimum of two nights, but this is not normally an issue here.
Dulverton, TA22 9QG
T 01398 323 197
www.marshbridgedulverton.co.uk

WINSBERE HOUSE

This homely bed and breakfast is endorsed by the Cyclists' Touring Club and sits a short distance south of Dulverton on the western bank of the River Barle. The only disturbance likely here is owls from the woodland.
64 Battleton, Dulverton, TA22 9HU
T 01398 323 278
www.winsbere.co.uk

WIMBLEBALL CAMPSITE

Spacious pitches, a cafe and fire pits for hire at Wimbleball Lake. The campsite is 6 miles into stage 6, so if you're keen on camping you'll need a bit more pedalling and some provisions from Dulverton.
Wimbleball Lake, Brompton Regis, Dulverton, TA22 9NU
T 01398 371 460
www.swlakestrust.org.uk/wimbleball-campsite

EAT

WOODS

This restaurant uses local produce, some sourced from the owner's farm on Exmoor; the adjoining, welcoming pub has a cosy fire and outdoor courtyard.
4 Bank Square, Dulverton, TA22 9BU
T 01398 324 007
www.woodsdulverton.co.uk

SUPPLIES

On Fore Street in Dulverton you will find a small **Co-op Food** supermarket with supplies for the next stage of your journey.

STAGE 5 CHULMLEIGH TO DULVERTON *157 / 1000 MILES*　　　CHALLENGING

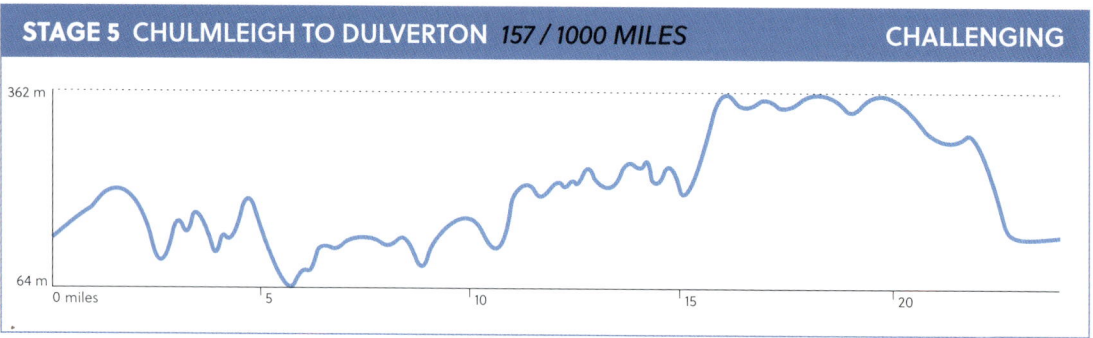

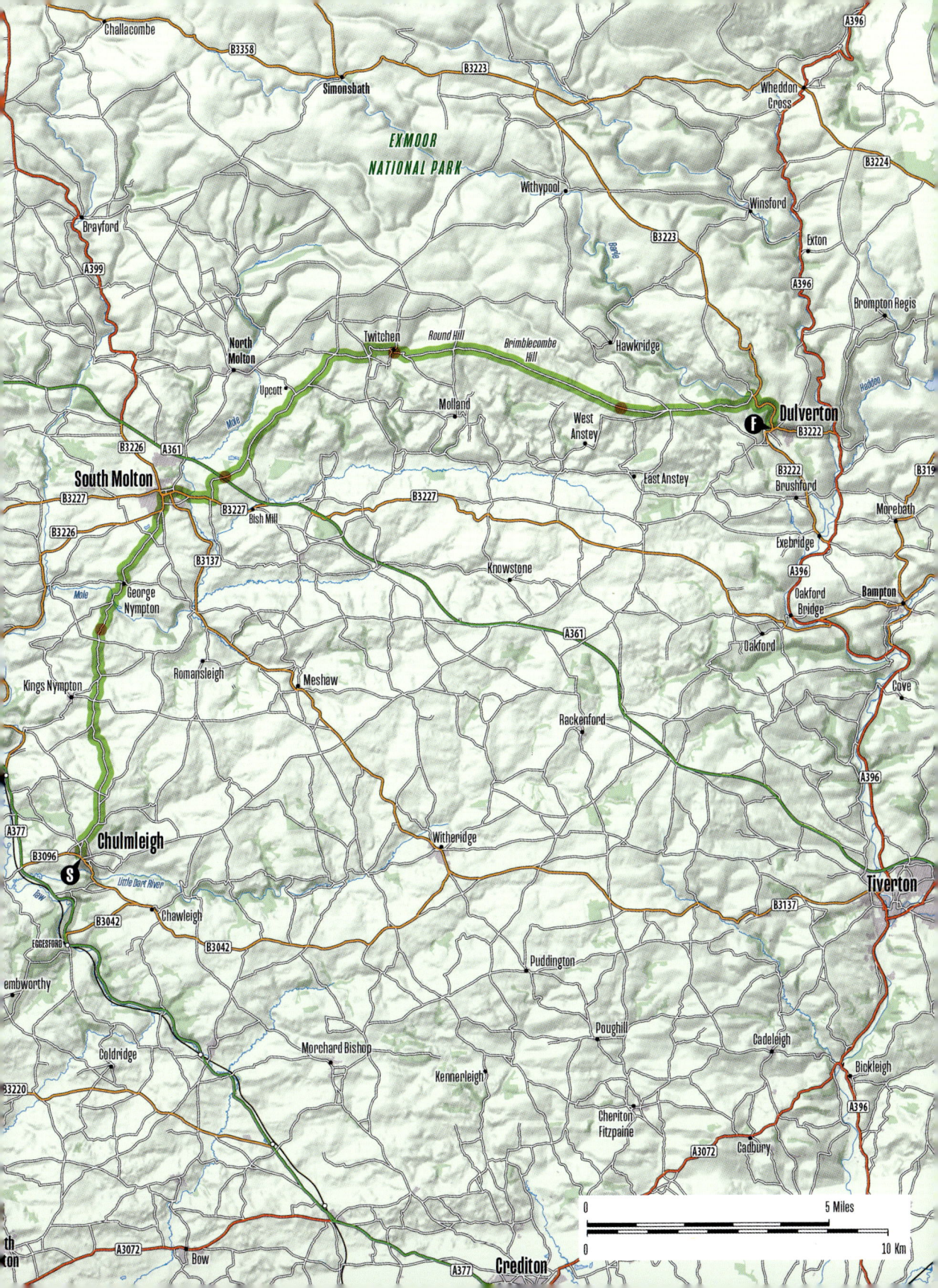

SOMERSET

STAGE 6

51 miles / 81km
750 metres ascent

DULVERTON TO GLASTONBURY

Streams, lakes and wetlands abound as you ride through the wooded Brendon Hills, once plundered for their iron ore. Reed beds rustle in the breeze as the mythical and mysterious Glastonbury Tor lures you on to the ancient 'Isle of Avalon', rising from the mists above the Somerset Levels.

A stage of two distinct halves – beginning with hills and ending with flat roads – this stage offers many surprises along the way. Slogging uphill, the sudden glint of Wimbleball Lake flashes through a gap, then as you rapidly descend you shoot across the bridge in the middle making you feel as if you are pedalling on water. Climbing up into the Brendon Hills you reach a height of over 400 metres; surprisingly this is the highest point in the route until stage 16 in the fells of Northern England. Even at the top of the hills their height won't feel apparent, but the undulating nature of the first part of the stage provides a clear contrast with the languid flatness of the Somerset Levels. The delightfully named Burrow Mump, as intriguing in appearance as Glastonbury Tor, appears first but it is the Tor itself which accompanies you across the Levels for most of the final part of the ride. While this is the longest single stage of the whole journey, the very flat final half ensures you arrive fresh into Glastonbury.

DULVERTON TO ELWORTHY

Leaving Dulverton head uphill, along the High Street, following the B3222 as it curves to the right at the top. A short, fast descent follows but don't let the kick up to the T-junction with the A396 take you by surprise. Turn right at the T-junction then almost immediately take a left fork on to a lovely lane, signposted *Brompton Regis*.

The road climbs for 2 miles to Beech Tree Cross. Turn right here then after around 500 metres turn right down

an unmarked lane. A green grass strip replaces the white line from earlier; this is as rural as you can find. Continue straight ahead at the give way at Mill Cross; as you gain height Wimbleball Lake comes into view and you rush downwards to cross the water. From the bridge it is yet another climb up. Turn left at the Robbery Gate junction. The dual radio station antennae on your right mark the highest point of your ride in the South West. Although the landscape feels modest compared to the open expanses of Exmoor, the road here actually reaches over 400 metres, a feeling that may go unnoticed as you ride hidden between the hedgerows.

On your right you will pass the Ralegh's Cross Inn, which was built in the 1850s to serve the miners in the area. Ralegh's Cross itself is a medieval stone cross named after the Ralegh family, and a landmark for travellers navigating the Brendon Ridgeway. As you approach the crest of the final hill, a magnificent vista opens up all around you as you begin to freewheel off the ridge to reach a crossroads. Continue straight ahead, with the road rising a little before descending more gradually.

ELWORTHY TO CREECH ST MICHAEL

Here at the foot of the Brendon Hills the farmland opens up, the distinctive deep red soil indicating the presence of iron oxide. The descent delivers you to a T-junction with the A358. Turn right for a short stretch before turning left into Bishops Lydeard. In front of a terraced

row of cottages in the centre turn left. Pick up the right turn 1 mile later signed to *Kingston*, and head back into the lanes beneath overhanging beech trees.

A little dog-leg at Mill Cross leads you to the edge of the village of Upper Cheedon. Along this road you will pass the entrance to Hestercombe; the elaborate formal gardens here were designed by Sir Edwin Lutyens, with a planting scheme designed by Gertrude Jekyll. At the sign welcoming you to *Cheddon Fitzpaine* turn left. One mile later, carry straight on by turning off the main route following the sign to *West Monkton* then after 800 metres turn right at a T-junction. On reaching a main road continue straight across, which is a through route for bicycles only. You emerge on the A38 close to a roundabout. Turn left at the roundabout; a cycle path is available. At a second roundabout, which handles traffic flowing in from the nearby M5 motorway, turn left (signposted *Creech St Michael*).

Passing over the M5 marks your entrance into the second, and flatter, half of this stage. Shortly after the M5, in Creech St Michael, you cross a canal, railway and two river channels. Immediately after crossing the second river channel, turn left on to Ham Road (signposted *Ham*) and then 800 metres later turn left on to White Street.

CREECH ST MICHAEL TO ASHCOTT

A series of right-angled turns trace the edges of the fields. Deep, water-filled drainage ditches alongside the road indicate you are now in a carefully managed wetland area. This unique, flat landscape is made by a complex network of rhynes and ditches.

Follow signs for *North Curry* and *Stoke St Gregory*. North Curry is pretty and well preserved; over 60 buildings in this small village are listed. You'll find a memorial to Queen Victoria in the middle of a junction; when you see this turn left. Continue on to Meare Green where you will find the Wetland and Willow Centre. The Coate family have been growing willow here since 1819; it's a great place to stop for a coffee and to discover more about this area.

Shortly after the Wetland and Willow Centre turn left following the sign for *Athelney*. A long drainage ditch accompanies the road on the left until you meet a T-junction; turn left here and then turn right on the A361 towards *Glastonbury*. The road takes a generous curve around the edge of Burrow Mump – a perfectly round hillock, rising above the Somerset Levels and topped with the ruins of St Michael's church. It's a smaller, possibly more peaceful and intimate, version of Glastonbury Tor. Following Burrow Mump is the village of Othery, which describes itself as 'an island in the Levels'.

With the flat roads it is not gradients but wind that can make a difference to your headway; the numerous right-angled turns around the field edges can often mean that you catch a strong side wind on a breezy day. Shortly after the village of Greinton, turn left up Pedwell Hill (where you start to climb), then turn right on to Pedwell Lane. Turn left on to the A39 then immediately turn right into the centre of Ashcott. At a T-junction with Whitley Lane at the end of Ashcott turn right.

ASHCOTT TO GLASTONBURY

After Ashcott you'll see your first glimpses of Glastonbury Tor, as the road picks its way between drainage ditches and wetland fields following Sustrans National Route 3. Turn right on to Back River Drove (leaving the Sustrans route) and turn left on to Porchestall Drove to eventually emerge in an industrial estate. Use the cycle path to escape the dead end of the estate and safely cross the A39. Continue straight ahead on Benedict Street with a line of terraced houses to your left and follow it to the end of the stage at the T-junction by the market cross, just in front of Glastonbury Abbey.

GLASTONBURY

Glastonbury is perhaps most widely known for hosting one of the most eclectic arts and music festivals in the world. The Glastonbury Festival is one of the few large festivals that hasn't totally capitulated to commercialism and is held most years on nearby Worthy Farm at the end of June. Even without the festival, the town is a lively, creative and spiritually diverse place to visit, with plenty of joss-stick-filled shops and interesting characters. If staying in Glastonbury, then the best time to visit Glastonbury Tor is very early in the morning so you can see the sun rise over the Somerset Levels. Even if continuing straight into the next stage it is worth a visit to the Red or White springs. Two different springs, one touched red with iron, the other white with calcites, rise within a few feet of each other from the caverns beneath Glastonbury Tor. These are believed to have healing powers.

SLEEP

THE CROWN
Completely refurbished in 2020, the building was previously a less than salubrious backpackers' hostel but now offers eight well-appointed rooms in the heart of the town overlooking the Cenotaph.
4 Market Place, Glastonbury, BA6 9HD
T 01458 837 870
www.crownglastonbury.co.uk

GEORGE & PILGRIMS INN
Not the most modern rooms, but it claims to be the oldest purpose-built pub in South West England so expect plenty of old beams. A long stone's throw from Glastonbury Abbey.
1 High Street, Glastonbury, BA6 9DP
T 01458 831 146
www.redcatpubcompany.com/inns/somerset/george-pilgrims

YHA STREET
Leave the route by turning right on to the A39 just before Ashcott to find the oldest YHA hostel still in operation today having opened in 1931. On the edge of the town of Street, the recently refurbished Swiss-style chalet also has camping pods and allows tents to be pitched in the grounds.
Ivythorn Hill, Street, BA16 0TZ
T 03453 719 143
www.yha.org.uk/hostel/yha-street

EAT

THE WHO'D A THOUGHT IT
You'll find classic pub food including Somerset sausages against a backdrop of antique memorabilia in this eighteenth-century inn. Also has accommodation.
17 Northload Street, Glastonbury, BA6 9JJ
T 01458 834 460
www.whodathoughtit.co.uk

SUPPLIES

Award-winning, old-school bakers **Burns the Bread** on the High Street in Glastonbury have sandwiches, savouries and cakes to fuel you on the open road. **Earthfare**, an eco-friendly grocer, is also on the High Street and **Morrisons** is the closest supermarket to the town centre.

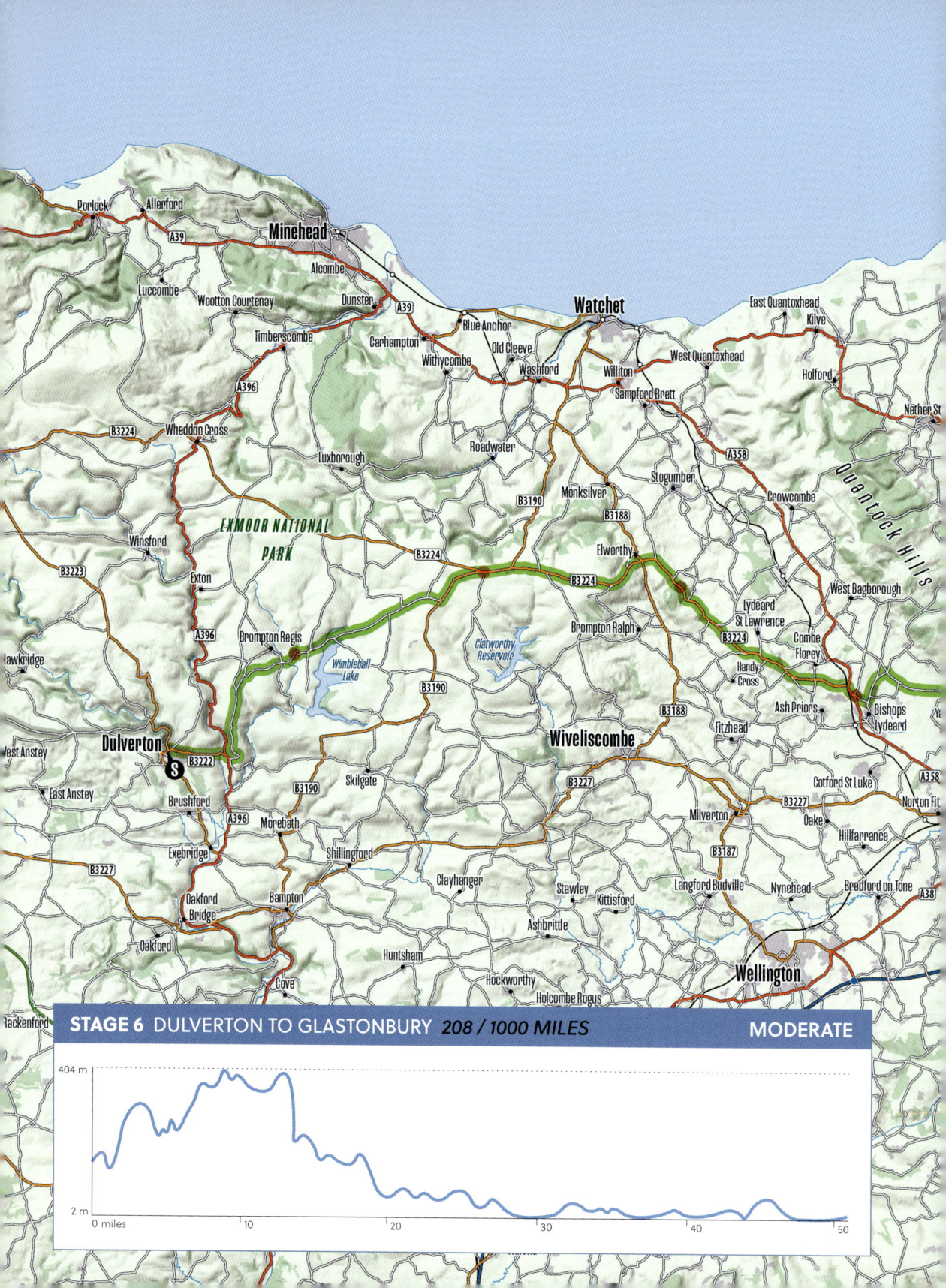

STAGE 6 DULVERTON TO GLASTONBURY *208 / 1000 MILES*   MODERATE

STAGE 7

27 miles / 44km
510 metres ascent

GLASTONBURY TO CHEW STOKE

Your legs will clearly tell you of the geological changes beneath your wheels as you transition from the low-lying wetlands of the Somerset Levels to the heights of the Mendip Hills. From the sublime grandeur of medieval Wells Cathedral to the rugged natural sculpture of Cheddar Gorge's limestone formation, this stage offers impressive views.

Starting with the flattest, straightest road imaginable and finishing with a twisting ascent up through the narrow slot of a gorge, Cheddar provides the first 'real' climb of the trip, one that will keep you working hard for a significant amount of time, but its towering rock walls make for a truly spectacular experience. Instead of the leg-burning roller-coaster of steep sharp undulations in Devon and Cornwall, this stage has a more sustained peak and trough, allowing you to find your rhythm. Despite the climb, this stage should feel a little easier than those preceding it as a real climb brings the first 'real' descent. Flying down towards Chew Valley Lake you will be grateful to gravity and Cheddar Gorge for the easy momentum that carries you virtually all the way to Chew Stoke.

GLASTONBURY TO WELLS

Facing the Town Hall and Abbey follow the High Street to your left, passing the Market Cross and the many eclectic shops. When you reach the end of the High Street turn left, heading out of town, towards *Wells*. Wells Road merges with the A39 at a roundabout on the edge of the town; a short section of cycle path runs along the right-hand side of the road to Wells. After 800 metres of cycle path turn right, to join one of the signature straight roads of the area.

Long Drove is a 2-mile, arrow-straight road; it is lined by a rhyne or drainage ditch on one side. The fields you cycle through are absolutely pan-flat; the light glinting

on the surface water and ditches gives the landscape a surreal luminosity. At the end of this straight road, turn left; this takes you between farms as you begin to climb. Hedges outline the zigzags of the road and after the miles of riding on the Levels the climb, although gentle, is enough to remind your lungs how to breathe deeply. Continue straight over at a slightly staggered crossroads.

Down the other side of the hill keep your eyes peeled for a right-hand turn, indicated by a blue sign for Sustrans National Route 3. Shortly after the turning you will catch your first glimpse of Wells Cathedral. At the T-junction turn left then look out for the blue Sustrans sign for *Wells* that takes you through an underpass under the A371 on the right. Follow the blue signs for *Wells* through the woods on a cycle path set back from the road, keeping an eye out for views of the Mendip Hills. The cycle path then runs right alongside the main road. At a large roundabout turn right on to Priory Road heading into the city centre.

WELLS TO WOOKEY HOLE

The LEJOG1000 route follows a principal road round a square left bend; to detour into the city centre and visit the Cathedral follow the *Light traffic only* sign and walk towards the High Street. Don't be put off by the word 'city'; Wells is no bigger than most market towns and is England's smallest city.

Twelfth-century Wells Cathedral is a masterpiece worth visiting; its west front contains one of the largest

galleries of medieval sculptures in the world. Its warm, yellow-toned stone turns golden in evening light and its majestic grandeur casts a calming feel to all those around. Vicars' Close, built in the fourteenth century, is believed to be the oldest continuously inhabited street in Europe.

Retrace your steps to rejoin the route on Princess Road, continuing to make use of the blue Sustrans signs as they lead you through a dead-end street to go straight over the main road at a light-controlled crossing and on to another residential road. Continue to follow the blue Sustrans signs as the houses soon give way to rural scenes and the road begins to climb. Wookey Hole Caves are full of ornate stalagmites and stalactites, but since becoming popular at the beginning of the twentieth century it has moved very much to the tacky end of the tourism spectrum! The caves and their history are still fascinating and the vintage penny arcade a kitsch novelty, but (unless cycling with children) you will probably want to give the plastic dinosaur park a swerve.

WOOKEY HOLE TO CHEDDAR

From the end of Wookey Hole High Street the road picks up a more rural feel again as you head in the direction of Cheddar. Around 500 metres after leaving Wookey Hole fork left, then rejoin the main Wells to Cheddar road

(A371) by turning right at the village of Easton. During 3 miles on the A371 you pass through the villages of Westbury-sub-Mendip, Rodney Stoke and Draycott.

Nearly every town and village we visit on this journey has some sort of war memorial; however, Rodney Stoke's sign proclaims it to be a 'Thankful Village', meaning it is one of only 53 parishes in England and Wales that welcomed home every one of their soldiers who served in World War I. It is a sobering thought. Nowhere in Scotland was so lucky and only 14 parishes are 'doubly lucky', losing no one in either of the world wars.

Stop at Warren's Farm Shop in Draycott for picnic supplies and the freshest local strawberries before taking a right fork along School Lane, just before the road narrows. If your day isn't under too much time pressure there is an excellent rustic cider barn just a little bit further along the main road, or buy a bottle for later – but you'll have to carry it up Cheddar Gorge!

CHEDDAR TO CHEW STOKE

In the town of Cheddar which guards the entrance to the famous gorge, turn right at a T-junction. Cheddar Gorge is liberally signposted with brown tourist information signs and once you are on Cliff Road, within the gorge, there really is nowhere else to go! At the bottom of the gorge there are some touristy shops, but The Original

Cheddar Cheese Company shop is definitely worth a look and a nibble if you are a cheese fan. After the shops and car parking the road gets steeper and scenery more wild, but after one steep and nasty corner the gradient eases off and you can enjoy the scenery more. The steeper the road and the further you get from Costa Coffee, the fewer people you see.

As you emerge from the top of the gorge it can feel a relief to be away from the claustrophobic pressure of the towering rock. After just over 3 miles of climbing from Cheddar, take the road forking off to the left and be rewarded with a gentler gradient and views of the Mendips. An occasional limestone outcrop rears up out of the green fields. At Cheddar Cross, follow a white fingerpost straight ahead towards *West Harptree*; the road begins to rise steadily again enabling you to ride along the flat tops of the Mendips.

Around 1 mile after Cheddar Cross at the next crossroads turn right, following the blue Sustrans signs. Continue to follow the blue signs taking a left turn downhill in the direction of *West Harptree*; this is the start of a long descent but be ready to brake as you are suddenly interrupted by the crossing of a busy A road. The road seemingly drops away in a short, very steep 12 per cent descent, however there are outstanding views of Chew Valley Lake on offer. The road passes

Herons Green Bay, with the cycle path running adjacent to the lake. It's often lively with birds along the shore, not in the least bothered by the road. The stage finishes at the first crossroads as you arrive in Chew Stoke.

CHEDDAR GORGE
Cheddar Gorge is England's largest canyon at 120 metres deep and 3 miles long. It was formed over a million years ago during a colder period when the meltwater coursed down the rock, cutting a deep groove through the limestone. Its caves have been offering shelter and fascination since prehistoric times. Cheddar Man, Britain's oldest complete human skeleton, was found here as well as much older Palaeolithic remains.

Tourism arrived in the caves with the railway in 1869; they soon became a popular attraction. The railway was known as the Strawberry Line, because it passed close by the many strawberry-growing fields in the largely south-west facing slopes on the Cheddar side of the valley. 'Strawberry Special' trains ferried the fruit by rail to all parts of the country, until the line was axed in the 1960s. The pub in Draycott is still known as The Strawberry Special. Don't leave Cheddar without enjoying both the cheese and the strawberries!

SLEEP

ORCHARD HOUSE
A warm, friendly welcome awaits you at Orchard House. Choose from bed and breakfast or self-catered accommodation – we recommend the breakfasts as the fresh home cooking uses produce from local growers and the garden.
Bristol Road, Chew Stoke, BS40 8UB
T 01275 333 143
www.orchardhouse-chewstoke.co.uk

THE BEAR & SWAN
Traditional eighteenth-century pub offering a luxurious country retreat. High-quality evening menu and a breakfast to look forward to.
13 South Parade, Chew Magna, BS40 8PR
T 01275 331 100
www.ohhpubs.co.uk

WALNUT TREE QUIET CAMPING
Beautiful countryside camping: there are no set pitches so the closest to wild camping you can get while still having a compost loo and hot shower. Campfires welcome. Also has shepherd's huts.
Walnut Tree Farm, The Street, Regil, BS40 8BD
T 01275 472 207
www.walnuttreeshepherdshuts.co.uk

EAT

THE STOKE INN
Good quality British-style pub food (and pizza) made from locally sourced ingredients. Sit in the bar and watch the food being prepared or get involved with some traditional pub games.
Bristol Road, Chew Stoke, BS40 8XE
T 01275 332 120
www.thestokeinn.co.uk

SUPPLIES
The nearest shop is the **Co-op Food** in Chew Magna. Stage 8 has more shops.

BIKE

BIKE CITY
Experienced mechanics just off the High Street in Wells. Closed Sunday and Monday.
8 Queen Street, Wells, BA5 2DP
T 01749 670 002
www.bikecity.biz

CHEDDAR BIKES
The heart of cycling in Cheddar Gorge. Workshop and spares.
Lower North Street, Cheddar, BS27 3HA
T 07864 329 840
www.cheddarbikes.co.uk

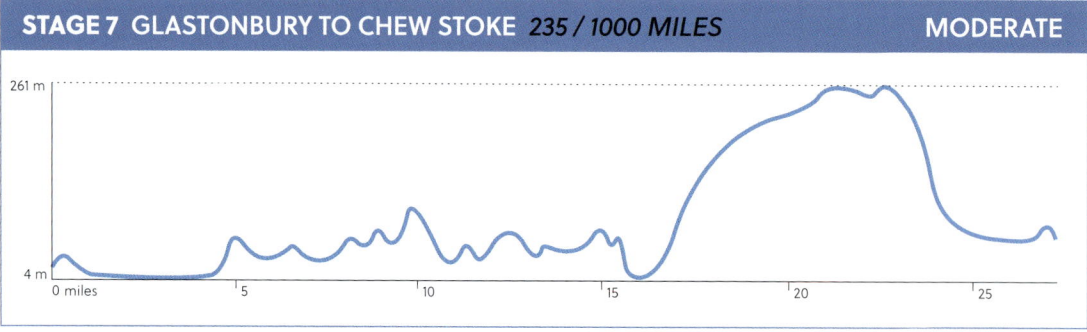

STAGE 7 GLASTONBURY TO CHEW STOKE *235 / 1000 MILES* **MODERATE**

WALES

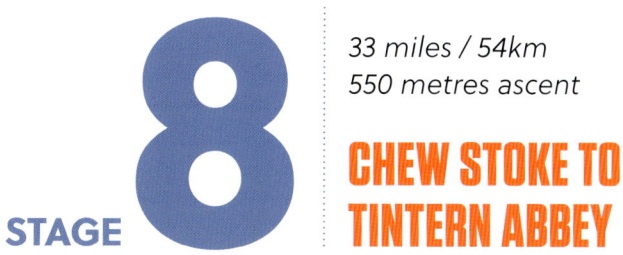

STAGE 8

33 miles / 54km
550 metres ascent

CHEW STOKE TO TINTERN ABBEY

Bristol is one of England's most underrated and bypassed cities. It is elegantly Georgian, but also artistic, lively and independent in outlook. Its innovative suspension bridge was a wonder of its day, and the open parkland of the Downs allows space for leisure. Crossing the River Severn into Wales takes you to the ancient castle of Chepstow, followed by a gentle saunter down to the River Wye to the romantic ruins of Tintern Abbey.

On a journey like Land's End to John o' Groats you really begin to appreciate beautifully engineered bridges and the safer, direct routes they provide for travellers. The Clifton Suspension Bridge is the first significant historic bridge of the industrial age the route crosses. It is swiftly followed by the giant Severn Bridge which straddles the River Severn allowing easy access between England and Wales. Despite passing through the city of Bristol, this section remains remarkably green and pleasant by opting to cross the parkland of Ashton Court and explore the Downs to the west of Bristol itself before heading into Wales. While slightly more downhill than uphill, the full reward doesn't come until you are cruising alongside the River Wye, a river that will become your constant companion for the next two stages.

CHEW STOKE TO LONG ASHTON

To leave Chew Stoke fork left on to Pilgrim's Way, signposted *St Andrews Church*. Splash through the ford; if the river is high there is a pretty footbridge. Just past a church turn left on to Scot Lane, part of the Avon Cycleway, and begin to climb between a few small cottages.

Despite only being a few miles from Bristol, birds sing in the hedgerows and the pungent aroma of a farmyard suggests no trace of the busy city just over the ridge. At the top of Scot Lane, a sharp left turn at a T-junction

encourages you steeply upward. In this network of narrow hilly lanes, bound by thick green hedges, it is easy to miss turns. A right-hand turn close to the top is marked by a blue Sustrans sign tucked deep inside the verdant hedgerow.

Follow the blue Sustrans signs until, instead of turning left, you carry straight ahead following the brown sign to *The Crown Inn* as the road rises up, before descending into Winford. Turn left at a T-junction with the B3130 to cycle through the village. This is a sharply undulating landscape despite being one of the flatter routes into Bristol.

Cross the A38 and follow the blue Sustrans sign; Hobbs Lane is marked as a dead end but cyclists can get through. It descends steeply to a gate at the bottom where the lane curves to the left. When you emerge amongst some residential houses, look for the blue signs and again cross the B3130 to pick up another minor road, Wildcountry Lane.

Sounds of the surrounding busy roads form a mild buzzing background track to your cycling. A busy A road passes beneath you as you cross a bridge, followed by a narrow bridge over a railway, until you arrive at Weston Road and turn right towards Long Ashton. Amongst the shops there is a distinctive row of almshouses. Endowed by Lady Emily Smyth of Ashton Court in 1902, over the front you can just make out the motto: 'Rest after toil, peace after stormy seas, doth greatly please'.

LONG ASHTON TO CLIFTON SUSPENSION BRIDGE

Continue through Long Ashton and straight across the road through the elaborate gates of Ashton Court; follow the road uphill. Take a left fork almost back on yourself at a junction. The route climbs up in a big loop past the fallow deer enclosure on the left to the top of a rise offering your first full view of Bristol. A straight, tree-lined road leads to the exit of the park, past Clifton Lodge and another ornate gate.

Emerging through the gate follow the blue cycle signs and pedestrian island to cross straight over the main road to the road diagonally opposite, a residential street of large houses which descends to Clifton Suspension Bridge. Bikes are free to travel across the bridge; use the cycle path to avoid the toll barrier. Take some time to dismount and look at the views towards Bristol on your right and the River Avon below.

The Clifton Suspension Bridge was designed and built by Isambard Kingdom Brunel. Aged just 24, it was his first major project, and he won the opportunity to do it through a design competition. He is credited with referring to the bridge as 'my first child, my darling'. Its presence across the tidal channel of the Avon Gorge was the idea of wine merchant William Vick, who left the money to the Society of Merchant Venturers to pay for a stone, toll-free bridge across the gorge. At the time of his gift the technology to make a suspension bridge did not yet exist, but he had faith in the ingenuity and rapid development of engineering. While the idea was sparked in 1754, the bridge was not fully complete until 1864.

CLIFTON SUSPENSION BRIDGE TO EASTER COMPTON

During the eighteenth and nineteenth centuries, wealthy Bristol merchants flocked to Clifton, transforming it into an elegant suburb of impressive Georgian buildings with expansive views across Bristol. From the suspension bridge turn left on to Observatory Road then left on to Clifton Down. Clifton Down and Durdham Down were once used for recreation by the wealthy of Clifton. Turn right then immediately turn left on to Ladies Mile, the dead straight avenue through the centre of the Downs once used for exercise on horseback or by carriage.

At the end of Ladies Mile at a T-junction you will see a huge 1950s water tower and a welcoming cafe, housed rather unusually in the former public toilets. Turn left here and pick the next right, Saville Road, to trace the edge of this green space. From here the route carefully picks its way through the residential areas and small villages that have merged into the wider Bristol conurbation. At the next crossroads turn left along Parry's Lane and at the junction left again. A cycle lane offers a little bit of extra space from traffic on this residential road.

Continue along Parry's Lane until a crossroads with Reedley Road where you turn right. Follow this pleasantly wide residential street until you meet a T-junction with Stoke Lane where the route turns right. At the traffic-light-controlled crossroads continue straight ahead, remaining on Stoke Lane.

Approaching a roundabout with a war memorial in the middle go straight ahead. Ride between the shops, pubs and restaurants then turn left on to Henbury Road. At the traffic-light-controlled crossroads continue

straight ahead, remaining on Henbury Road. Gradually the residential areas spread out; a high wall to your left contains the grounds of the Blaise Castle Estate. Turn right at a mini-roundabout along Station Road, followed by a left turn at the next mini-roundabout along Avonmouth Way. Cross over the railway and then the M5. Shortly after the motorway turn right along Berwick Lane. Follow Berwick Lane and look out for blue cycling signs to the *Severn Bridge*. At the next T-junction turn left on to the B4055.

EASTER COMPTON TO SEVERN BRIDGE

After the village of Easter Compton fork right to Pilning railway station. Pass underneath the railway line before forking left (signposted *Pilning*). Around 1 mile later turn right towards *Northwick*; keep following signposts to the village to cross the M4 motorway. When you reach the busy A403 carrying traffic to the Severn Bridge on leaving Northwick, follow the cycle path to your right then cross straight over the road following the sign to *Old Passage*. After 1 mile with some spectacular views of the Severn Bridge turn left (following blue Sustrans signs) on to the bridge.

SEVERN BRIDGE TO CHEPSTOW/CAS-GWENT

The Severn is the longest river in the UK and has the second largest tidal range in the world. The Severn bore is a wave of up to 2 metres in height created by the rising tide combined with the funnel shape of the river. The wave it creates can reach speeds of up to 16 kilometres per hour, making it an irresistible challenge to surfers and paddleboarders.

Riding across the bridge is a bracing experience – as a mere cyclist you feel insignificant compared to the biting southwesterly wind, and the reverberations of the bridge give you a feeling of vulnerability that vehicle drivers do not experience. With an expansive vista to the estuary and over the other bridge across the Severn there is plenty to distract you from the height and movement of the bridge! At the end of the bridge you drop down off the raised section and follow the cycle path sign through an underpass, creatively decorated with graffiti, welcoming you to Chepstow and Wales.

The cycle path brings you into the back of a housing estate; turn left at a T-junction then exit the roundabout in the direction of *Bulwark*. Continue straight ahead over three roundabouts until you reach a T-junction

with the A48. Turn right, heading downhill towards Chepstow. Soon afterwards, turn left by a distinctively painted pink house following the signposts for the *Town centre*; this leads to the stone arched gateway of the original fortified walls.

CHEPSTOW/CAS-GWENT TO TINTERN ABBEY

Chepstow – which means 'marketplace' in Old English, or Cas-Gwent 'castle of Gwent' in Welsh – has always been a place of significance for both protection and trade. Chepstow Castle was commissioned by William the Conqueror just a year after the Battle of Hastings, making it the oldest surviving post-Roman castle in Britain. The fortifications and building work continued with Chepstow Port Wall, built in the thirteenth century.

To leave Chepstow turn left on to Welsh Street, immediately in front of the stone arched gateway that leads to the centre of town. From here it is uphill to a roundabout; turn right on to the A466 following the signpost for *Tintern*. Initially a straight, wide and modern-feeling road, it narrows and begins to imitate the curves of the River Wye after the village of St Arvans.

Thick woodlands of beech, oak and hazel line the roadside, frequently obscuring any chance of a snatched view of the river below. From here to Tintern the road is predominantly downhill, with just an occasional section of uphill to break your meandering flow. Arriving in Tintern you will have enough momentum to freewheel gracefully to the front of the dramatic ruins of Tintern Abbey where the stage is completed.

TINTERN ABBEY

Tintern Abbey was founded in 1131 by Cistercian monks; it was initially a timber building but as their prestige and patronage from wealthy landowners grew so did their architectural ambitions. The new abbey was begun in 1269 and became a masterpiece of Gothic architecture. But Henry VIII's English Reformation led to the dissolution of the monastery, and it slowly descended into a majestic ruin.

In the eighteenth century several movements stirred at once. Organised tourism in the Wye Valley began to grow and artists and writers began to celebrate the picturesque and romantic. William Wordsworth's 1798 poem, *Lines Composed a Few Miles above Tintern Abbey*, added to the already burgeoning tourist traffic to the area. While not as busy as it was in its heyday of tourism, it has remained an iconic site for visitors ever since.

SLEEP

THE WILD HARE
Elegant rooms in a lovely pub serving delicious evening meals and hearty breakfasts. Each room is individually decorated and promises a sumptuous stay and good night's sleep.
Main Road, Tintern, NP16 6SF
T 01291 689 205
www.thewildharetintern.co.uk

PARVA FARMHOUSE
Enjoy a night's rest in a former seventeenth-century farmhouse, eat in the Michelin-Guide-listed restaurant and wake up to a delightful view over the river or garden. Secure bike storage available.
Tintern, NP16 6SQ
T 01291 689 411
www.parvafarmhouse.co.uk

BEECHES FARM CAMPSITE
Found on the opposite side of the river, this delightful site offers traditional camping on a hilltop with a wonderful view down on to Tintern Abbey. Advance booking required.
Miss Grace's Lane, Tidenham Chase, NP16 7JR
T 07791 540 016
www.beechesfarmcampsite.co.uk

EAT
There are several pubs within sight of Tintern Abbey, including **The Anchor Inn** which has outdoor seating.

THE FILLING STATION CAFE
Much loved by cyclists – it even has its own LEJOG signpost.
Main Road, Tintern, NP16 6SF
T 07770 544 592

SUPPLIES
While you can buy a limitless number of gifts, postcards and knick-knacks, finding basic food supplies in Tintern is harder. Llandogo, a few miles into stage 9, has a convenience store.

BIKE

BLACKBOY HILL CYCLES
Bristol has dozens of bike shops, but this is closest to the LEJOG1000 route and one of Bristol's oldest bike shops.
180 Whiteladies Road, Clifton, Bristol, BS8 2XU
T 01179 731 420
www.black-boy-cycles.co.uk

MUD DOCK
The epicentre of the Bristol cycling scene, located a couple of miles off-route in the heart of Old Bristol just off Queen Square. Great cycle cafe with outdoor terrace and workshop.
40 The Grove, Bristol, BS1 4RB
T 01179 292 151
www.mud-dock.co.uk

STAGE 8 CHEW STOKE TO TINTERN ABBEY *268 / 1000 MILES*   MODERATE

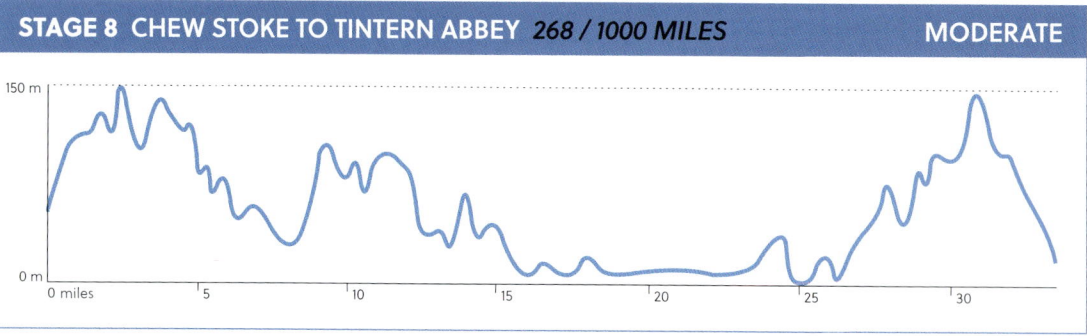

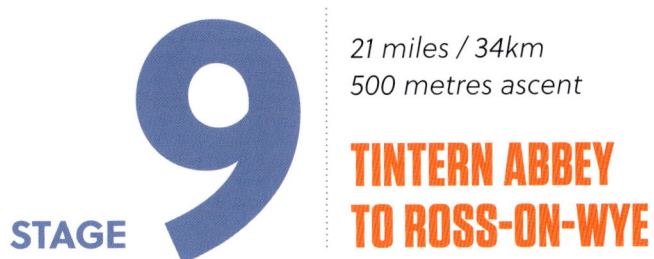

STAGE 9

21 miles / 34km
500 metres ascent

TINTERN ABBEY TO ROSS-ON-WYE

Following the curves of the River Wye through the lush Wye Valley Area of Outstanding Natural Beauty makes for a pleasantly flowing start to the stage. After leaving Wales to return to England, the long climb up to Symonds Yat Rock provides a viewpoint so picturesque it inspired a movement of art and tourism.

The start and end of this stage is passed at river level, interrupted midway by the climb up to Symonds Yat Rock with its stunning view of the great meander bend. For the first 8 miles the road and river travel in parallel; woodland edges rich with bluebells and garlic scent the air in spring. On the opposite riverbank rises a forest of beech, oak, ash and lime. At Symonds Yat Rock, in a spot that has attracted thousands of visitors to pause and absorb the natural scenery, birds of prey float above you, while brightly coloured specks of kayakers paddle the river below. Following the rush of the descent back down to river level, a Norman castle catches the eye before entering the narrow streets that lead to the heart of the market town of Ross-on-Wye.

TINTERN ABBEY TO REDBROOK

Following the curves of the River Wye the route takes you past Parva Farm Vineyard, the oldest commercial vineyard in Wales. It was planted in 1979 with 17 different grape varieties and is believed to be on the site which was used by the Cistercian monks of Tintern Abbey to cultivate vines hundreds of years ago.

Mimicking the curves of the river you can still see evidence of its tidal nature in the mudbanks at the sides. While small and peaceful now, the village of Llandogo was once a busy loading point for the wide, flat-bottomed 'trows' that carried goods from the riverside villages along the Wye to the markets of Bristol,

but the arrival of trains reduced the need for boats on this stretch of the river.

Bigsweir Bridge, with its distinctive symmetrical white railings, carries you to the other side of the Wye and into England. In the woodland to the left a carpet of bluebells emerges in early spring, the floral scent competing with sharpness of wild garlic. It's not until the village of Redbrook, 8 miles into the stage, that the route turns right away from the river. It is at this point that you meet the Welsh–English border again. For around 900 metres you cross back into Wales before re-entering England and the county of Gloucestershire.

REDBROOK TO SYMONDS YAT

Once you leave the River Wye behind a gradual and continuous climb begins. Are you riding this section at night? If so, don't read the rest of this paragraph. On your right you will pass Swanpool Wood; here you may find the apparition of a mother cradling her child, who rise from the waters of Swan Pool and then vanish. If that doesn't sound scary enough, the ghost of a dog, which is sometimes said to be headless, comes down from one of the old limekilns nearby and walks around the pool.

Watch out for a very easy-to-miss left-hand turn on the outside of a right-hand bend. The gradient begins to steepen and a sweeping series of two hairpin bends touches on a 10 per cent gradient. At the crossroads continue straight over, following the signpost to *Symonds Yat*. Turn right on to the A4136 at the next

junction towards *Gloucester*. Shortly afterwards, turn left (following the signpost to *Symonds Yat*); follow this residential road until you spot a left fork, again signposted to *Symonds Yat*.

SYMONDS YAT TO ROSS-ON-WYE

The entrance to the Symonds Yat Rock car park and viewing spot is fairly unobtrusive, opposite a handful of residential homes. However, it is worth deviating from the route for a few minutes to explore this part of the Wye Valley. From the top of Symonds Yat Rock it is a rush downhill to be reunited with the River Wye, as the road cuts through the middle of a great meander bend. The steep descent begins as soon as the road passes under a footbridge and the gradient only lessens as you enter Herefordshire.

Crossing the river at the northern end of the meander needs some caution as the single-track bridge leaves little space for a car and a bike to pass. The narrow lane continues until you reach a T-junction where the right-hand turn takes you towards *Ross-on-Wye*. The next crossing of the Wye is at Kerne Bridge; this is a popular spot for swimmers and kayakers, as it is an easy entry point into the river and many tours start or finish their paddling here.

Immediately after the bridge turn left on to the B4234 at a T-junction towards *Ross-on-Wye*. You can catch a glimpse of Goodrich Castle; one of the best-preserved Norman castles in the country, it was originally built to control a key access point between Monmouthshire and Ross-on-Wye. As the road bends to the right in front of the church in Walford, turn left on to a minor road for a more pleasant ride into Ross-on-Wye. After around 900 metres turn right down an unmarked lane; high hedges hide bright green fields and tops of greenhouses peer out, producing vegetables on the fertile farmland. Turn left then right on a housing estate on the edge of Ross-on-Wye as buildings begin to cram out the fields.

Turn left on to the B4234 into Ross-on-Wye, descending slightly down old narrow streets towards the well-preserved Market House.

ROSS-ON-WYE

The Wye Valley is an Area of Outstanding Natural Beauty and Ross-on-Wye is its economic centre. One of the oldest buildings in Ross-on-Wye, the Market House, was built between 1650 and 1654 replacing the older, probably wooden, Booth Hall. It has its origins in the twelfth century when King Stephen granted the right to hold a market in the area; this stimulated the economy and encouraged trade. Markets are still held here on Thursdays and Saturdays; the shop above the Market House sells products made by local craftspeople and artisans, seamlessly carrying on the heritage of the town.

BIRTH OF TOURISM

Ross-on-Wye has resonance for guidebook writers as it is here the first real tourism guide was created. William Gilpin was a pioneer of organised tourism; in 1770 he took a boat trip along the River Wye and he wrote *Observations of the River Wye*, the first ever British tourist guide. Gilpin went on to publish guidebooks to picturesque destinations such as the Lake District and encouraged tourists to seek out specific vantage points from which to view pleasing scenery. His writings influenced the popularity of English landscape painting and inspired the Romantic poets, creating a movement which became known as 'the picturesque'.

Visit the vantage spots he recommended today, and you will find a throng of tourists vying for the perfect Instagram shot. The method of capturing the scene may have moved on but the principles of viewing, framing and controlling the landscape would be familiar to the painters of the late eighteenth century.

SLEEP

KING'S HEAD HOTEL
This fourteenth-century hotel retains many of its old oak
beams and an original fireplace. Make sure to check out the
library – it is stacked full of books and comfy armchairs which
you may struggle to get out of after a day's riding.
8 High Street, Ross-on-Wye, HR9 5HL
T 0800 801 098
www.kingshead.co.uk

ROYAL HOTEL
Four centuries younger than the King's Head and, although
part of the Greene King chain, there is plenty of character.
Many rooms have views of the River Wye and the surrounding
bucolic countryside.
Royal Parade, Ross-on-Wye, HR9 5HZ
T 01989 565 105
www.greeneking-pubs.co.uk/pubs/herefordshire/royal-hotel

ROSS ROWING CLUB CAMPING
Camping at the rowing club which is a popular launch point
for canoe trips. Has toilet access, phone charging lockers and
if you're lucky enough to be in town on a sunny Friday and
Saturday the alfresco club bar may well be open.
Metcalfe Close, Ross-on-Wye, HR9 7DD
www.rossrowingclub.co.uk/camp-here

EAT

No3
Modern European menu and cocktails if you are looking for
a break from beer-battered cod and steak and ale pie pub
menus.
3 Gloucester Road, Ross-on-Wye, HR9 5BU
T 01989 564 997
www.no3rossonwye.com

SUPPLIES

Truffles Delicatessen on the High Street in Ross-on-Wye
does sandwiches and other treats for your picnic. There are
several supermarkets near the town centre.

BIKE

REVOLUTIONS@ROSS ON WYE
Anything and everything you ever need for cycling as long as
you're not here on Sunday when everyone is out riding, and
the shop is closed.
48 Broad Street, Ross-on-Wye, HR9 7DY
T 01989 562 639
www.revolutionsatross.co.uk

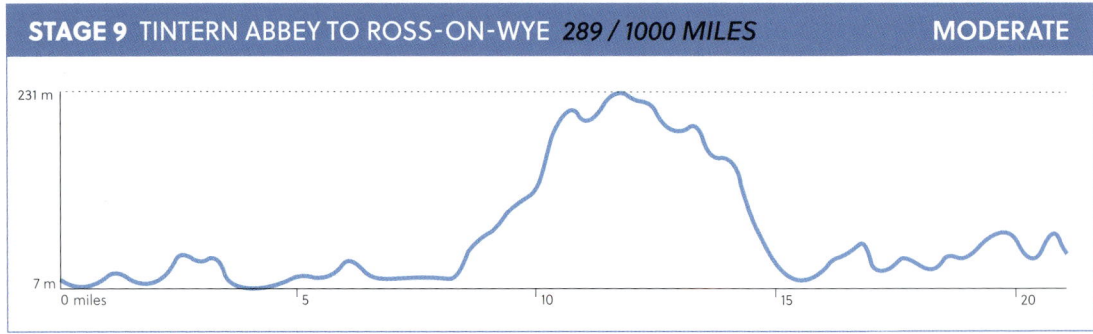

STAGE 9 TINTERN ABBEY TO ROSS-ON-WYE *289 / 1000 MILES*   **MODERATE**

HEREFORDSHIRE & SHROPSHIRE

Ancient orchards, medieval woodland and wild-flower meadows are interspersed with the fertile agricultural land which makes Herefordshire such a foodie heaven. Farm shops and artisan producers close to the land may have proliferated across the country, but here it is a way of life to be deeply rooted in the soil, not a pretension.

The first 10 miles of this stage follow the River Wye, which has provided a near constant backdrop to your pedalling for almost 40 miles. Here its character remains nonchalantly meandering, continuing to provide picturesque cycling with temptingly serene tributaries that invite hot and tired cyclists to relax in pristine wild-swimming spots. Turning away from the river, as you pedal northwards through Herefordshire there is Hampton Court Castle to explore, a wealth of food producers and an artisan cider maker. A mainly agricultural landscape, much of the fine produce of Herefordshire and Shropshire makes its way to the tightly woven streets of Ludlow with its ancient half-timber buildings. Within the heart of the 'old town' streets which radiate out from its castle, market stalls overflow with the bounty of the richly fertile land.

ROSS-ON-WYE TO FOWNHOPE

With your back to the Market House, head down the one-way Broad Street in search of Herefordshire countryside. Carry straight on at two adjacent mini-roundabouts then fork left on to Brampton Street. The road rises slightly crossing a bridge over a dual carriageway on the edge of town. The route descends steeply down a winding lane to the River Wye; take care as the high, earth-banked bramble hedgerows can make visibility difficult.

The lane caresses the banks of the River Wye for just over 1 mile, passing through the hamlet of Hole-in-the-Wall – a short section but beguiling in its picture-postcard, pastoral beauty. Canada geese can often be seen gliding along the water, kingfishers darting and dancing by the riverbanks and the occasional swan sauntering by.

The road climbs and plummets northwards cutting off the corners of the meanders on the Wye; sometimes the river is nearby but a steep drop below you, at other times it is much further away. Just under 7 miles into the stage a viewpoint allows you to peer through the woodland to the gold and green patchwork of the Wye Valley and the Black Mountains and Wales beyond. A 16 per cent downhill delivers you back to river level.

FOWNHOPE TO HAMPTON COURT CASTLE

Continue straight on until you reach the village of Fownhope where you turn left, joining the B4224 which takes you to the smaller village of Mordiford. In Mordiford turn right, signposted *Dormington* and the *Elgar Route*. If you have just missed the turning you will find yourself crossing the River Lugg on a sixteenth-century bridge, one of the oldest in Herefordshire, just before the Lugg's confluence with the Wye. Normally the river is content with flowing through just two of the nine arches, but in times of flood all are called into use. The view from the bridge is said to have influenced composer Edward Elgar's *Elegy for Strings.*

Around 1 mile north of Mordiford turn left then shortly afterwards turn right along Longworth Lane. Continue straight across the A438; after 800 metres turn left then immediately right across the A4103 in Withington, a growing commuter village for the nearby city of Hereford. Further north in Withington turn right then immediately left. Just over 1 mile later at Cross Keys, cross the A465 by turning right then immediately left. Just over 2 miles after Cross Keys turn right to merge on to a more major road signposted *Leominster*, which will deliver you to the village of Bodenham Moor around 2 miles later. In Bodenham Moor turn left on to the A417, signposted *Leominster*.

After soaking up the delights of the quiet lanes of Herefordshire, from Bodenham Moor the 7 miles to the town of Leominster are on more major roads. Just under 2 miles along the A417 you will notice the double-turreted gate guarding the driveway to Hampton Court Castle to your left.

HAMPTON COURT CASTLE TO LUDLOW

The way to Leominster is well signed (turn right on to the A49 then turn left on to the B4361) but if you're lost ask for 'Lemster'. Locals will give you a look if you pronounce it 'Leo-Minster'. Newton Court Cider offers another welcome distraction after Hampton Court Castle. Situated 400 metres after you turn on to the B4361, fresh craft cider is served up from barrels in the tasting room which backs directly onto the orchards. Often overlooked in favour of Ludlow, Leominster is a pleasant market town; it sits on the River Lugg and has a sprinkling of half-timbered houses. Follow the main road to the left at the first roundabout in the town then turn right at the next roundabout. After a set of traffic lights, the road curves to the right with the town centre tucked on the inside of the curve. At a mini-roundabout after passing the town centre take the exit to your left on to the B4361 signed *Richards Castle*.

The remaining 10 miles of the stage are spent ever so gradually climbing with a more pronounced rise just

before Ludlow. The road is wide but most of the traffic now travels on the A49 to the east enabling a real sense of peaceful yet purposeful progress northwards after wandering the lanes of the Wye and Herefordshire. Slightly off route to the left at the small village of Richards Castle, a pre-conquest yet Norman-style crumbling castle is tucked behind the church. After Richards Castle the route enters Shropshire rising for a mile before descending to a stop sign. Turn left following the signpost for *Ludlow*, arriving at the stage end by crossing the River Teme on Ludford Bridge which guards the southern entrance to the town.

LUDLOW

It's worth taking a bit of time to explore the bustling lanes of Ludlow. Continue straight on after crossing the river, rising uphill past Georgian town houses. Enter through Broadgate, which is the only remaining gate of the town's seven medieval gates. Originally famous for its castle, built in a near-impenetrable location atop a river cliff, Ludlow is now perhaps most famous for its independent foodie traders. Ludlow Food Festival, which is held in September, is one of the country's original foodie celebrations and sees over 100 independent traders pitch up from both sides of the border in the castle grounds and beyond. Continue on to Market Street and Castle Square to pick up some delicious food to fuel your day and appreciate the best view of the castle.

If you want some respite from the tourists and tight lanes of the town, Linney Riverside Park offers wild swimming in the river meanders below the town with the majestic castle ruins providing the backdrop.

SLEEP

FEATHERS HOTEL
One of around 500 listed buildings in Ludlow and probably the most iconic. Creaky ancient floorboards, timber beams and crammed full of Jacobean furniture with over 400 years of history it is worth a drink in even if you're not staying. Pick one of the rooms in the older building for the best character if possible.
24–25 Bull Ring, Ludlow, SY8 1AA
T 01584 875 261
www.feathersatludlow.co.uk

THE CHARLTON ARMS
Next to the Ludford Bridge as you ride into the town. Many rooms have river views; if your muscles need a treat check into the Othello Suite with its private terrace and hot tub.
Ludford Bridge, Ludlow, SY8 1PJ
T 01584 872 813
www.thecharltonarms.co.uk

WHITCLIFFE CAMPSITE
Great views overlooking Ludlow are your reward for the short uphill cycle or walk back from town. Slightly sloping site next to Mortimer Forest with access to parks and the river nearby.
Whitcliffe, Ludlow, SY8 2HD
T 01584 872 026
www.northfarmludlow.co.uk/whitcliffe.html

EAT

BISTRO SEVEN OF LUDLOW
A gastronomic destination of national repute. Nearly every establishment in Ludlow understands quality local produce, so standards are high whatever your budget.
7 Corve Street, Ludlow, SY8 1DB
T 01584 877 412
www.bistro7ofludlow.co.uk

DRINK

LUDLOW BREWING CO.
Head here for your après-vélo drink with a tasty bar snack. Open till 5.00 p.m. (6.00 p.m. on a Friday) to the north of the historic centre, it's definitely worth the few extra pedal strokes. They are used to welcoming local cyclists to their carefully crafted beer tap and visitor centre in a beautifully restored railway engine shed.
The Railway Shed, Station Drive, Ludlow, SY8 2PQ
T 01584 873 291
www.theludlowbrewingcompany.co.uk

SUPPLIES
Head to the market or one of the numerous bakeries to stock up for the next stage. There are also a few supermarkets in the town.

BIKE

PHILL PROTHERO CYCLES
Small, no-nonsense store in the heart of Leominster.
The Buttercross, Leominster, HR6 8BN
T 01568 611 222
www.cyclesofleominster.co.uk

EPIC CYCLEWORKS
Town centre bike shop (bike viewings by appointment only) with a workshop.
7–8 Tower Street, Ludlow, SY8 1RL
T 01584 705 034
www.epic-cycles.co.uk

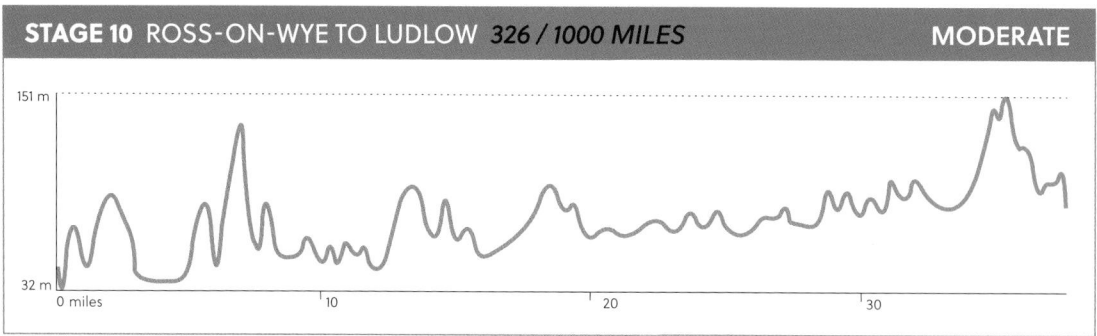

STAGE 10 ROSS-ON-WYE TO LUDLOW *326 / 1000 MILES* — **MODERATE**

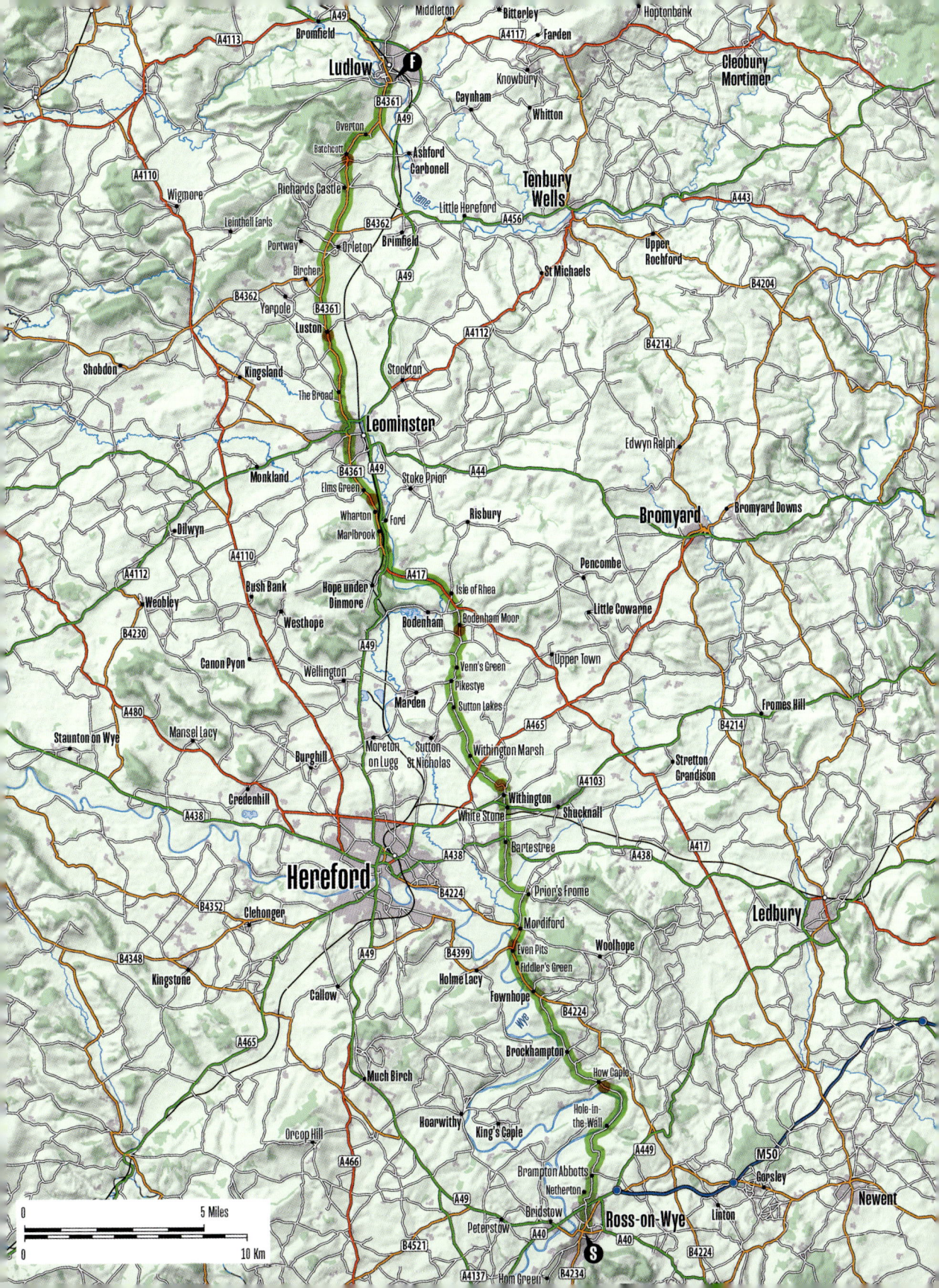

STAGE 11

LUDLOW TO IRONBRIDGE

Shropshire is one of the least populated of England's counties but its landscape is one of the most varied. From dense woods to rolling pasture and unusual limestone escarpments, landscape forms an integral part of the county's unique scenery. One of the greatest features of this stage is the man-made monument of the great Iron Bridge, spanning a deep, narrow gorge.

From a medieval castle to the birthplace of the Industrial Revolution, this stage is a journey through time as much as place. Riding from medieval Ludlow and finishing in industrial Ironbridge, you will encounter many of the unusual features of the Shropshire landscape that have formed the basis for its industry and agriculture. Wenlock Edge, a steep-sided limestone escarpment, has inspired painters and poets with its wild, exposed, blustery ridge, and contrasts with the milder, rolling green fields of pasture elsewhere on this stage. While few and far between, the villages and towns have their own stories – when visiting Much Wenlock, you will discover the connection between this medieval town and the modern Olympics. Finally, flying downhill to the River Severn you will arrive at the Iron Bridge, slotted in its narrow gorge, that gave both name and impetus to the growth of a village.

LUDLOW TO BROADSTONE

Having crossed the medieval Ludford Bridge at the end of stage 10, follow the road as it bends round to the right. As the road curves around the edge of the town centre and the castle, the residential streets are filled with large Georgian properties. North of the town centre take a right fork off the main road by a mustard-coloured timber-framed house. Turn right at a T-junction then, immediately after passing under the railway line, turn left at a mini-roundabout on to

Fishmore Road. By the time you pedal across the bridge over the A49, the town is behind you and only wide open expanses of farmland line the road. Surrounded by rolling hills and woodland views, follow this gentle road to a handful of houses at Lower Hayton and beyond to Peaton. You will notice in your legs, if not with your eyes, that the road is now starting an almost imperceptible drag upwards. In the small hamlet of Peaton, follow the road as it curves round to the left and then turn right, following the signpost to *Tugford*.

Just under 1 mile after Tugford turn left, following the signpost to *Broadstone*. A vista of patchwork farmland continues to open up all around you with the limestone escarpment of Wenlock Edge becoming fleetingly visible in the distance, above the hedgerows. A small bridge over a brook signals your arrival in Broadstone; shortly afterwards turn right at a T-junction on to the B4368.

BROADSTONE TO WENLOCK EDGE

Around 900 metres after leaving Broadstone, turn left, signed *Longville*, heading towards Wenlock Edge. (At this point, if you wish to avoid the climb up to Wenlock Edge you can continue straight ahead and follow B roads all the way to Much Wenlock, but you would be missing out on the narrow limestone escarpment and its vistas.) At around 18 miles long, Wenlock Edge runs from Craven Arms to Ironbridge. The limestone edge was formed in a tropical sea around 425 million years ago; if you are lucky it is possible to find pieces of coral along the edge.

Its steep slopes are now covered with dense deciduous woodland and carpeted with wild flowers in spring. As you head along the road, the climbing becomes even more noticeable, and occasionally challenging, as you head up on to the ridgeline.

The road descends a little into Longville in the Dale on the far side of the ridge. Turn right at a T-junction in the village and climb through a pocket of woodland back on to the ridge. While riding along the road you will have a sense of there being a drop to your left, but you really need to get off your bike to gain the full impression. Look out for lay-bys with worn limestone steps and footpaths that will allow you to peer over the edge and see the view off the ridge. One of the best, but busiest, access points is from Wenlock Edge car park in Presthope.

The pronounced shape of Wenlock Edge means that the top of the ridge catches the weather. It is both wild and exhilarating to feel the full force of the wind blow through you. It's stirred many writers and artists; you may want to (re)acquaint yourself with A.E. Housman's poem *On Wenlock Edge*.

WENLOCK EDGE TO IRONBRIDGE

Once you have had your fill of Wenlock Edge, continue along the ridge road to Stretton Westwood, where the road takes a welcome downward trend towards the town of Much Wenlock. After descending, turn right at a T-junction with the A458 in Much Wenlock then, on the outside of a right-hand bend, turn left, following the signpost for the *Town centre*. This leads you along the High Street, bringing you out directly opposite the part-timbered medieval Guildhall.

Much Wenlock is a medieval town which has grown and developed into a delightful mix of medieval, Georgian and Victorian buildings. A short stroll from the town centre are the dramatic ruins of Wenlock Priory, on the site of the even older St Milburga's Abbey from around AD 680. Sports fans may not have heard of Much Wenlock, but it played a major part in the nineteenth-century revival of the Olympic Games. It is the home town of Dr William Penny Brookes, the founder of the Wenlock Olympian Society and thought to be an inspiration for the modern Olympic Movement. This is why one of the London 2012 Olympic Games mascots was named Wenlock (if you ever need the answer to a very niche pub quiz question).

Turn right in the centre of Much Wenlock. Leaving the town there is a small amount of climbing still remaining, but you know it is over when you start seeing increasing numbers of houses as you approach Benthall; from here the route heads downhill all the way into Ironbridge. Be careful not to pick up too much speed, as there is an easy-to-miss left-hand turn (signposted *Ironbridge*) soon after the start of the descent.

As you drop into the gorge the road steepens and tightens until the final, very tight right-hand bend which may have you testing your brake limits if you have picked up too much speed. Turn left into the car park, go past the Toll House and over the magnificent Iron Bridge itself.

IRONBRIDGE

Erected in 1779, Iron Bridge was the world's first bridge made of iron and gave the village its name. Ironbridge and the surrounding area have a wealth of attractions for anyone interested in engineering and the Industrial Revolution – from the Museum of The Gorge and the Coalbrookdale Museum of Iron to Blists Hill Victorian Town, there is plenty to explore. But, for the weary cycle tourist who just wants to relax, there are plenty of places for a decent meal, possibly a pint, and some lively music.

THE BIRTHPLACE OF THE INDUSTRIAL REVOLUTION
Although there were already a few dwellings and industries in the area before the Iron Bridge existed, the town really took off with its display of engineering ingenuity. The Tontine Hotel, situated opposite the bridge, was built in 1780; its location was specifically chosen to afford visitors a view of this wonder of the Industrial Revolution. A tontine was a way of raising capital investment; you buy into a tontine alongside many other investors. The entire group is paid at regular intervals; as your fellow investors die, or leave the tontine, their share of the payout gets redistributed to the remaining survivors. In a tontine, the longer you live, the larger your profits. Being one of the two final investors would be a nervous position to be in! You will see another tontine hotel in Peebles, later in the trip.

With the museums and bridge itself the only reminder of an industrial past, nature has again asserted itself in Ironbridge. The river and woodland edges of the gorge are now a place of tranquillity and clean air which would have been unrecognisable to those working in the heat of iron foundries and kilns.

SLEEP

VALLEY HOTEL
Listed Georgian country house hotel next to the River Severn. On-site restaurant. Quiet yet close to the many pubs and Ironbridge's live music scene at weekends.
Buildwas Road, Ironbridge, TF8 7DW
T 01952 432 247
www.thevalleyhotel.co.uk

IRONGORGE CAMPING
Pedal up the private road to this tranquil site with fire pits, pods and great views over the surrounding countryside. Find the entrance a short distance into stage 12.
Strethill Road, Coalbrookdale, TF8 7EY
T 01952 433 047
www.irongorgecamping.co.uk

YHA IRONBRIDGE COALPORT
Good quality youth hostel housed in part of a nineteenth-century red-brick china factory looking out over the banks of the River Severn.
High Street, Coalport, TF8 7HT
T 03453 719 325
www.yha.org.uk/hostel/yha-ironbridge-coalport
....

EAT

WATER RAT
Seasonal, quality pub food cooked fresh to order.
Buildwas Road, Ironbridge, TF8 7BJ
T 01952 433 193
www.waterratironbridge.com

DRINK

THE MALTHOUSE
Craft ales, cocktails and world food opposite the river. Also has rooms. There is a quiz on Thursdays and live music on Fridays and Saturdays, helping Ironbridge compete with Inverness for the liveliest place en route to John o' Groats.
Wharfage, Ironbridge, TF8 7NH
T 01952 433 712
www.themalthouseironbridge.co.uk
....

SUPPLIES

ELEY'S OF IRONBRIDGE
Handmade pork pies for your pannier made using a secret recipe. The company has been in the same family since it was set up in the 1960s.
13 Tontine Hill, Ironbridge, TF8 7AL
T 01952 432 504
www.eleysporkpies.co.uk

There is also a **Co-op Food** a short distance into the next stage.
....

BIKE

PEARCE CYCLES
Early in the stage tucked away on a country lane just north of Ludlow you'll find this great family-run bike shop.
Fishmore Road, Ludlow, SY8 3DP
T 01584 879 288
www.pearcecycles.co.uk

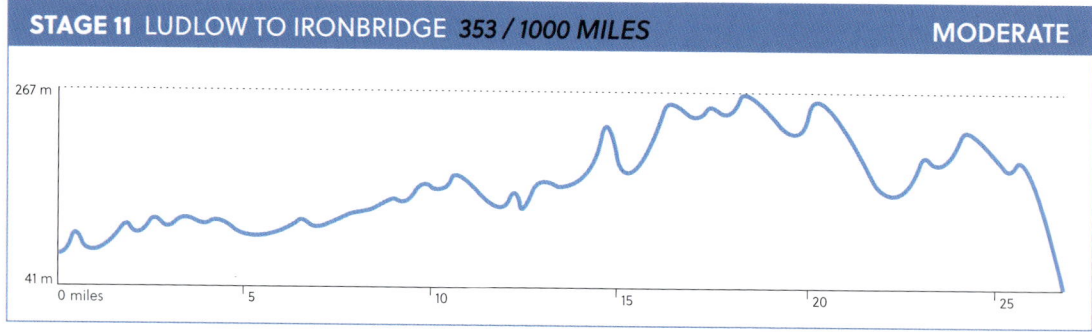

STAGE 11 LUDLOW TO IRONBRIDGE *353 / 1000 MILES*   MODERATE

267 m

41 m

0 miles   5   10   15   20   25

STAGE 12

IRONBRIDGE TO MARKET DRAYTON

25 miles / 39km
350 metres ascent

Shropshire's varied landscape continues to provide scenic delights. Rising above the flat Shropshire Plain, The Wrekin, despite its relatively diminutive height, is a distinctive landmark in this area of otherwise flat, fertile, agricultural land. The rounded hills, valleys and forests seen from the top are said to have inspired J.R.R. Tolkien's descriptions of 'The Shire' in The Lord of the Rings, as he walked here frequently.

A front-loaded stage with the majority of climbing packed into the first 4 miles, the climb begins as soon as you turn away from the river and ascend out of Ironbridge Gorge, passing through Coalbrookdale, where the iron that built the famous bridge was smelted. From the top of the climb The Wrekin's distinctive volcanic shape comes into view. A long descent follows, between the edge of The Wrekin and the smaller Ercall hill. Much of the remainder of the stage is an amble through quiet pastoral lanes, small villages and isolated woodland pockets to arrive at Market Drayton. 'Draitune' was originally a Saxon settlement and appeared in the Domesday Book, a trading post for produce from the good agricultural land that surrounds it. In the thirteenth century, the town was granted a charter to hold a market and, as a result, the name changed to Market Drayton; the Wednesday market continues to this day.

IRONBRIDGE TO LITTLE WENLOCK

From the end of the famous bridge turn left and follow the river through Ironbridge; turn right on to Station Road, where you can see cooling towers up ahead. Station Road becomes Darby Road as you cycle past the brick arches that mark the entrance to the Ironbridge Gorge Museum. As you approach the T-junction there are railway arches to your right but don't pass under them, turn left towards *Little Wenlock*, and continue climbing to leave the industrial sites of Coalbrookdale behind you.

The narrow road continues steeply upwards but keep pushing on – this is the only significant climb of the stage. Occasional breaks in the hedges allow you to look back down on to the cooling towers below but more spectacular views await you at the top. Pass over the A4169 on a bridge and turn left at a T-junction, signposted *Little Wenlock*, shortly after you arrive in Little Wenlock itself. Continue through the village and turn left in front of the pub.

LITTLE WENLOCK TO WROCKWARDINE

As you emerge at the top of the climb the view of The Wrekin hill, which the steep sides of the narrow road had been concealing, is revealed. Disappointingly, despite its appearance, The Wrekin is not an extinct volcano as popularly believed, although it is made of volcanic rock deposits. It is topped by an Iron Age hill fort; once home to the Cornovii tribe, it was built around 400 BC. On a clear day, you can see 17 counties from The Wrekin's 407-metre summit, making it an obvious place for a stronghold.

After around 1 mile of descending, fork left on a road that has no entry but is permitted for cyclists. Cross over the M54 motorway and almost immediately after turn left on to Roman Road towards *Wrockwardine*. This section of Roman road was part of Watling Street, one of the most significant Roman arterial roads. Shortly afterwards, turn right on to Drummery Lane towards *Wrockwardine*.

WROCKWARDINE TO MARKET DRAYTON

In Wrockwardine turn right at the give way and follow the road passing by the church on your left through the village and on towards *Admaston*. Turn right at a T-junction then pass over a railway bridge into Admaston. After leaving Admaston, turn left, following the signpost to *Shawbury*. After just over 1 mile turn right along a road signposted *Long Lane*. After 800 metres turn right at a T-junction and then turn left on to the A442.

A couple of miles on the busy A442 is an unfortunate necessity; turn right in Waters Upton (signposted *Great Bolas*) to quickly return on to quieter lanes. This marks the almost entirely flat, mid-section of the ride. Follow the classic fingerpost pointing in the direction of *Eaton on Tern* for enjoyably easy narrow lanes surrounded by farmland. This gentle bucolic riding continues through Ollerton; turn left in the village, following the signpost towards *Stoke on Tern*. In Stoke on Tern turn right at a T-junction then turn left along Warrant Road. The back lanes are briefly and rudely interrupted by a dog-leg right-then-left crossing of the A41.

Around 1 mile after crossing the A41 the lane rounds a broad, sweeping left-hand bend by a farm; continue along the road, gently rising and falling, all the way to a bridge over the almost stream-like, youthful River Tern, which rises to the north-east of Market Drayton. Immediately after crossing the stone bridge, you are into a residential area. Follow Kilnbank Road, keeping an eye out for the interesting, exposed sandstone rock that edges the narrow road as it climbs slightly towards the centre of the town. At the end of Kilnbank Road as you squeeze between buildings, turn right at a T-junction.

The stage ends at a mini-roundabout on the corner of Frogmore Road and Shropshire Street. A stroll round town will reveal Market Drayton's prosperous history in the quality of its building from the Stuart, Georgian and Victorian periods. Only one house – Cotton's House on Shropshire Street – remains from the seventeenth century, as nearly the whole town was destroyed by fire in 1651.

GINGER AND SPICES

Warming, spicy gingerbread is one of the products that Market Drayton has proudly produced for over 200 years. It is connected to the history of 'Clive of India', a Market Drayton school boy who became an 'Empire Builder', twice serving as a Governor of Bengal (1758–1760 and 1764–1767).

While he is remembered in the town as a famous former resident, his reputation as a ruthless military commander and greedy speculator is not necessarily one to be celebrated. However, his connections to India may have been the beginning of the more wholesome tradition of baking gingerbread – it is said that he brought the spice and the idea back with him. The first recorded mention of gingerbread being made in Market Drayton was in 1793; by the early twentieth century there were four rival bakers. Today, Billington's still flourishes, using the original 'secret' recipe from 1817.

SLEEP
TUDOR HOUSE HOTEL
The best hotel in town but also the only hotel in town. The hotel is one of the oldest buildings in Market Drayton – it was built in 1653, shortly after a town fire in 1651. No independent website.
1 Shropshire Street, Market Drayton, TF9 1PD
T 01630 652 880

CASTLE INN
To the west of Market Drayton, this hotel has 11 rooms and a restaurant with a good reputation locally.
Bletchley, Market Drayton, TF9 3RZ
T 01630 638 246
www.castleinnbletchley.com

ABDO HILL FARM
Campsite with glamping pods to the south of Market Drayton. There is a fish and chip restaurant and take away nearby for your evening dining option.
Rosehill, Market Drayton, TF9 2JG
T 07928 910 091
www.abdohillfarm.co.uk
....

EAT AND DRINK
THE RED LION
Flagship brewery tap of the adjoining Joule's Brewery. The original Joule's house sits over an ancient aquifer, the water source for all the ales. Locally sourced bar meals. Pork is from their own herd at Fordhall Farm and is reared on the brewery's spent grains. If you are here on a Friday, you may chance upon complimentary sausage rolls at the bar.
Great Hales Street, Market Drayton, TF9 1JP
T 01630 652 602
www.joulesbrewery.co.uk
....

SUPPLIES
FORDHALL FARM SHOP
Follow Shrewsbury Road slightly off route out of town to reach England's first community-owned farm, including a shop and cafe with plentiful supplies for the day's riding.
Tern Hill Road, Market Drayton, TF9 3PS
T 01630 317 531
www.fordhallfarm.com

Alternatively, for a shop on the route there are supermarkets in the centre of Market Drayton.
....

BIKE
RACE TIME REPAIRS
Based in Market Drayton, this is one of a growing number of mobile bike services which comes to you. Included here as there are no bike shops in Market Drayton – they may be able to help you to keep pedalling northwards.
T 07484 828 171
www.racetimerepairs.co.uk

STAGE 12 IRONBRIDGE TO MARKET DRAYTON *378 / 1000 MILES*   MODERATE

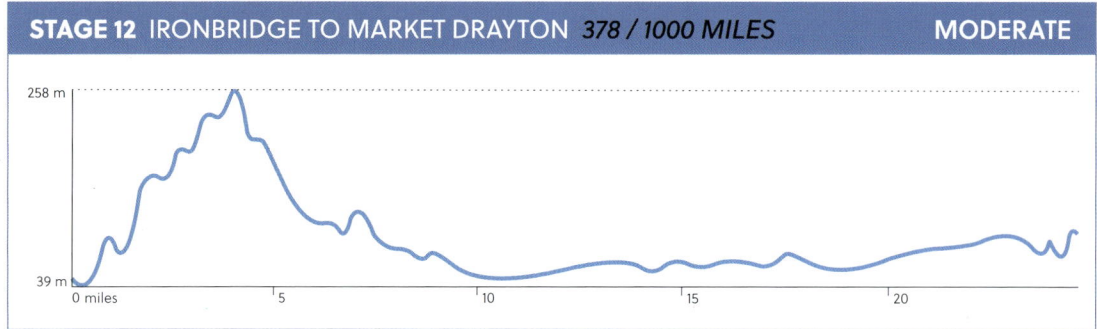

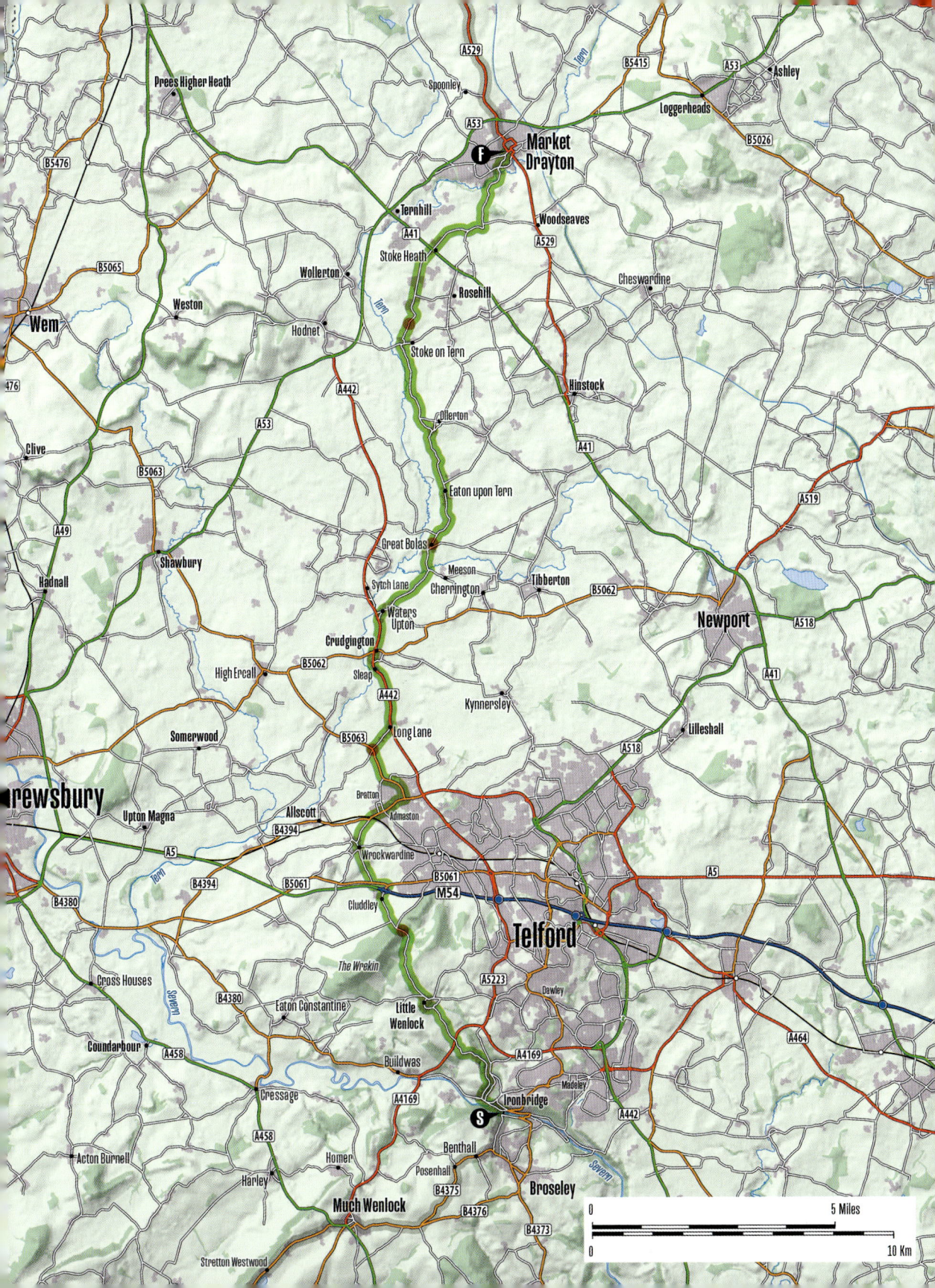

CHESHIRE & LANCASHIRE

STAGE 13

34 miles / 55km
200 metres ascent

MARKET DRAYTON TO KNUTSFORD

Amid a network of canals discover the 'wich' towns of Cheshire where salt was gathered and the making of cheese is still celebrated. Find medieval architecture in unexpected places and enjoy tranquil farmland between the busy towns of the North West.

A stage of gentle riding that leaves Shropshire behind and enters Cheshire, mimicking the route of the Shropshire Union Canal, you first pass near Adderley Locks which are just a warm-up for the infamous 15 locks that follow on the Audlem Lock Flight, which accommodates a drop of 28 metres over a 1.5-mile stretch. Canals are as much a feature of the Industrial Revolution as the Iron Bridge which we passed earlier, and what was once a regularly navigated place of work is now an enjoyable challenge for those who enjoy their leisure time on canals. LEJOG1000 uses a network of lanes to link small villages and the larger towns of Nantwich and Middlewich, maximising the time spent in the rural spaces in between. For many drivers on the M6, Knutsford is best known for its service station, but this does the real town of Knutsford a disservice – it is an old market town with a strong sense of local identity.

MARKET DRAYTON TO AUDLEM

Weave your way out of Market Drayton towards the ring road. Head along Frogmore Road and turn left at the first mini-roundabout on to Cheshire Street (the A529). When you meet a larger roundabout with the ring road go straight ahead, staying on the A529 and following the sign for *Audlem*. This is a broad road, with fields interspersed by occasional houses and farms, running almost perfectly straight until a right-angle bend just before Adderley village.

A mile or so before Audlem you leave Shropshire behind and enter Cheshire. When you reach a T-junction at Audlem, turn left towards *Whitchurch* on the A525 to follow the route. (If you wish to detour to explore Audlem, turn right here to cross over the Shropshire Union Canal to reach the town. The Old Priest House coffee shop is popular with cyclists; you can purchase a quarter of sweets, weighed out from their glass jars in the traditional way. Or head to the canal to watch narrow boats navigate the locks.)

AUDLEM TO NANTWICH

Around 800 metres after leaving Audlem, turn right towards *OverWater Marina*. You can't see the marina from the road but a short detour down the track allows you to see the boats in their moorings.

The route crosses a bridge over the Shropshire Union Canal giving a clear perspective on how well engineered and perfectly straight the canal is as it stretches out to either side of you. Rolling along this quiet back lane feels a world away from the busy parts of Cheshire where commuters charge around the lanes.

Turn right at a give way towards *Nantwich*, then pass Nantwich Lake. Shortly afterwards, turn left (following the sign for *Nantwich town centre*) then pass over a railway line at a level crossing. Nantwich is believed to have been a salt-producing centre from the tenth century or even earlier; in hand with this was cheese production and leather tanning, both of which use salt.

While the route skirts the edge of Nantwich by turning left at a small roundabout, you might want to detour and explore further by continuing straight ahead here instead; the town centre is a lot more attractive than the outlying residential areas suggest. Distinctive black and white timber-framed Tudor buildings line the main streets, built after the town was nearly destroyed by fire. Queen Elizabeth I personally donated money and rallied the country to raise more money to help rebuild the properties of the 900 people made homeless. Queen's Aid House, a magnificent Tudor property, can be seen on the High Street.

To continue on the LEJOG1000 route passing around the town, go straight ahead at a set of traffic lights then turn right, following the sign to the *Swimming Pool*. After passing the pool pick up the cycle path to your left, following the sign to *Chester*. The cycle path ends after around 900 metres; turn left then immediately afterwards go straight ahead at the roundabout signed *Church Minshull*.

NANTWICH TO SWAN GREEN

The route passes large, open-plan fields edged by the occasional ancient oak which has withstood the progress of the agricultural industry. Church Minshull interrupts the rural landscape, now just a small collection of houses

and a church but once a place where blacksmiths and craftsmen worked to supply the needs of the farming communities. Turn right at the mini-roundabout in Church Minshull, cross the canal and then turn left signed *Minshull Vernon*.

The rural idyll ends as you turn left on to the A530 towards *Middlewich* – another 'wich' town that can attribute its economic growth to salt extraction. It was founded by the Romans who originally gave it the name 'Salinae', whereas 'wich' or 'wych' is believed to be an Old English term for a brackish spring. Built within the confluence of three rivers and with three major canals passing through the town, it was once a busy place for water traffic. At a large triangle of streets which functions as a roundabout, follow signs to the *Town centre*. As you leave town you cross the Trent and Mersey Canal.

At a major roundabout turn left on to Centurion Way (a nod to the Roman Road nearby), following the signpost for *Knutsford*. Shortly afterwards, turn right on to Byley Road (again following the signpost for *Knutsford*). Byley is a tiny hamlet with a scenic position amongst the fields and brooks; tall purple wild flowers highlight the edges of the watercourse, speedwell and frothy cow-parsley complete the picture.

Continue straight ahead (following the signpost for *Knutsford*), past Shakerley Mere, a small lake and

country park on the site of a former sand quarry. A remarkably tranquil place given that it is within sight of the M6, which you shortly cross over en route to the next village of Swan Green.

SWAN GREEN TO KNUTSFORD

Swan Green and Lower Peover are two almost-connected small villages with a traditional pub in each.

In Lower Peover, St Oswald's Church can be reached by detouring up The Cobbles. While the oldest part of the building is the tower built in 1582 the font inside is much earlier – reputedly it was brought to the church from Norton Priory in 1322 as part of the dissolution of the monasteries. It is easy to take for granted how many of our British villages have ancient buildings such as this and the amount of care required to preserve them. Reaching a T-junction turn left on the A50 towards *Knutsford*; the road here can be busy as traffic makes its way into Knutsford. Turn right at the traffic lights by the railway station and then turn left, signposted *Town centre*, to complete the stage.

Knutsford is home to many independent shops and restaurants; it has resisted the homogenisation that has afflicted so many large towns on the periphery of big urban areas. The town was the inspiration for the novel *Cranford* by the English writer Elizabeth Gaskell and has a huge mix of architecture – Steven Spielberg somehow even managed to make it look like Shanghai when he filmed *Empire of the Sun* here. For fans of the quirky and historic bikes, the Penny Farthing Museum (handily incorporated into a coffee house) in the centre of town is worth a visit – it hosts an impressive collection of penny farthings and early bicycles.

SLEEP

THE ANGEL
Centrally located traditional pub offering great quality
accommodation and good food. Beers from independent
Manchester brewery Joseph Holt.
96 King Street, Knutsford, WA16 6HQ
T 01565 651 165
www.joseph-holt.com/pubs/angel-king-st

BOUNDARY PARK
Campsites close to Knutsford are thin on the ground and
this site has only limited facilities – no toilets or showers.
It is affiliated with the Camping and Caravanning Club so
call ahead to book if you're not a member as you will need
to join.
Chelford Road, Ollerton, Knutsford, WA16 8TA
T 01625 860 893
www.campingandcaravanningclub.co.uk

EAT

ROSE AND CROWN
Traditional British pub-style food done exceptionally well.
You can have a pint and a snack through to a full meal. For
evening meals booking is recommended. Also has rooms.
62 King Street, Knutsford, WA16 6DT
T 01565 652 366
www.knutsfordroseandcrown.co.uk

DRINK

PROJECT 53
The tap room for The Mobberley Brewhouse which started
from a basic DIY brew-kit and became a top-100-rated
independent brewery. Also serves artisan gins, home-made

pizza and deli-boards for snacking on as you work your way
round the beer pumps.
15 Minshull Street, Knutsford, WA16 6HG
T 01565 655 787
www.project53.bar

SUPPLIES

The centre of Knutsford is well represented by supermarket
chains including **Booths**, a premium chain in Northern
England. For a few extra miles **Waugh Brow Farm** has a farm
shop and a snack bar.

BIKE

ROCK GARDEN CYCLES
Comprehensively kitted out workshop with the possibility of
mobile call-out service.
Marsh Bank Works, Marsh Lane, Nantwich, CW5 5HH
T 07891 491 835
www.rockgardencycles.co.uk

BIKE BENCH
Fast and fair cycle care, a very short distance off route in the
village of Byley.
Byley Warehousing, Moss Lane, Byley, CW10 9NG
T 01606 832 202
www.bikebench.co.uk

BIKES N GEAR LTD
If none of the other shops in cycle-mad Cheshire have sorted
you out, head here in the centre of Knutsford.
31 King Street, Knutsford, WA16 6DW
T 01565 750 273
www.bikes-n-gear.co.uk

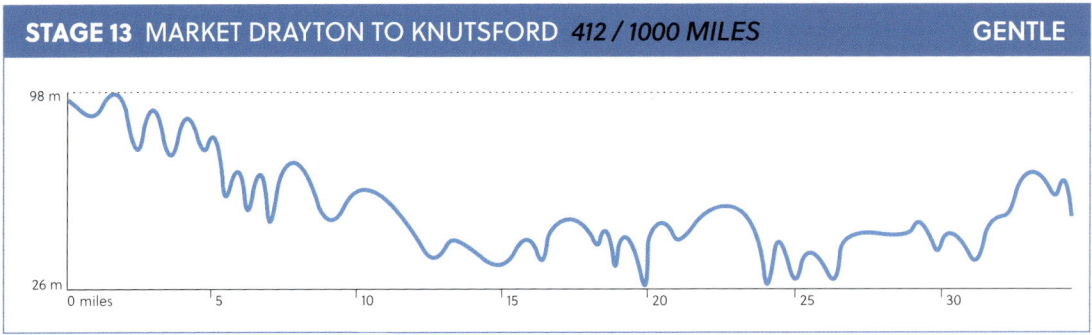

STAGE 13 MARKET DRAYTON TO KNUTSFORD *412 / 1000 MILES*   GENTLE

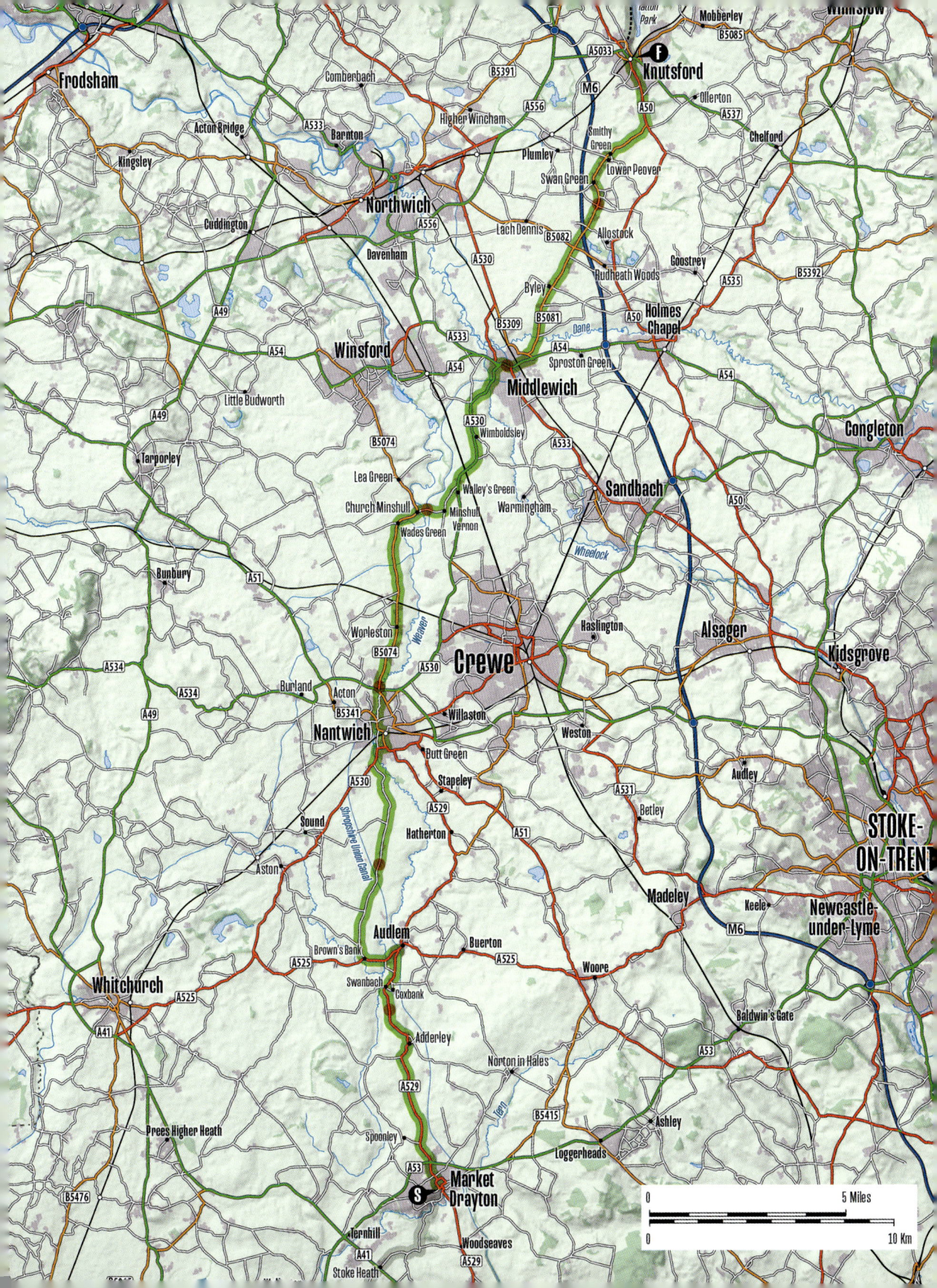

14

28 miles / 45km
250 metres ascent

KNUTSFORD TO BLACKROD

Tatton Park offers a beautiful start to one of the most urban stages of the entire thousand-mile route, showing that even in the most built-up areas of Britain pockets of natural beauty can still be found. Urban expansion has merged small towns and villages together; discovering their individual identities is part of the character of this stage.

A relatively flat and easy day in terms of the physical terrain as you pick your way through the towns and sprawl of the busy North West. While this isn't a destination that you would choose for a day ride, the route seeks out the quietest roads and finds the places of peace and interest along the way. Miles of rural lanes between fields and ancient hedges belie the location between major motorways. Even so, the clues to how urban the area is are still there – fields are interrupted by the march of electricity pylons and birdsong silenced by the sound of planes coming in to land at Manchester Airport. With canals, toll bridges, railways, motorways and overhead planes, this stage demonstrates the changes in transportation across 300 years in the industrial North West, and the towns you pass through tell their own stories of financial prosperity, loss and tragedy.

KNUTSFORD TO HEATLEY

Start by continuing your journey through Knutsford on King Street and then turn right at the entrance for Tatton Park. The gates to the park have set opening times – check online for details. Outside of opening hours you can divert around the western side of the park. Tatton Park is a huge expanse of just over 1,000 acres of parkland and gardens providing valuable green space for visitors to explore in an otherwise built-up area. Owned by the Egerton family from 1598, the 'new' mansion seen in the grounds today was built in 1716.

Maurice, the last Lord Egerton, gave the mansion and gardens to the National Trust on his death in 1958.

Tatton Park is a beautiful place to cycle; fork right to emerge at the northern end of the park at the Rostherne entrance. Continue straight ahead on to Rostherne Lane then turn left in Rostherne village, following a blue Sustrans sign for the Cheshire Cycleway.

A series of small villages now appear as isolated hamlets, their occupants most likely commuting to Manchester or Warrington. In Bucklow Hill turn right at the T-junction, then take the second left turn. After just over 2 miles, turn right at a give way on to the B5159. When you reach Heatley turn right on to the A6144 then take the next left signed to *Warburton*.

From Heatley there is the option for a 1.5-mile detour along the Trans Pennine Trail to visit Dunham Press Cider. This small orchard has been in the same family for over 100 years, on land that has been growing apples for over two centuries. They are the only cider maker in the North West solely using their own apples.

HEATLEY TO LOWTON

Warburton is the final village we pass through on the southern side of the Manchester Ship Canal; Warburton Toll Bridge is the only route across the River Mersey and the Manchester Ship Canal between the M6 and M60. A toll bridge predates the canal by a couple of years. Originally a toll bridge spanned the River Mersey but when the river was diverted for the canal works,

the original course dried up. The Manchester Ship Canal Act 1890 paved the way for a new high-level cantilever bridge. The toll has remained at an inflation-busting 12 pence since 1890.

Once across the bridge the route meets the old Manchester Road (A57); turn right and shortly before it becomes a dual carriageway fork left through the village of Hollins Green. Turn left at a T-junction to reach Glazebrook. Across the fields you can see the red-brick outlines of the backs of the terraced houses and estates where they expanded outwards, nibbling away at the green edges. The height of the bridge over the M62 gives you a bird's-eye view of the traffic below.

It is easy to overlook the history of towns and villages in this area, submerged as they are beneath layers of road networks and new buildings, but the clues are there to see as you cycle through them. In Culcheth turn left at the mini-roundabout into the village and right at the next mini-roundabout to leave. The rows of terraced houses and the street name Daisy Bank Mill Close on your left are a reminder that there was once a cotton mill here. On the right is a bungalow that still has some resemblance to the gatehouse it once was.

Leigh Golf Club, glimpsed through the trees, was once Kenyon Hall and owned by Sir Jabez Johnson Ferguson, a wealthy cotton manufacturer from Manchester. Nearly everywhere has its history interwoven with its present.

Approaching the junction in Lowton the roads can feel busy with traffic, particularly around rush hour. Turn right then immediately left at the traffic lights. Go straight ahead at the next set of lights over the East Lancs Road dual carriageway which connects Liverpool and Manchester. The traffic dissipates again as it is syphoned off east and west by the large trunk roads.

LOWTON TO ABRAM

In built-up areas navigation can be difficult as towns merge together with no distinct boundaries. Signs, aimed at car drivers, indicate the direction of large distant cities rather than the next village a couple of miles away. Between Lowton and the crossing of the Leeds and Liverpool Canal at Abram, the route goes straight ahead on the primary road at each junction.

Abram was recorded as a settlement as early as the thirteenth century, but its growth, and the majority of the terraced homes you see as you cycle through,

are from the industrialisation of the nineteenth century. Hemmed in by the canal and railway line and home to several collieries, it would have been a dust-filled and smoky place to be. In 1908 an explosion in one of the mines, the Maypole Colliery, killed 75 men and boys, leaving 44 women without husbands and over 120 children without fathers. Such a horrific loss in a small town had a lasting and profound impact; Abram Heritage and History Group still regularly hold a commemoration. Some victims are buried in the churchyard, but many more remain within the mineshaft.

ABRAM TO BLACKROD

Abram merges into Platt Bridge; turn right at the roundabout in the centre signposted to *Hindley*, the next significant town. There is a small gap between settlements here. In Hindley there is a large, traffic-light-controlled junction to negotiate – go straight over towards *Bolton*, then fork left at the next mini-roundabout. Hindley railway station is at the edge of the town; after passing this the views become more scenic for a short distance. From now on, the road almost imperceptibly climbs up to Blackrod, which is on the top of a small rise.

At a T-junction in Aspull turn left, tracing the edge of the churchyard. A right turn takes you between two large sections of open grassland and towards a housing estate; follow the road around to the left to neatly avoid Aspull's busy one-way system. Emerge at a T-junction with a parade of shops in front of you; turn right to follow the same road to the stage end at the next T-junction on the southern tip of Blackrod.

BLACKROD

Blackrod stands on an ancient Roman road; its name in Old English would have meant a bleak or dark clearing in the forest. Slightly higher than the surrounding countryside, it would have been an easy marker in the landscape for navigation. Roman remains found suggest it was once a stopping point of importance. When industrialisation arrived, work increased and by the end of the nineteenth century there were over 1,000 miners working in the pits at Blackrod. When many of the pits closed in the 1930s, it created severe hardship for the town.

SLEEP
BOLTON WHITES HOTEL
With pitchview rooms this is a novel hotel for the night and a must for genuine football fans.
De Havilland Way, Bolton, BL6 6SF
T 01204 673 610
www.boltonwhiteshotel.co.uk

MERCURE BOLTON GEORGIAN HOUSE HOTEL
With views over the Pennine countryside, relax with your cosy robe and in-bedroom coffee machine.
Manchester Road, Blackrod, BL6 5RU
T 01942 330 012
www.mercurebolton.co.uk
....

EAT
THE RIVINGTON GRILL
Restaurant with local produce and a comfortable lounge bar make this pub and grill a relaxing stop at the end of the day.
Station Road, Blackrod, BL6 5JF
T 01204 696 027
www.therivingtongrill.co.uk
....

SUPPLIES
A good-size **Spar** convenience store in Blackrod has everything you need to restock your supplies.
....

BIKE
BICYCLE CENTRE
No-nonsense, old-school sales and repairs. No website.
2 Bank Buildings, 1 Walthew Lane, Platt Bridge, WN2 5DB
T 01942 862 843

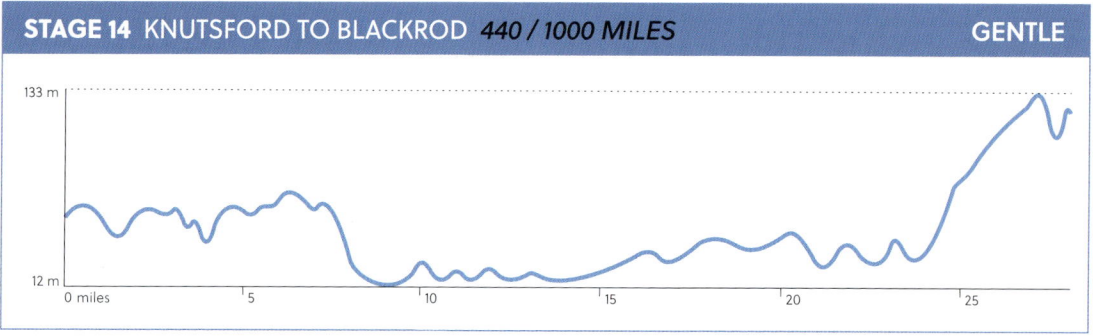

STAGE 14 KNUTSFORD TO BLACKROD *440 / 1000 MILES*   GENTLE

133 m

12 m

0 miles   5   10   15   20   25

STAGE 15

15

20 miles / 32km
490 metres ascent

BLACKROD TO MELLOR

Threading its way through the industrial North West, between coalfields and canals, passing great Victorian-built reservoirs and old textile mills, this stage charts the fortunes of an area transformed from rural dwellings to industrialisation and urbanisation. Now, city dwellers return to the countryside seeking out the peaceful green spaces between modern motorways and urban sprawl.

This is a short but lumpy stage with a series of staccato climbs and very little flat riding. Given how close the route is to major roads and cities, the roads are quieter and more picturesque than the previous stage. However, being urban doesn't mean it is lacking in interest or in scenery. The joy in this section is finding the between spaces and edge-lands, the old roads forgotten by traffic funnelled on to bypasses and motorways. If anything, the pleasure taken from climbing above Rivington Reservoirs and surveying the placid waters and bracken-covered hillside is enhanced by the distant flashing glints of motorway traffic and the smog rising up from the towns below. The pleasure being that you are 'here' and not 'there'. From canal-side to moorland, this stage shows that even in one of the most built-up areas you'll cycle through on this journey, green spaces survive.

BLACKROD TO WHEELTON

Turn left on to Manchester Road to go through the town of Blackrod. As you cycle along you can tell from the selection of ages and style of the housing a little of the history of the town and how it has been added to piecemeal as its growth accelerated and declined through the ages. Turn left at a T-junction with the A6 then almost immediately turn right on to a surprisingly quiet and rural road that takes you under the M61 motorway and continues uphill straight across the A673.

Despite the hum of the motorway, the scenery around contrives to make the area feel a long way from the densely urbanised areas close by. At the crest of a small hill, you just spot to your right the mound of Rivington Pike. The road drops down to pass alongside the M61; although hidden from view, it makes its proximity known with the rumble of tyres on tarmac.

Turn right away from the M61 as the road tries to take you back across the motorway into the arms of the urban sprawl. You approach Rivington Reservoirs by riding across the dam for Anglezarke Reservoir. The reservoirs have provided water to Liverpool for over 150 years. Water from the scheme first made its way to the city in 1857; it was the biggest network of reservoirs ever built at the time it opened and the first to filter its water supply. It became a model for reservoir systems all over the world.

From water level a testing climb will give your legs a workout, but also provide the opportunity to look across the reservoir to hazy towns beyond and offers a different perspective on the area you have just cycled through. At the top of the moorland climb the road bends to the left, descending all the way to the northern end of Anglezarke Reservoir, behind the picturesque Waterman's Cottage.

Turn right towards White Coppice along gentle lanes, then turn left in the small village following the sign towards *Wheelton*. Turn right at the next junction, again following the sign towards *Wheelton*. Passing the

Church of St Barnabas in Heapey marks the top of a long drag and you can freewheel down to the dog-leg straight-across junction on the main road that takes you into Wheelton.

WHEELTON TO MELLOR

Wheelton's centre has tiny sloping streets; some of the terraced houses give the impression of neighbours leaning on each other for support as they make their way up the hill. Turn left in the centre of Wheelton, passing the clock tower to your right. At the end of the village the route meets the Leeds and Liverpool Canal. The Top Lock is a good place to break your journey as the locks are a fascinating reminder of the canal linkage, once vital to trans-Pennine industrial canal traffic, in their difficult descent from the higher reaches of the Leeds and Liverpool Canal to the lower regions of West Lancashire.

Turn right over the canal at the locks and pedal slightly uphill, remaining parallel to the M61 on your left. Turn right at the T-junction to avoid crossing the motorway. In the village of Brindle turn right at the church. Shortly after passing over the M65 turn left on to Hillhouse Lane; from this approach the hill is in your favour. As the road flattens out, a right-hand turn on to a private road which is part of the Lancashire Cycleway takes you to the village of Hoghton.

In Hoghton turn right and then right again on to the A675, followed almost immediately by a left turn that takes you quickly back into the mesh of lanes. Only slightly off the route and found by continuing along the main road is Hoghton Tower. Built in 1565 on the site of a much older fort that dated back to 1109, it is now a visitor attraction with the tower, gardens and cafe open to the public.

Around 900 metres after Hoghton turn right on to Goosefoot Lane. This leads you to Samlesbury Bottoms where, once you cross the small stream in the 'bottom', the only way is up for the next mile. Part way up you'll find a four-way junction; continue straight ahead along Further Lane, signposted to *Mellor*. We imagine it is called Further Lane after all the cyclists asking 'how far to the top?' and getting the reply 'just a little further'.

After passing Stanley House – an early-seventeenth-century manor house now a luxury hotel – take a short dog-leg (right then left) over the A677, then climb into Mellor, where the stage ends at a T-junction next to the Millstone Inn.

MELLOR

Mellor is situated on a high ridge, as no doubt your legs have informed you, overlooking the low-lying area of the Fylde, the Ribble Valley and Blackburn. Mellor Moor was

FOOTBALL FACTORIES
Not only are we deep in England's manufacturing heartland but also a stronghold of football. The first set of football rules were drawn up at Cambridge University and the FA Cup, introduced in 1871, was initially the preserve of the nobility. But in 1883 Old Etonians lost the FA Cup final to a five-year-old club called Blackburn Olympic. Five of the 12 founder members of the Football League were clubs from Lancashire mill towns: Accrington, Blackburn, Bolton, Burnley and Preston were towns where population had swelled dramatically as men moved to work at the many mills. Football was unifying and provided a much-needed social outlet for those working long, hard hours in the burgeoning new industries.

once the site of a Roman encampment, an outpost of the one at nearby Ribchester. In the nineteenth century Mellor's population dropped as villagers headed to Blackburn and other areas for work. Now the population is growing again as the movement is reversed with city dwellers moving into the surrounding countryside seeking a rural life within commutable distance.

SLEEP

STANLEY HOUSE HOTEL & SPA
If your body is in need of a massage as you come closer to the halfway point of your journey, consider treating yourself at this boutique hotel and spa complete with its own brasserie.
Further Lane, Mellor, BB2 7NP
T 01254 769 200
www.stanleyhouse.co.uk

MILLSTONE INN
Comfy rooms with fresh milk for your tea, delicious biscuits to enjoy and AA Rosette cooking for your evening meal at this seventeenth-century coaching inn right at the stage end.
Church Lane, Mellor, BB2 7JR
T 01254 813 333
www.millstonemellor.co.uk

MYRE EDGE FARM
If you prefer a bed and breakfast, this one is a short distance into (and a short detour from) the next stage. With only two rooms in this cosy farmhouse, you are assured of a personal service.
Showley Road, Clayton-Le-Dale, BB1 9DR
T 01254 814 140
www.myreedgefarm.co.uk

EAT

TRADERS ARMS
The Millstone Inn has great dining options, but head to this Thwaites pub at the other end of the village if you want a change of scenery.
77 Mellor Lane, Mellor, BB2 7EW
T 01254 812 478

SUPPLIES

In Mellor, **Frank Littler & Sons** is a small butchers and deli selling cold meats, cheese and bread for your sandwiches. Alternatively, there is a **Spar** convenience store in the centre of the village.

BIKE

GIANT BLACKBURN
Around 3 miles east of Mellor on the edge of Blackburn, this busy bike shop has an experienced team who service all bike brands.
491–501 Whalley New Road, Blackburn, BB1 9AU
T 01254 662 440
www.giant-blackburn.co.uk

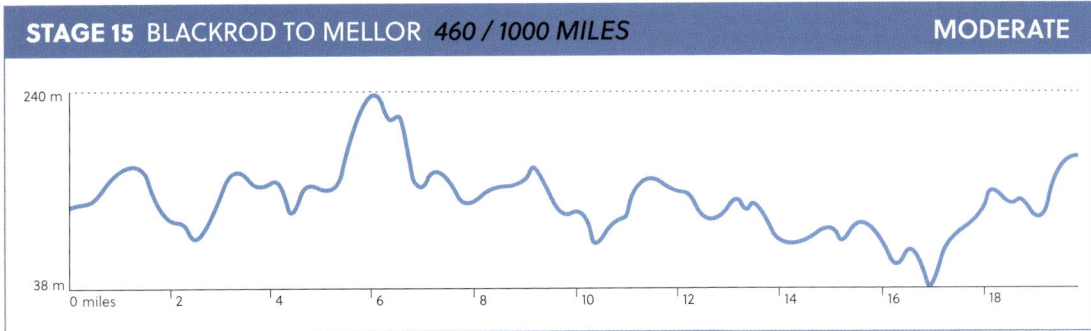

STAGE 15 BLACKROD TO MELLOR *460 / 1000 MILES*   **MODERATE**

STAGE 16

MELLOR TO HIGH BENTHAM

31 miles / 50km
910 metres ascent

Your journey really starts here. The climbs are bigger, the landscape more dramatic, and the roads are handcrafted for the cyclist. Welcome to the rural North. With the industrial North West behind you, the route changes character again and a new style of riding emerges, featuring more metres of climbing per mile than any other stage.

Leaving Mellor and skirting around the northern edges of Blackburn is your final contact with deeply urban cycling in England – from the moment you leave Clitheroe the route becomes a feast of spectacular open vistas, wild fellsides and exposed, hilly terrain. The twin challenges of Waddington Fell and the Cross of Greet announce themselves as the first proper peaks and passes of the journey, and offer the highest point of the route in England. This is the first stage with several long, sustained climbs, and the most challenging since the early stages of the South West. By now your legs and body are attuned to the daily repetition of cycling and you will feel ready for the fresh challenges ahead. An exhilarating descent from high moorland into the wide expansive views of the Three Peaks of the Yorkshire Dales follows. This is a day of cycling you are unlikely to forget.

MELLOR TO CLITHEROE

The first 4 miles of the 10 to the town of Clitheroe are spent on a ridgeline to the south of the Ribble Valley before descending into the valley itself. Turn right on to Mellor Lane with the war memorial to your left and the Millstone Inn to your right as you pedal. The road descends slightly; after just over 2 miles you arrive at a busy crossroads with a station and supermarket to your left. Many larger suburban pubs have struggled to survive in recent times and this convenience store in the shell of a pub is an indication of that. Here you are on

the northern fringes of the cotton mill town of Blackburn. Continue straight across the main road at the traffic lights, climbing slightly with the pint-sized Parsonage Reservoir off to your right; fork left following the sign for *Whalley* and a blue Sustrans sign for route 91. Arriving at a T-junction with another reservoir straight ahead on the horizon, turn left continuing to follow Sustrans National Route 91.

Over the next 3 miles you gradually descend, losing 150 metres in altitude, to reach Whalley, famous for the ruins of its fourteenth-century Cistercian abbey. A very tight left-hand switchback announces your arrival on the edge of Whalley. Turn right at the abrupt T-junction at the bottom. Follow the principal road through the town, which then takes you under the A59 Whalley Bypass. The village of Barrow is sandwiched between Whalley and Clitheroe. It is home to the flagship showroom of Ribble Cycles, one of Britain's oldest cycling brands established in 1897 in nearby Preston.

On leaving Barrow the road reaches a T-junction with the A671; turn left here and pedal for under 2 miles to reach Clitheroe town centre. Clitheroe is the largest market town in the Ribble Valley; great views of the valley can be enjoyed from the keep of Clitheroe's twelfth-century castle. Off to your right as you ride into Clitheroe you may spot Pendle Hill, which rises to a height of 557 metres.

Pendle Hill and its surrounding villages were the setting for dramatic witch trials in 1612. Witchcraft was

widely feared but also a fascination for many. The early 1600s were a time of much superstition and religious persecution with the Protestant James I, having just survived the Gunpowder Plot, not particularly keen on this Catholic corner of rural Lancashire. The Pendle Witches were accused of practising witchcraft and were convicted to be hanged based on the testimony of a nine-year-old child. A few decades later, George Fox climbed Pendle Hill and experienced visions of 'great people to be gathered', which led him to found the Quaker movement.

CLITHEROE TO SLAIDBURN

From Clitheroe the first 'real' climb on LEJOG1000, Waddington Fell, lies in wait. In Clitheroe follow the one-way system, keeping right when the entrance to the castle is up to your left. Turn left at a crossroads with two minor streets, following the symbol for the railway station. Take your next right, then turn right again at the end of the road. Finally turn left to head out of Clitheroe on the B6478, following the signpost for *Waddington*. After crossing the River Ribble on leaving the town, it is 1 mile to the village of Waddington, passing Waddow Hall.

Waddington village marks the gateway to the Forest of Bowland Area of Outstanding Natural Beauty. The village is also thought to have been a royal hunting ground in Norman times; the spectacular surrounding scenery

dominates the rest of the stage as you leave the mill towns and villages behind for open landscape and space.

From the village it's a straight 3-mile climb to the cattle grid at the top at 352 metres, averaging around 6 per cent with a short steep kick at 10 per cent near the top. This is real climbing in real hill country and the vastness of the views afforded from the top have not been experienced on this route since Exmoor. From the top, it's a steeper more snake-like descent for 2 miles to reach the village of Newton, then a rise and descent into Slaidburn, a picture-perfect village. The cafe is rarely without cyclists pausing for cake and a brew.

SLAIDBURN TO HIGH BENTHAM

Leave Slaidburn by turning left at the war memorial opposite which there is a functional village water tap, a rarity in Britain and perfect for thirsty cyclists. This left turn is signed *Bentham via Quiet Lane* and indeed you are more likely to see cyclists, hill farmers and gamekeepers than too many cars. The Cross of Greet climb lies between you and the end of the stage in High Bentham – this is the highest point of the route in England topping out at 427 metres. From Slaidburn, the 6 miles to the top also includes a slight descent as, after passing Stocks Reservoir to your right, the road drops to cross the River Hodder before following the river virtually to its source in the high, heather-coated grouse moorlands near the Cross of Greet. After crossing the river, the climbing is

gradual through a bracken-blanketed fellside which slopes gracefully down to the river. The summit is announced by the clanging of a cattle grid beneath your wheels, interrupting the moorland calm.

The sense of space, openness and limitless vistas of the top is given stark, brooding definition by the limestone outcrops of the Three Peaks of the Yorkshire Dales. The solitude also makes for a perfect place to spot a hen harrier, an increasingly rare bird of prey.

At the summit, after crossing the cattle grid, look for a stone on your right by the side of the road. There is a square hollow in the stone which not everyone agrees was the foundation stone for a cross which gave its name to the pass. The hollow could be a plague hole, where money would be washed to prevent the plague being passed by traders from one region to another.

The descent starts steep and quick, but has one short climb in its middle section before descending again past a huge, imposing boulder off to your left. At 5 metres high, the Great Stone of Fourstones has a staircase carved up it and ancient and some more modern rock art markings. The stone marks the border between Lancashire and North Yorkshire and was likely a meeting place through the ages. Stories vary, but the boulder was supposedly thrown at England in anger by the Irish giant Finn McCool, who also had time to build the Giant's Causeway in Northern Ireland. The rock being a glacial erratic is a more likely explanation, deposited at the end

of an ice age when glacial ice retreated. The view from the top of the Yorkshire Three Peaks is exhilarating.

Crossing the River Wenning and a railway line in quick succession followed by a short rise leads you to the crossroads at the centre of the small town of High Bentham and the end of a queen of a stage.

YORKSHIRE THREE PEAKS

Forget Scafell Pike, Snowdon (Yr Wyddfa) and Ben Nevis, this version is the true Three Peaks to many Yorkshire folk. If you are feeling energetic, it is a popular walking challenge to summit the trio of hills in a day: Whernside, Ingleborough and Pen-y-ghent.

Making the most of the terrain, the 3 Peaks Cyclo-Cross is Britain's biggest and toughest cyclo-cross race. It's no surprise the roster of winners includes some top fell runners as much clambering and carrying is needed as well as great bike handling skills. As there is a lot of slipping and sliding down the descents, it also helps to have a support crew holding some spare wheels for the inevitable snakebite punctures if you're serious about competing.

John Rawnsley was the founder of the race and organised the first 50 events, competing in 45 of them himself, and winning the first one. He was also a keen fell runner and completed the route at least 100 times before he died. Despite being without doubt the world's hardest cyclo-cross event and being oversubscribed year after year, it remains a grassroots event, loved (and equally hated) by every rider tough enough to give it a go.

SLEEP

COACH HOUSE
Here you will find comfortable rooms named after the
surrounding landscape.
Main Street, High Bentham, LA2 7HE
T 01524 262 432
www.coachhousebentham.co.uk

STACKSTEAD FARM
A shepherd's hut, camping pods, bunk barn or a place to
pitch your tent. Not your average campsite, as there is access
to a sauna, gym and indoor pool for a small fee. A short
detour from the route towards Ingleton.
Ingleton, LA6 3HS
T 01524 241 386
www.stacksteadfarm.co.uk

EAT

The **Coach House** (see SLEEP) does home-made pub food
and has a regularly changing specials board.

SUPPLIES

The small **Co-op Food** in High Bentham will have bars and
bananas to keep you going into Cumbria.

BIKE

THE GREEN JERSEY CYCLING CLUB
The cycling hub of the Ribble Valley with a wide range of
essentials to keep most bikes on the road and a workshop for
repairs. Brews are also available.
Old Shawbridge Sawmill, Taylor Street, Clitheroe, BB7 1LY
T 01200 427 630
www.thegreenjersey.cc

RIBBLE CYCLES
Flagship showroom of Britain's most iconic cycling brands
which stays true to its roots in the Ribble Valley.
Barrow Brook Trade Park, Barrow Brook, Clitheroe, BB7 9BQ
T 01200 441 581
www.ribblecycles.co.uk

STAGE 16 MELLOR TO HIGH BENTHAM *491 / 1000 MILES*   **CHALLENGING**

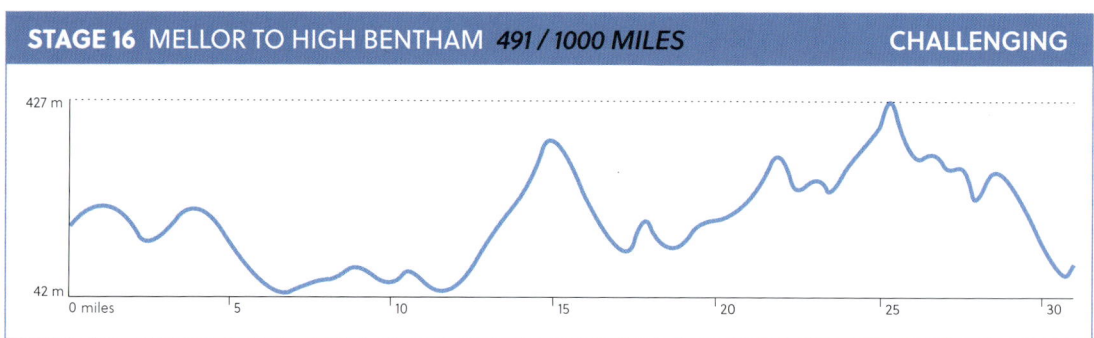

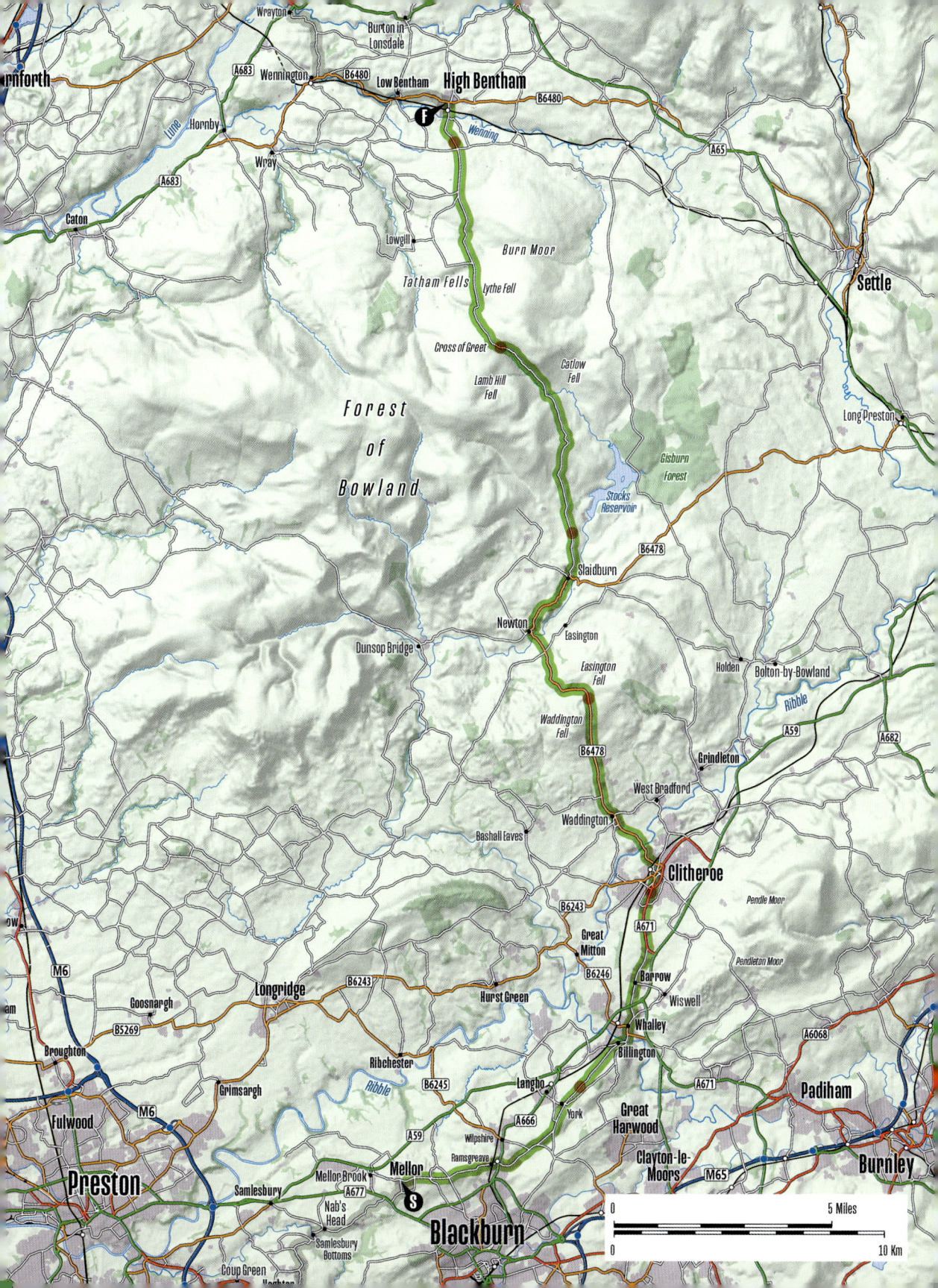

CUMBRIA

STAGE 17
HIGH BENTHAM TO SEDBERGH

22 miles / 36km
380 metres ascent

Starting in North Yorkshire and ending in Cumbria, the final English county.
With only one beautiful, but testing, climb, this stage is one to savour.
Not least because of tipping the scales – at the end of this stage
you'll be nearer to John o' Groats than Land's End.

Barbondale, the only climb on this stage, provides absolutely everything you could want from a bike ride in microcosm. It has a long gradual entry to the valley, traversing a fellside with occasional stone walls, which are typical of this area. Then there is the grand reveal of its dramatic ice-carved steep edges, distinctive scooped river bottom and thin ribbon of road climbing away from the beck until it disappears out of sight on the horizon. A long, but never very steep climb draws you upwards away from the valley bottom. Where at first you feel dominated by the towering hillside opposite, you eventually view it as an equal. When you rattle across the final cattle grid to attain the top you are rewarded with a panoramic view of the Dales laid out at your feet. A skill-testing descent drops you into Dentdale. It is the perfect ride, a complete test of bike-handling and fitness.

HIGH BENTHAM TO DEVIL'S BRIDGE

Turn left on to the B6480 along the main street of High Bentham to reach Low Bentham, where the route crosses the River Wenning twice in quick succession. For the next couple of miles, the road companionably follows alongside the river. In Wennington the route follows an unsigned right-hand turn along Spout Lane. Across Cumbria, 'spout' is used to describe waterfalls, most often those with a high but narrow drop; it is a word you will spot frequently on maps and in place names.

Around 1.5 miles after Wennington, continue through the hamlet of Wrayton. Turn right on to the A683 at a T-junction by a stone bus shelter. A large imposing gateway and gatehouse marks the entrance to Thurland Castle. Originally built in the fourteenth century, the castle was destroyed in a Civil War siege; the ruins were incorporated into a grand manor house in the nineteenth century. It is now luxury apartments but retains its moat and portcullis entrance.

The road takes you through Tunstall and Nether Burrow, two distinct villages each with their own pub and a handful of stone-built houses. Turn left at a T-junction on to the A65; shortly afterwards turn right to take you to Devil's Bridge on the outskirts of Kirkby Lonsdale.

DEVIL'S BRIDGE TO BARBONDALE

Kirkby Lonsdale's twelfth-century stone bridge is a well-known landmark attracting motorbike riders, walkers and families. The story goes that the bridge was built by the Devil for an old woman who needed to collect her cow from the other side of the water. The pact made was that the Devil would take the soul of the first body to cross it. When it was complete, the Devil waited expectantly, but the cunning old woman threw some bread across and her little dog chased after it, cheating the Devil of his human soul. You can see the Devil's handprint in the centre of a stone at the apex of the bridge.

William Wordsworth in his *Guide to the Lakes* (1810) recorded the view from St Mary's Church in Kirkby

Lonsdale as being of note, but it was art critic, social theorist and poet John Ruskin who gave his name to it in 1875. From Ruskin's Viewpoint there are stunning views across the meander bend in the River Lune to the fells behind. It is undeniably beautiful. Ruskin's reaction verged on the rapturous: 'I do not know in all my country, still less in France or Italy, a place more naturally divine.'

From Devil's Bridge the route climbs slightly to the small village of Casterton; after passing the entrance to the Casterton Sedbergh Preparatory School, turn right on to a narrow lane which works its way up towards the fell edge. Turn right over a stone bridge then immediately turn left, signposted *Dent*. A narrow strip of tarmac between the lofty green fronds of bracken leads to the open fell. At a T-junction follow the fingerpost pointing in the direction of *Dent*.

BARBONDALE TO GAWTHROP

A short fast descent takes you down to the level of Barbon Beck and, as the road curves round, a cleft between two hillsides appears. Bit by bit the road rises, tantalising with hidden dips as it stretches away towards the skyline and the full dramatic curved shape of this ice-carved valley reveals itself. South-east facing, the light

plays across the valley side that towers above the road on the opposite side of the beck in the early part of the day, while the lower section by the steam holds the light and warmth long into a summer's evening. Calf Top, the highest point of the fell, was recently reclassified as a mountain after a measurement showed it to be higher than the requisite 2,000 feet (609.6 metres).

Barbondale is a climb that draws you on; gradually more of the surrounding fellsides appear until the summit offers a panoramic view of the intersection between Barbondale behind you and Dentdale with Aye Gill Pike ahead. While the climb up through Barbondale is long, the descent into Gawthrop on the other side is a steep corkscrew that rapidly spirals down to an old stone bridge. It is a descent to approach with caution rather than daredevilry.

GAWTHROP TO SEDBERGH

A left turn at the abrupt T-junction at the bottom means that rider and river run parallel, both heading towards Sedbergh where the River Dee joins the River Rawthey. With the dark presence of Combe Scar to the left, the road twists up and down between farm buildings, flirting with the river. A short, flat section of the road matches up with a wider, shallower section of the river.

Here you might see the silhouette of a heron or the flit of a kingfisher between the trees.

Almost 3 miles after leaving Gawthrop, turn right to cross the river on a stone bridge, then turn left at a T-junction to join the road towards Sedbergh just beneath Moser Hill. It's a tricky turning as the road is steep and you approach it with no momentum. As the road kicks up again, a view of the Howgill Fells appears, framed by the trees on either side of the road. In the foreground you will notice the distinctive octagonal shape of the Pepperpot.

The original Pepperpot building is over 100 years old and was part of the now demolished Akay Estate. The building is now owned by Sedbergh School; it has recently been restored. Built on a small mound, it enjoys far-reaching, 360-degree views from its upper windows. A perfect spot for enjoying the evening sun or stargazing over the fells. In 1948 a passing cow fancied surveying the grazing and managed to ascend the stairs; a picture was published in the *Westmorland Gazette* of it looking out from a window. It took five men with ropes to get it down again.

Cross over the River Rawthey on the stone bridge at Millthrop and pass Sedbergh School chapel and sports fields to arrive at the end of the stage by the entrance to

DENT
A visit to Dent and its cobbled streets is a worthwhile detour. Just 1 mile along Dentdale from Gawthrop takes you to this charming village. With white-walled stone cottages and narrow streets, it is like stepping back in time. Dent has had two major exports in its history: Dent marble and textiles.

Dent marble is unique in that its deep black surface is covered with the white outlines of fossils. It has been exported worldwide; it can even be found in a fireplace made in 1843 for the Winter Palace in St Petersburg. The rocks and features surrounding Dent inspired Dent's most famous son, Adam Sedgwick, one of the founders of modern geology. A large lump of pink Shap granite in the centre of Dent is engraved with his name.

The Terrible Knitters of Dent – terrible because they were so astoundingly fast – were famous around the Dales. Until the nineteenth century knitting was a cottage industry and women, children and even men would knit in every spare moment. Knitters were brought yarn by merchants who returned to collect the mittens, socks, stockings, hats and jackets they knitted and took them off to sell at a market.

St Andrew's Church to your left and the narrow one-way main street to your right. Standing at the stage end in Sedbergh you are now closer to John o' Groats than Land's End.

SLEEP

THE BLACK BULL
Enjoy a night of luxury in a beautiful hotel room furnished
with custom-made toiletries designed by the Sedbergh Soap
Company.
44 Main Street, Sedbergh, LA10 5BL
T 01539 620 264
www.theblackbullsedbergh.co.uk

DALESLEA
Lovely comfortable rooms, a hearty breakfast, and the perfect
position with fell views and a short walk to the centre of town.
Station Road, Sedbergh, LA10 5DL
T 01539 621 789
www.dalesleabnb.co.uk

FARM & FELL
Traditional working farm campsite with absolutely outstanding
views. Hot showers, toilets and washing-up facilities, plus a
fire pit for every pitch so you can make the most of the star-
filled dark skies.
Birks Farm, Birks Lane, Sedbergh, LA10 5HQ
T 07894 739 232
www.farmandfell.co.uk

EAT

The Black Bull (see SLEEP) is a multi-award-winning
fine dining pub with great food but without the stuffy
atmosphere. Enjoy inspired cooking from head chef
Nina Matsunaga, who specialises in seasonal food with
a nose-to-tail cookery style.

DRINK

KIRKBY LONSDALE BREWERY
A slight diversion from the route but worth it to see Kirkby
Lonsdale and grab a pint at The Royal Barn. With a signature
brew called Singletrack, you know that the team here are
keen on cycling, as well as making excellent craft beer.
New Road, Kirkby Lonsdale, LA6 2AB
T 01524 271 918
www.klbrewery.com

SUPPLIES

In Sedbergh there is independent butcher **The Meat Hook**,
bakery and deli **The Three Hares** and greengrocer **Powells** to
provide you with everything you might need. The traditional
ironmongers **J.B. Rycroft Ltd** may surprise you with what
problems they can solve.

BIKE

ESCAPE BIKE SHOP
If you are really in need of spares then head north out of
High Bentham via the village of Burton in Lonsdale, taking
care on the busy A65.
Kirksteads, Westhouse, Ingleton, LA6 3NJ
T 01524 241 226
www.escapebikeshop.com

POLKA DOT CYCLES
If you need help with a mechanical give them a call if you're
within 10 miles of Sedbergh.
T 07887 780 629
www.polkadotcycles.com

STAGE 17 HIGH BENTHAM TO SEDBERGH *513 / 1000 MILES*   MODERATE

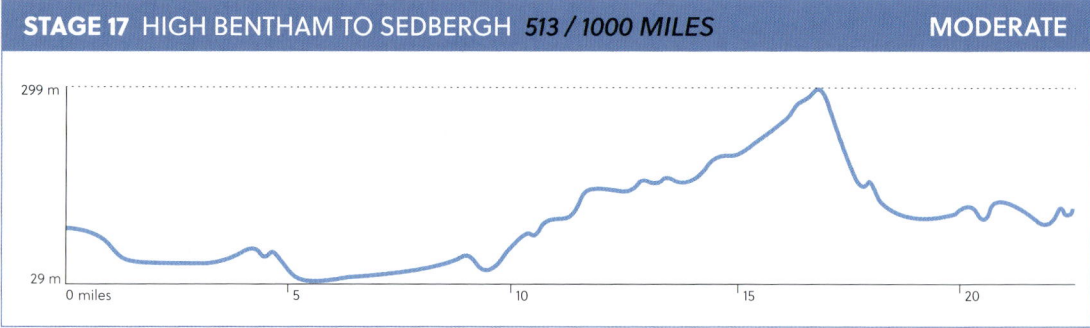

Howgill
Cautley
A683
Arant
Haw
B6257
Sedbergh
A684
A684
Garsdale
F
Millthrop
Long Rigg
Killington
Reservoir
A684
A684
A683
Lune
Dentdale
Aye Gill
Pike
M6
Middleton
A683
Gawthrop
Dent
Cowgill
Weather
Ling Hill
Yorkshire Dales
National
Park
Calf Top
B6254
Barbondale
Great
Coum
Old Town
Barbon
Crag Hill
Long Hill
Whernside
Lupton
A65
Casterton
Ribblehead
Kirkby Lonsdale
A683
Hutton Roof
High Biggins
Chapel-le-Dale
Whittington
Over Burrow
A65
B6255
Ingleborough
Nether Burrow
A683
B6254
Tunstall
Ingleton
A683
Wrayton
Burton in
Lonsdale
B6480
Wennington
Low Bentham
High Bentham
B6480
Hornby
S
A65
A683
Wenning
Wray
Lowgill

0   5 Miles
0   10 Km

THE HALFWAY POINT | SEDBERGH

The halfway point is a significant moment in any journey – from now on you are closer to John o' Groats than Land's End. Halfway also marks a distinct change in the landscapes and style of riding you can expect from the remainder of the route. Sedbergh, England's Book Town, is the perfect place to stop and take stock of the journey so far.

Breaking your LEJOG1000 journey in the vibrant market town of Sedbergh sets you as part of a great tradition of travellers, as it has been a meeting point for trade routes for centuries. Now walkers and cyclists pass through on long-distance routes across the Pennines and Dales – Sedbergh is a place used to welcoming visitors who arrive under their own leg power. Stock up on supplies, enjoy a relaxing meal and a drink, rummage through the many bookshops. Or simply appreciate the peace that can be found at the foot of gently rounded Howgill Fells as you relax and recharge for the second half of your journey.

BOOK TOWN

Sedbergh, though small, is a true town, one of a dying breed which has the three essentials of salvation, education and damnation – a church, schools and pubs. It is a fully functioning independent town with everything else you need from the post office to a weekly market, a butcher, a baker, and probably a candlestick maker, as it is also a centre for arts and crafts.

As you might expect from England's Book Town, almost every shop has a small area dedicated to book sales, often themed to fit with the shop. You can buy books on fishing and seafaring with your fish and chips or get some gardening inspiration at the florists. A 'book shelter' in the old stone-built bus stop on Main Street is a popular place to sit and watch the world go by as well as picking up a book or two.

The crowning glory of the Book Town is the magnificent Westwood Books, stocking over 70,000 books across two floors, mainly second-hand with some new and some antiquarian; it is a place to lose yourself for hours at a time. If you purchase too enthusiastically you can arrange to have them sent home to save your legs from the added weight!

FIELD TO FORK

Surrounded by fells, woods and rivers, there is a close relationship between the landscape and food in Sedbergh. The award-winning local restaurants and pubs actively seek out food that has been produced within a few miles of the town. Foraged foods are frequently on the menu and the local butcher's shop prides itself on locally sourced meat. A regular weekly market on a Wednesday provides freshly baked bread, fruit and vegetables, fish, meat and British cheeses.

CRAFT AND HERITAGE

Once a centre for woollen textiles, Sedbergh had at one point several mills close by. Farfield Mill, built in 1837, was the last to close and is now a heritage centre where you can discover the history of textiles, weaving and knitting in the area. An exhibition centre showcases a wide variety of arts and crafts from both local and international artists.

Weavers, artists and craftsmen can be found in small shops and workshops throughout the town carrying on the great traditions of the area.

18

STAGE

31 miles / 50km
520 metres ascent

SEDBERGH TO LANGWATHBY

Sandwiched between the Lake District and the Yorkshire Dales, the Howgill Fells have been dubbed 'hidden' so often that they started to emerge from the shadow of their more famous neighbours with in-the-know visitors being rewarded with uncrowded open spaces. The rounded yet imposing fells rise to the north of Sedbergh before the Eden Valley provides verdant green fields and comforting lanes below the towering wall of the North Pennines.

This is a full day spent on the bike in the greatest county of them all: Cumbria. North of Sedbergh, the route joins a railway line and the M6 in squeezing through the upper reaches of the Lune Valley, which acts as an approachable gateway around the seemingly impenetrable Howgill Fells. Whereas most people whizz along the M6 or speed up the West Coast Main Line, gasping at the open expanses of fells, the route feels a world away on the other side of the river, tucked snugly into the Howgill Fells with only sheep and the odd tractor for company. A climb up Orton Scar changes the perspective entirely, with the open expanses of the Eden Valley flanked by the imposing North Pennines. The stage ends at Langwathby, the crossroads of cycle touring and an obligatory rest stop for any discerning coast-to-coast cyclist, as well as end-to-end riders.

SEDBERGH TO ORTON

Cycle for a short distance along Main Street from St Andrew's Church then turn right on to Howgill Lane, which skirts the western slopes of the Howgill Fells. Look out for Lockbank Farm on your right as the road bends sharply to the left to sample home-made ice cream, with a great view along the Lune Valley. Pedalling away from Sedbergh, the double-pointed roof of Sedbergh's old railway station can be seen to the left.

The rise out of Sedbergh tops out as a track heads up the fell of Winder to your right, which watches

reassuringly over Sedbergh. Ahead, the eastern fringes of the Lake District National Park and the first glimpse of the M6 and the Lowgill Viaduct, which used to carry trains to Sedbergh, come into view. Howgill Lane plummets down and rises back up twice in quick succession. The second climb out of the hamlet of Howgill is steep and punchy for the first 100 metres, cocooned between high hedgerows. The only company to look out for is likely to be a tractor or farmer on their quad bike attending to their sheep. The smooth, rounded Howgills dominate the landscape to the right, carpeted with bracken on the lower slopes and purple dashes of heather higher up towards the skyline. You might be fortunate enough to see paragliders hurling themselves off the side of the Howgills.

The low hum of the M6 is a world away here on the eastern side of the River Lune. A cattle grid and short steep pull uphill announce the disappearance of hedgerows and the arrival of open grazing land, passing the paragliders' landing area, a patch of grass kept like a manicured lawn thanks to the hungry fellside sheep. As you look up the slopes of the Howgill Fells, the native fell ponies can be spotted in the bracken.

Entering the Lune gorge, the railway line, the M6, the A685 and the river all fight for space in this vital artery, the path of least resistance for logistics between Scotland and England. Squeezed into this narrow valley high above the eastern bank of the Lune is also the sinuous quiet rolling road that is Howgill Lane.

Although the M6 gets closer and its lorries louder, on the slopes above the opposing riverbank it feels a world away as your main concerns are probably the generous dollops of sheep poo lying on the lane. A 1.5-mile stretch of classic open fell road comes abruptly to an end with a cattle grid and sharp left-hand bend over a beck, emerging into a drystone-wall-lined lane which descends down over the River Lune to a lone farmstead (Low Borrowbridge) where you keep right to stay on the lane as opposed to turning into the farmyard. Continue on the road underneath the railway line and motorway before turning right on to the A685 following the signpost to *Tebay*.

Tebay is perhaps most famous for its services on the M6 which even had its own television documentary, charting the rise of a nearby farming family as they developed a huge farm shop services stuffed full of local produce. From Tebay, which originally grew as a railway village, go straight ahead at a roundabout and then it's just over 2 miles of gradual uphill to reach the village of Orton, entering the Westmorland Dales along the way. Curiously, after expanding its area by nearly 24 per cent, the Yorkshire Dales now encompasses more of the historic county of Westmorland, which had nearby Appleby-in-Westmorland as its capital. Appleby is famous for its

Horse Fair, the largest in Europe, which is sacrosanct in the travelling community calendar. In June you may see proudly groomed horses pulling bowtop caravans making their way through Orton to the fair.

ORTON TO CROSBY RAVENSWORTH

The Yorkshire Dales are synonymous with limestone, and you will be acquainted with the rock shortly with a wall of it to climb up called Orton Scar just north of the village. The climb starts just past Bullflatts Farm and lasts for around 1 mile; the reward is glorious views of the Eden Valley to the north and looking back to the Howgills in the south. The sky above Orton Scar is often filled by murmurations of starlings, which swoop and dance above the limestone pavement attracting birdwatchers from afar.

At the top, go over a cattle grid then turn left (signposted *Crosby Ravensworth*) to start descending gently downhill. Orton Scar marks the watershed between the Lune and the Eden. Dominating the skyline like an impenetrable wall to the north-east are the North Pennines with Cross Fell, at 893 metres and the highest peak in England outside the Lake District, and next to it Great Dunn Fell, at 848 metres with its domed radar station which is accessed by what is said

to be the highest paved road in England. It is the closest mountain the UK cyclist has to Mont Ventoux, as riders from far and wide strive for an unsurpassable Strava time on the UK's highest segment. The area even boasts the only named wind in the UK, the Helm Wind, a strong northeasterly to rival the Mistral of France's Rhône Valley.

CROSBY RAVENSWORTH TO LANGWATHBY

After 3 miles of rolling descent from Orton Scar the route arrives in Crosby Ravensworth where open fells give way to the re-emergence of hedgerows. The Butchers Arms is a community-owned pub which even has an espresso van making an appearance on some summer days. Although the pride of the village is the 'book shelter', an old bus shelter stuffed full of novels and, if you're lucky, huge home-grown courgettes. The rural idyll and sense of community is alive here in the Eden Valley, with a heavenly welcome extending to visitors with free Wi-Fi and toilets in the village church.

Maulds Meaburn, a meandering mile down the road from Crosby Ravensworth, is spliced in two by a picturesque stream by which sit a couple of swings, making an inviting place to stop for a picnic. Turn right over a stone bridge on leaving Maulds Meaburn then, after 2 miles, turn left at a T-junction into King's

ENGLAND'S FINEST RAILWAY

Saved from ruin in the late 1980s and famed for its tunnels and stunning viaducts higher up in the Yorkshire Dales, you don't have to be a trainspotter to appreciate the beauty and amazing feat of engineering that is the Settle to Carlisle Railway. The line to the south of Langwathby rises to the highest mainline station in England above the village of Dent (350 metres above sea level). The Midland Railway Company, fed up with waiting for cooperation from its rivals for a slice of the Anglo–Scottish travel market, set about building its own line in 1869. The result was a spectacular railway and the last in Britain to be built by gangs of 'navvies', who toiled in tough conditions without the aid of any heavy machinery to construct 14 tunnels and over 20 viaducts. Makeshift towns sprung up to house the workers, including Jericho near the Ribblehead Viaduct. Over 100 men were killed during the building of the viaduct, with unstable wooden cranes and gunpowder blasts accounting for many.

Meaburn. This is cow country now, and a pause may be needed to let a herd laden with milk mooch nonchalantly across the lane to the parlour. Turn left at a T-junction after King's Meaburn then fairly swiftly afterwards turn right, signposted *Temple Sowerby*.

The route briefly heads to the north-east, straight at Cross Fell and the imposing North Pennines. Pass underneath the A66, then turn left into the village of Temple Sowerby, with the quietness of its main street due to a new bypass.

After Temple Sowerby, turn right (signposted *Culgaith*); the road climbs steeply over a level crossing into the village. The route rolls alongside the Settle to Carlisle Railway with the mountain of Blencathra, or Saddleback as it is more commonly known due to its distinctive shape, guarding the entrance to the northern Lake District off to the west. Continuing north, the land drops away to the west to the River Eden in the bottom of the valley. Arriving in Langwathby, turn left on to the A686. The stage finishes next to the Shepherds Inn. On a summer's day it's a great meeting point for cycle tourers as thousands pass through the village on the C2C cycle route, which crosses Northern England from the Irish Sea to the North Sea, each year.

SLEEP
SHEPHERDS INN
Heartbeat of the village and stopping point for coast-to-coast cyclists with six rooms.
Langwathby Bridge, Langwathby, CA10 1LW
T 01768 881 463
www.shepherds-inn.co.uk

BANK HOUSE FARM
A camping field overlooking Sunny Gill Beck with a shower block and a full breakfast available in the farmhouse. Just under 2 miles north of Langwathby in the next stage.
Little Salkeld, CA10 1NN
T 01768 881 257
www.c2c-cycle-accommodation.co.uk

EAT
The **Shepherds Inn** (see SLEEP) do pub classics in the evening if you're staying and sandwiches until 5.00 p.m. if you're passing. If it's sunny head to the tables on the village green for a post-ride ale.

SUPPLIES
Pick up some fuel for the next stage at **Langwathby Stores** at the northern end of the village green.

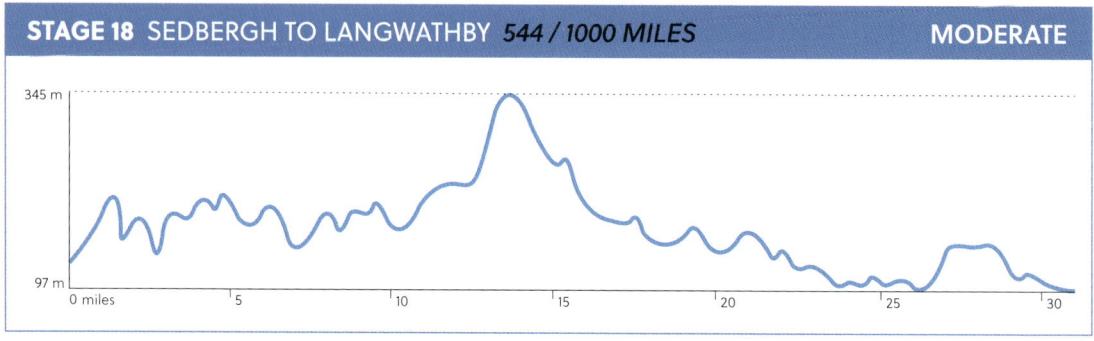

STAGE 18 SEDBERGH TO LANGWATHBY *544 / 1000 MILES*　　　　**MODERATE**

STAGE 19

LANGWATHBY TO BRAMPTON

21 miles / 33km
320 metres ascent

Welcome to the Garden of Eden. The River Eden, which rises within the Yorkshire Dales and saunters into the sea at the Solway Firth, has carved a valley of great fertility and beauty. An unfussy farming landscape lying between the rugged North Pennines and the at-times overdressed, beautified Lake District.

A busy cross-section of the country for cycling with the first few miles spent amongst cyclists completing their coast-to-coast crusades, rolling northwards you leave the coast-to-coasters behind and enjoy a freewheeling frolic down the Eden Valley. Each rise rewards with enticing views to Scotland and a suggestion of the remaining, final, country of the journey still ahead. Here in these rural backwaters the importance of hospitality is made clear. Hamlets which are little more than clusters of farms and cottages still support lone local hostelries, the heartbeat of the community. In these hidden away villages, off the beaten tourist track, it is hard to believe you are still in the same county as central Lakeland. The choked lanes, second-home owners and tea towels emblazoned with Wordsworth's famous verses seem a world away.

LANGWATHBY TO KIRKOSWALD

Turn right, crossing Langwathby village green, and ride past the post office to follow Salkeld Road to Little Salkeld, heading under the railway line just before the hamlet. For the first 3 miles of this stage, the route follows the same tyre tracks as the C2C cycle route. Little Salkeld has its own working watermill painted in pink, one of only a handful of working watermills remaining in the country. On leaving the hamlet, the road bends to the right and rises upwards towards the dark imposing ridge of the North Pennines. The route passes the

entrance to Long Meg and her Daughters, the second largest (by diameter) stone circle in the country – William Wordsworth wrote: 'Next to Stonehenge it is beyond dispute the most notable relic that this or probably any other country contains.' Long Meg is the tallest of the 69 stones, standing at nearly 4 metres high.

Around 1 mile after the entrance to Long Meg, follow the road as it curves to the left to reach the small village of Glassonby. After Glassonby, the road swoops downhill towards the River Eden; as you rapidly lose height to cross one of its tributaries you can hear the water effortlessly and serenely flowing over rocks on the riverbed. The towering ridgeline of the North Pennines looms large to your right. To the east, the grey asphalt road of Hartside Pass curves its way to the top of the ridge. Hartside often features in the Tour of Britain; however, LEJOG1000 remains in the serene Eden Valley.

Just before entering Kirkoswald, you may catch a glimpse of the remaining tower of the old castle off to your right, looking down on the rest of the ruins of the former castle site. The castle was ransacked by Scottish raiders led by Robert the Bruce in 1314 before being rebuilt. On entering the village, turn right at the T-junction (signposted *Brampton*); from here it is 15 carefree miles on the same road until the end of the stage. The village gets its name from its church, St Oswald's. Oswald, King of Northumbria, toured the pagan north looking for converts to Christianity in the seventh century. The belfry is in an elevated position,

separate from the church, so the sound could resonate more pertinently to summon the parishioners to worship, or to warn of marauding Scotsmen.

Riding up through the village, the jumbled jigsaw of fine Georgian buildings and old cottages of varying shapes and sizes are seemingly stacked up on each other, with a welcoming pub on each side of the road. Until recently, Kirkoswald had three pubs all within a short distance of each other; the local pub is a vital institution of community, a place of socialising and solace for many.

KIRKOSWALD TO CASTLE CARROCK

The next settlement is aptly named High Bankhill, an indicator of what happens next as the road keeps climbing away from the River Eden. The 5-mile stretch from Kirkoswald to the farming community of Croglin is mainly gradual climbing, with a couple of short descents, to reach an altitude of around 210 metres. The route criss-crosses through a landscape of fields enclosed by a tapestry of moss-covered walls and hedgerows. Sweet-smelling hay perfumes the lanes as you ride. Stray straw gives a soft comfy crush under your wheels where it has drifted from the carefully stacked bales.

Saying hello to a busy farmer is an art in itself. It seems to be all about the timing of the 'nod'. The nod is a

recognition as you pass, but not to be employed a moment too soon. Local farmers seem to have spent years perfecting this subtlety. The less movement in the head, the more authentic the nod. The road drops amongst a shady avenue of trees crossing a narrow humpback bridge which marks as a hello from the village of Croglin. Many small villages in this area, like Croglin, are still devoted to farming: cattle and crops on the fertile valley slopes to the west and sheep farming on the eastern fellside. Move along the route northwards which remains at the foot of the North Pennines, passing through another fellside community, Newbiggin, and bypassing a third, Cumrew, which cuddles closely to the contours of the fell which bears its name.

Continuing past Cumrew, the Pennine Ridge, which has been seen throughout the stage, begins to taper as the Scottish Borders approach. On a clear day, the border city of Carlisle can be spotted, along with the mouth of the River Eden as it empties into the Solway Firth, the large, often sandy, estuary separating Cumbria from the hills of South West Scotland. The road undulates with short rollers before descending pleasantly to Castle Carrock. After many miles with hills for company, there is a revitalising sense of renewal as the more open borderland stretches away to the horizon.

To your right as you enter Castle Carrock a small reservoir appears which keeps Carlisle in drinking water and provides a habitat for a variety of waterfowl. Carlisle has had more than enough water, suffering major floods in 2005 and then again in 2015. In 2015 the city's new flood defences were unable to cope with the volume of water cascading off the high fells into the River Eden catchment. During December 2015 with the Eden overflowing, time stood still in the Warwick Road area of the city. Tinsel on Christmas trees remained in carefully decorated bay window displays at the end of January as the area took on an eerie apocalyptic feeling before residents set about restoring their homes and lives.

CASTLE CARROCK TO BRAMPTON

On entering Castle Carrock you are encouraged to 'please dance' by the sign, a reference to Music on the Marr. The 'Marr' is the village green where, along with other venues, an annual music festival was held every year until recently, with folk and many other musical styles represented. Castle Carrock will disappoint castle enthusiasts as the term is thought to have referred to a fortified manor house, of which very little remains.

This pleasant village signifies the end of the fells; from here the land feels more tamed with woodland, small pastures and a sanitised semi-rural landscape

CYCLING THE C2C
For the first 3 miles on leaving Langwathby, LEJOG1000 shares its route with the distinctive blue signs of the C2C. The C2C to many means 'Coast to Coast' but it was actually designed as the 'Sea to Sea'. The route is a 137-mile slice of Northern England from Whitehaven or Workington on the Irish Sea to Tynemouth or Sunderland on the North Sea, crossing through the northern fringes of the Lake District, tackling the hills of the North Pennines and then descending on old wagonways turned cycling paths through the old coalfields of County Durham.

The C2C holds a special place in the heart of many cyclists. It is long enough to be a challenge, but short enough to feel accessible. It is often an adventurous junior or reluctant teenager's first multi-stop adventure and taste of life on the open road. Or perhaps an older new rider looking for inspiration in a physical challenge.

in the form of Brampton Golf Club. Farming still takes place of course, but within commuting distance of Carlisle and with the high fells receding into the rear view, many village dwellers are just as likely to earn a screen-bound living as they are to live off the land.

A 90-degrees left-hand bend leads you out of Castle Carrock past Brampton Golf Club. Hidden behind the trees to your right is Talkin Tarn, a 'kettle-hole' glacial

lake fed by underground streams now used for water sports and a fine place for a picnic. After the club house, enjoy a leisurely downward gradient all the way into Brampton, crossing a level crossing over the Carlisle to Newcastle railway line before descending further into town.

Brampton was constructed in a hollow formed by glacial action. A network of now grassed-over gravel ridges, or kames, deposited during the dying days of a glacial period secludes the town from view until the last moment. The stage ends on the cobbled Market Place by the fine octagonal Moot Hall, standing proudly amongst a square of local sandstone buildings. Originally built in the seventeenth century, the existing structure has stood since 1817. The lower floor was originally for trading; there are some sadistic-looking stocks on one side of the building.

SLEEP

HOWARD ARMS
Traditional pub with warm hospitality. The large breakfast will set you up nicely for the day, and there is secure storage for your bike.
Front Street, Brampton, CA8 1NG
T 01697 742 758
www.howardarms.co.uk

SCOTCH ARMS MEWS
This former pub is now a bed and breakfast. It offers great accommodation with a breakfast buffet and secure bike parking.
35 Main Street, Brampton, CA8 1SB
T 07786 115 621
www.thescotcharmsmews.co.uk

CAMPING AT BANKS
Back to basics campsite for cyclists and walkers in the village of Banks a few miles into the next stage. A compost loo and drinking water is all you get.
Newgate House, Banks, Brampton, CA8 2JH
T 07838 225 108
www.campingatbanks.com

EAT
Home-cooked food at the **Howard Arms** (see SLEEP) is probably the best option in town.

SUPPLIES
Cranstons Brampton Food Hall on Front Street in Brampton is a renowned Cumbria butcher which also stocks great deli treats for the riding ahead. There is also a small **Co-op Food** in the town centre.

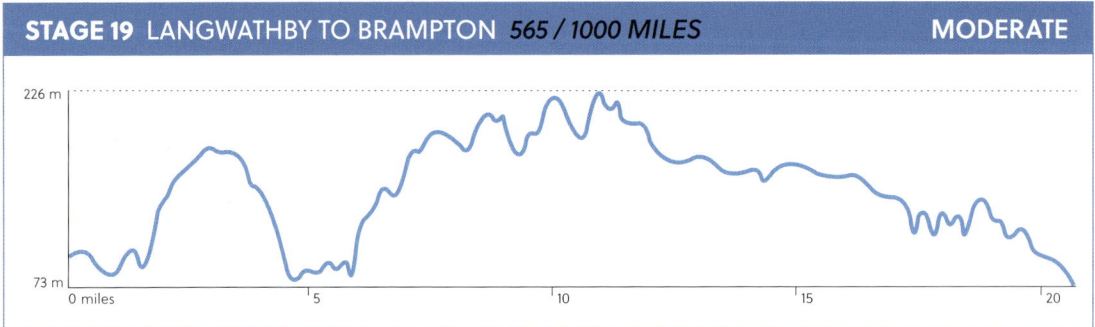

STAGE 19 LANGWATHBY TO BRAMPTON *565 / 1000 MILES*   MODERATE

SCOTTISH BORDERS & LOWLANDS

STAGE 20

20

25 miles / 41km
540 metres ascent

BRAMPTON TO LANGHOLM

Crossing through the border country you will receive a warmer welcome than those arriving from the south have in times past. Picking your way past sites of extraordinary historic interest, this border crossing can be wild and exposed in places with long stretches between settlements, giving you a taste for the terrain that contributed to the border's turbulent history.

Windswept hillsides, dark forests and narrow glens create a feeling of mystique as you make your way into Scotland on this constantly undulating stage. An optional short detour is worth it to see Hadrian's Wall, an astounding feat of engineering. It's the best-known and the best-preserved frontier of the Roman Empire, and Banks East Turret is the most intact observation tower in the western sector of the wall. While the borderland has been aggressively fought over, back and forth, for centuries with the Scottish border at times stretching further south than it does now, there is little more than a 'Welcome to Scotland' sign to inform that you have entered the most northerly nation of Great Britain. Like many travellers before you, Langholm is the first town you encounter within Scotland and a gateway to the delights of Scottish cycling that awaits.

BRAMPTON TO HADRIAN'S WALL

After passing the Moot Hall on your right, turn right down a narrow road squeezed between buildings, then turn right again at a T-junction on to Main Street. After around 300 metres fork left alongside a triangular-shaped green, following the signpost to *Lanercost*; this road has the lovely name of The Swartle. Crossing the River Irthing, you can see the well-preserved packhorse bridge to the side, which was constructed around the year 1724 by four local stonemasons. There is a carved inscription on each side of the bridge stating 'this bridge is not safe for tractors'.

As you enter Lanercost, have a look for the raised relief on its unusual road sign. Lanercost Priory looks like a haven of tranquillity, but its 800-year history has seen much unrest. Its proximity to Hadrian's Wall meant it was at risk of frequent attack during the Anglo–Scottish wars. The priory was dissolved by Henry VIII, although the church remained in use which probably protected the priory from becoming ruins. It is worth exploring the well-preserved buildings of the priory.

Leaving Lanercost the road bends to the left and starts to climb; part way up the climb turn left, following the signpost for *Askerton*. (If you want to get a better view of Hadrian's Wall, continue straight on at this junction – it does mean a little bit more climbing but if you are into historic landmarks, it is not one to miss. Standing here, looking south towards the Pennines, you have to feel for the soldiers stationed here on this windswept upland.)

HADRIAN'S WALL TO THE BORDER

Back on the route the road continues to rise a little, crossing the course of Hadrian's Wall, and then descends taking you down to a stone bridge. Continue along this lane, going straight ahead at a crossroads towards *Askerton*. Around 800 metres after this, turn left (signposted *Kirkcambeck*); after a further 800 metres turn right at a T-junction on to the B6318. The road bends round to the right in front of St Kentigern's Church.

St Kentigern, also known as St Mungo, is of Scottish origin. He was an illegitimate child, so he and his mother

were cast adrift on the Firth of Forth, eventually pitching up at the monastery of St Serf where he was educated. He left Scotland to spread the word of Christianity and many of the parish churches on his route south bear his name. He is the patron saint of, amongst other things, those accused of infidelity.

At the Crossings Inn turn left towards *Hethersgill*, then turn left on to another lane. It's a bit of an upwards drag on this section with farmland either side and the hills of the Scottish border on the distant horizon. As the road descends and you start to pick up pace, be ready for a right-hand turn towards *Penton*. The road features wide sweeping bends and further along a lovely little stone bridge forms an S-bend that snakes you across the river.

When you arrive at a T-junction with a low, stone slate-roofed building opposite, turn right; shortly afterwards turn left (following the signpost for *Longtown*). Turn right at the next junction, then turn left to rejoin the

B6318 (following signposts for *Penton* again) as the road zigzags its way through the field system and farmland.

A short but brisk descent sweeps you down to Liddel Water and flings you across a bridge into Scotland. Once over the bridge a sign announces your entry into the third and final country of this tour.

THE BORDER TO LANGHOLM
From river level the road climbs steeply upwards; at the crossroads take the left then right dog-leg towards *Langholm* and continue to climb. A patch of conifer woodland marks the top of the climb. The road continues to undulate; farmland is interspersed with patches of dark, foreboding woodland.

A long, somewhat gradual descent through thick woodland down to a stone bridge marks the start of the final small climb of this stage. Once the top is attained you can roll gently down to ride alongside the waters

of the River Esk. A delightful canopy of trees filters pale green light as the river sparkles beside you (on a sunny day at least). Turn right on to the A7 into Langholm; the stage ends on the High Street outside of the grand Library Building.

LANGHOLM

As a southern gateway to Scotland and just a few miles over the border, Langholm has always attracted visitors, some more welcome than others. Romans, invading English armies and Border Reivers have all made their presence felt. Langholm had a period of wealth and industry in the seventeenth century as a mill town, earning the local name of 'Muckle Toon'; it is now a popular stopping point for people following the A7 towards Edinburgh as the first taste of Scotland.

BORDER REIVERS
All along the Anglo–Scottish border from the late thirteenth century to the seventeenth century, homes and livestock were at risk from the Border Reivers. The Reivers – or raiders – came from both sides of the border and were indiscriminate about the sovereignty of the land they raided from. Reiving was, for many, the only way of survival – steal from others and protect your own possessions. It was a brutal way of living with very little families could do to protect themselves or their stock. Often a raid would be swiftly followed by a counter-raid, as people tried to retrieve their goods. The crowning of James VI of Scotland as King of England in 1603 largely brought an end to the Border Reivers, although horse thieving was still a problem until a little later.

SLEEP

ESKDALE HOTEL
The largest of the hotels in Langholm but still small and intimate in approach. Right in the centre complete with dining room, library and lounge bar.
Market Place, Langholm, DG13 0JH
T 01387 380 357
www.eskdalehotel.co.uk

BORDER HOUSE B&B
Cosy, family-run bed and breakfast with classic Scottish shortbread thrown in. The garage at the back is perfect for bike storage.
28 High Street, Langholm, DG13 0JH
T 01387 380 376
www.border-house.co.uk

EWES WATER CARAVAN AND CAMPING PARK
A short distance north along the A7, this site is adjacent to the rugby club. Hot showers, toilets, dishwashing and laundry facilities are underneath the main stand.
Langholm Rugby Club, Milntown, Langholm, DG13 0DH
T 01387 381 670
www.ukcampsite.co.uk/sites/details.asp?revid=15277

EAT

The **Eskdale Hotel** (see SLEEP) offers restaurant and bar food, as do the **Douglas Hotel** and the **Crown Hotel**.

SUPPLIES

Langholm offers some good options. **Pelosi's Corner Cafe** in the Market Place is popular with locals hanging out on a nice day and offers takeaway sandwiches. **Townhead Baker** on the High Street does traditional macaroni pie. There is also a **Co-op Food**. Whatever you choose, take something with you as amenities on the remote next stage have sporadic opening hours.

BIKE

MORRISONS
A classic combination of vehicle and bike repairs. Don't expect high-end parts, but they may be able to help you keep your bike on the road.
23 High Street, Langholm, DG13 0JH
T 01387 380 476

STAGE 20 BRAMPTON TO LANGHOLM *590 / 1000 MILES*   **MODERATE**

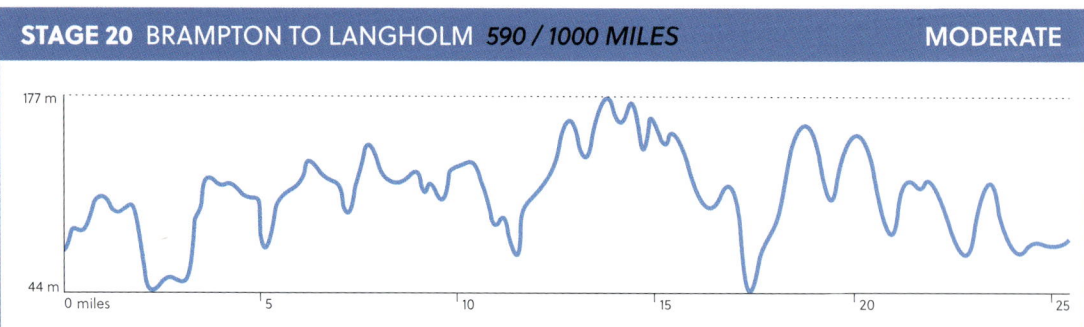

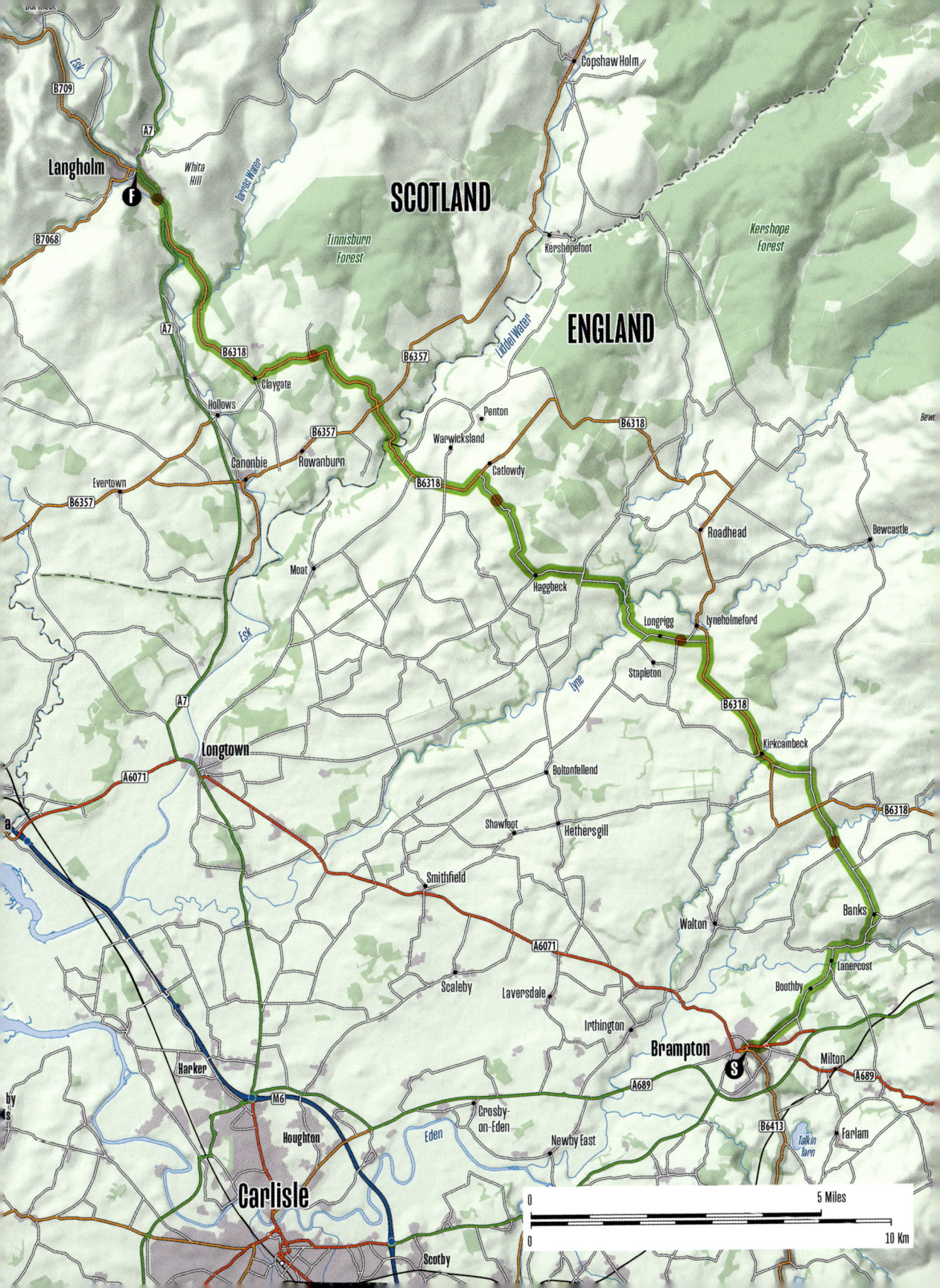

21

STAGE

50 miles / 80km
950 metres ascent

LANGHOLM TO PEEBLES

Scotland starts here. On this border foray and the first stage of your journey entirely in Scotland you will experience exhilarating riding with not a soul around. The variety and depth of interest in this landscape is often overlooked by people rushing to the Highlands.

With few settlements, this stage instead serves up four climbs to act as mental checkpoints to be ticked off in your head. Long open stretches with little to distract from the views make it easy to get into your own rhythm as the miles tick peacefully by. Managed woodland and sheep farming are the only signs of industry that can be seen from the saddle. With limited expectation of traffic, many roads are single-track, with passing places to avoid the occasional logging truck or tractor. Following the course of the River Esk you will discover Eskdalemuir, a place where Buddhists find peaceful contemplation and cyclists will find endless miles of quiet quality roads. Finishing deep in the heart of the Scottish Borders, Peebles enjoys a proudly picturesque setting on the banks of the River Tweed. The gentle(ish) climbs, endless open landscape and near deserted roads make it harder to find a better 50 miles of riding on the whole route.

LANGHOLM TO ESKDALEMUIR

Continue along the High Street and leave Langholm by turning left to cross the bridge over the River Esk, following the signpost for *Eskdalemuir*. The B709 follows the Esk for a time, before climbing through woodland then descending back down to and following the river. Just under 8 miles into the stage, the road curves to the right over a stone bridge and climbs away from the river, steeply at first then more gradually, as you gain 130 metres over the course of 2 miles. This is the first of

four climbs in this stage, but most offer friendly gradients and gloriously empty roads. Occasional timber waggons, with fresh-cut logs heading into the paper mills of Northern England, sometimes pass at keen speeds, delivering a waft of fresh pine as well as wind turbulence.

The road descends back down into the valley. The lack of fences on either side of the road adds to the sense of freedom and openness; you might feel somewhat insignificant in this landscape of bracken and forests. As the road begins to flatten you may notice an oval ring of 12 stones off to your left called the Loupin' Stanes. The tradition of local lads 'louping' (leaping) from one to the other of the two largest stones was abandoned after a leg was broken – definitely not recommended for this journey as there is still the majority of Scotland to be cycled.

In the valley bottom the White Esk is crossed before you reach Eskdalemuir, from where it is just over 1 mile further along the route to reach Kagyu Samye Ling Monastery and Tibetan Centre, the first Tibetan Buddhist centre to have been established in the West. The prayer flags fluttering in the breeze greeting you by the roadside are certainly an unusual sight.

The monastery previously ran a quirky vegetarian cafe on site ideal for the curious passing cyclist. It was a fascinating place, with cosy cushions and meditative music, but you did have to remain pretty zen when hunger struck and you wondered if the waiter had gone to Tibet to prepare your toastie, which often took half

an hour to arrive. At the time of writing, the most recent guru decided more time should be spent on Buddha and less on business, so the cafe has closed. Luckily locals have recognised the scarcity of a good coffee in these remote borderlands and in Eskdalemuir you will find the Old School Hub and Cafe. The hub enables people to access the internet, exchange goods and quaff quality cake all under one roof – a vital asset in such a remote area.

ESKDALEMUIR TO MOUNTBENGER

The road climbs gradually for the 6 miles beyond Eskdalemuir and is the first experience of passing places on this route, with many more to come in the Scottish Highlands. On these single-track roads with designated passing places etiquette is important; if followed it elicits friendly encouraging nods but if not it can lead to being nearly nudged off the road by a tetchy passing tradesman.

The important thing to remember is to read the road ahead and anticipate where you will need to pull over (the passing places are mostly marked with white signs) and wait in a passing place, not forgetting to pull over and let traffic behind you pass. A polite standoff can often ensue with both parties waiting and then deciding to go at the same time. The polite wave in response to etiquette can be comforting and reassuring on these remote roads and a distraction from lethargic legs. The top of the climb at 334 metres in altitude – it is announced by a cattle grid and a sign welcoming you to the Scottish Borders.

The road descends for around 6 miles to the small village of Etterick, before flattening out for 4 miles. Shortly after the Tushielaw Inn, turn left (staying on the B709; signposted *Innerliethen*) to start the penultimate climb of the day. A gradual 2-mile climb with Tushielaw Beck below you to the left leads to the top of the highest of the hills you will be conquering in the Scottish Borders at 376 metres. You are rewarded with a 4-mile carefree descent down the sheepfold-filled valley to the Gordon Arms Hotel in Mountbenger at the crossroads (where the B709 meets the A708), where you continue straight ahead.

MOUNTBENGER TO PEEBLES

The final, 3-mile climb takes you to 354 metres – nearly the same altitude as the last hill – and is followed by a flowing 4-mile descent. Hedges and fields re-emerge and take over from forestry at Kirkhouse near the bottom of the descent. Turn left at a sandstone war memorial, following the signpost for *Traquair*. Traquair is said to be Scotland's oldest inhabited house. There are antique-filled rooms and sloping floors as well as a maze and small brewery. The Bear Gates which guard

the entrance to the impressive tree-lined driveway have remained unopened since Bonnie Prince Charlie passed through them for the last time and won't be reopened until a Stewart monarch reclaims the throne in London; in the meantime, entry is by a side gate.

From the sandstone war memorial, Peebles is just 7 miles away along the B7062; although there is little climbing compared to the rest of the stage, the minor undulations as the road rises above and then drops down to the River Tweed can be felt at the end of a long stage. On arriving in Peebles, the road sweeps to the right crossing the River Tweed into the town centre, to reach a mini-roundabout marking the end of your border raid.

PEEBLES

If you are passing through the town in June, you may see the Beltane Festival which has its origins in fifteenth-century paganism and is held every year to celebrate the return of summer. Peebles and nearby Innerliethen have more recently been put on the map by mountain biking. Firstly, by the trail centre development at nearby Glentress Forest, but more recently by the dedication of locals at 'the Golfie', a heaven of handcrafted, home-made singletrack trails which dive down towards Innerliethen Golf Club from the wooded slopes above. The Tweed Valley often has hosted the cream of the

BUDDHA AND THE BORDERS
In 1967 two Rinpoches (religious teachers) established the first Tibetan Buddhist centre in the Western world at Eskdalemuir. The Kagyu Samye Ling Monastery and Tibetan Centre was named after the first Buddhist monastery to be established near Lhasa, Tibet, during the eighth century. The initial aim was to promote awareness of the compassion of Buddhism and the importance of human understanding. The development has had the added benefit of bringing employment to the area around Eskdalemuir as well as continuing the tradition of Tibetan sacred art in the most unlikely of places.

The monastery has had many visitors, those interested in learning about Buddhism or simply seeking a quiet retreat, but one of the most famous was David Bowie, who had a connection with the founding Tibetan monks when they were still in London and visited Scotland when the monastery was first established. He considered taking up holy orders, but a monk persuaded him to stick to music, or so the story goes.

On the left-hand side of the road before the monastery seek out Fairy Hill for quiet contemplation and solace in the woods on a softly cushioned carpet of moss.

world's mountain bike talent for the Enduro World Series, but is also a go-to for many mountain bike weekend warriors.

SLEEP

PEEBLES HYDRO

An iconic local landmark. This resort-style hotel has everything you require including a jacuzzi, sauna and steam room – just what the aching muscles need. Its imposing grandeur may suggest a snobby welcome, but the receptionists are relaxed and there is a bike store and bike wash at the back of the hotel.
Innerleithen Road, Peebles, EH45 8LX
T 01764 651 846
www.peebleshydro.co.uk

TONTINE HOTEL

Right in the centre of Peebles with a great view over the River Tweed from the grand dining room, where a delicious breakfast is served.
High Street, Peebles, EH45 8AJ
T 01721 720 892
www.tontinehotel.com

GLENTRESS FOREST LODGES

On the outskirts of Peebles, these camping pods and camping pitches are near the well-known mountain bike location of Glentress, one of the 7stanes trail centres. Shower block, indoor reception area, drying room and bike storage – this is worth the mile or so of off-route riding.
Glentress, Eshiels, EH45 8NB
T 01721 721 007
www.glentressforestlodges.co.uk

EAT

CROWN HOTEL

There are rooms here but stick to the food. First impressions are they are a bit tight on the chips but the home-made burgers are juicy and perfectly cooked.
54 High Street, Peebles, EH45 8SW
T 01721 720 239
www.sites.google.com/view/the-crown-hotel

DRINK

THE BRIDGE INN

Cosy pub with plenty of real ales and a snug complete with dartboard round the back of the bar.
Port Brae, Peebles, EH45 8AW
T 01721 720 589
www.thebridgeinnpeebles.co.uk

SUPPLIES

You'll find fresh quiches and sausage rolls among a wider range of deli items at **Coltmans** on the High Street in Peebles. There are also a number of supermarkets in the town.

BIKE

BSPOKE CYCLES

All your servicing and spares needs, even a shop dog.
Old Tweeddale Garage, Innerleithen Road, Peebles, EH45 8BA
T 01721 723 423
www.bspokepeebles.co.uk

STAGE 21 LANGHOLM TO PEEBLES *640 / 1000 MILES*   MODERATE

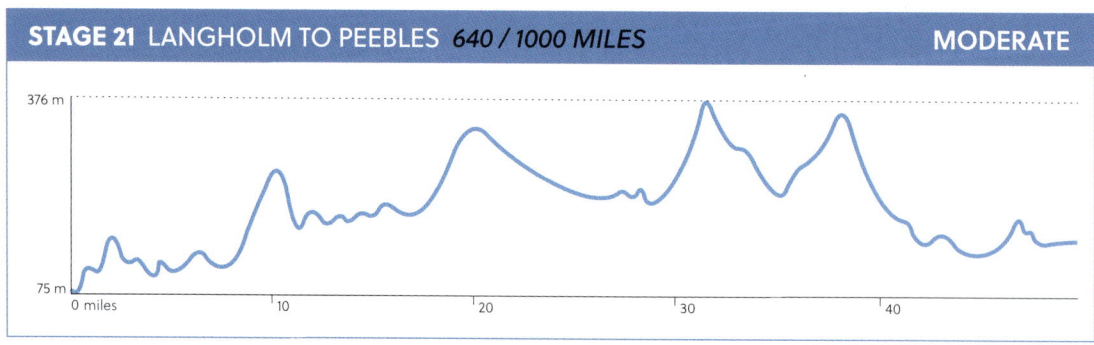

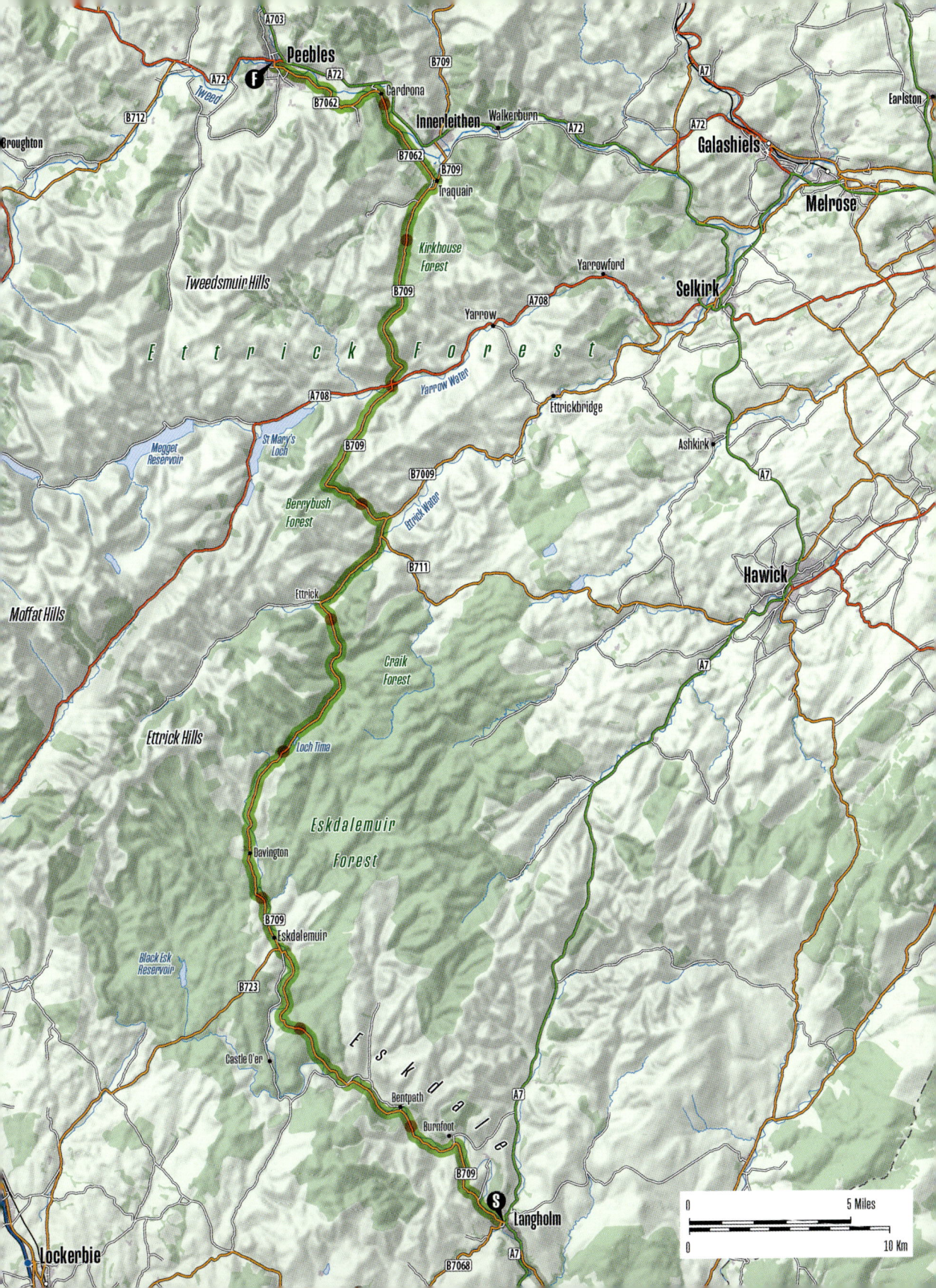

STAGE 22

22

36 miles / 58km
440 metres ascent

PEEBLES TO QUEENSFERRY

Calming riding in the shadow of the Moorfoot Hills is a world away from the bagpipes and the bustle of Edinburgh's Royal Mile, but as the Borders fade into the background the volcanic pinnacle of Arthur's Seat announces itself above the city of Edinburgh and invites further exploration.

Whether you are a seasoned visitor to the Scottish capital or discovering it for the first time, there is plenty to see. You need only give a cursory glance down an alleyway in the Old Town to see its 400 years of history or stay for hours to better appreciate the architectural accomplishment of the Georgian New Town or to take a deeper delve into one of Edinburgh's watering holes. While extensive urban areas are often seen as an obstacle a cyclist wants to escape from and rush through, Edinburgh does not leave you longing for open space and views as both are served up in abundance. Arriving at Queensferry brings you to three extraordinary feats of engineering: the iconic bridges, three parallel lines spanning the Firth of Forth, directing you across the water to the next chapter of your journey.

PEEBLES TO LASSWADE

From the mini-roundabout just up from the bridge in the heart of Peebles turn left on to the A72 following the sign for *Glasgow*. After around 250 metres turn right, following the sign for the *Golf Course*. Pass the houses of northern Peebles and then through fields to reach the A703. Turn left; the road rises imperceptibly alongside the modest river channel of Eddleston Water through the village of Eddleston, surprisingly home to what is claimed to be the largest three-dimensional outdoor relief map in the world.

The Great Polish Map of Scotland is a 1:10,000-scale three-dimensional topographic model of the whole of Scotland with incredible detail including all the islands, curves and gradients of this mountainous nation. The map was commissioned by Jan Tomasik, a Polish hotel owner who was stationed in Scotland during World War II; it was built in the 1970s by Polish employees of the Jagiellonian University of Kraków and hotel staff. The map, which sits in the grounds of the Barony Castle Hotel, was built to deal with queries from hotel guests about Scottish geography. It was abandoned and condemned to disappear in the undergrowth for years before recent restoration revealed its incredible detail.

Around 2 miles further north on the A703 turn right (signposted *Temple*); a gracefully arched switchback bend lined with willowherb takes you uphill on a minor road into this quiet corner of the Scottish Borders, sheltered by the ridgeline of the Moorfoot Hills to the south. The climb is rewarded with views of the Pentland Hills, a patchwork of small squares of scotch pines huddled together, heathland and the occasional hill farm.

Shortly after passing Gladhouse Reservoir, turn right on to the B6372 (signposted *Temple*); the road begins to pitch and roll, descending gradually. The feeling of space, stillness and solace belies the closeness to Scotland's capital city. Dropping into a glade of deciduous woodland the road descends more steeply; you may catch a glimpse of the Old Temple Kirk through the trees off to your right.

The hamlet of Temple derives its name from the

Knights Templar; this well-known military order had their Scottish base in the area between the twelfth and fourteenth centuries. Fork left on to a minor road at a junction where there is a triangle of grass. The minor road rises for a short distance before continuing to descend.

The route emerges from woodland into wheatfields and passes through the hamlet of Carrington. Around 18 miles after leaving Peebles rural riding is about to be replaced by Edinburgh and its environs. At a crossroads with a churchyard ahead, turn left on to the B704 to enter the twin settlements of Bonnyrigg and Lasswade. After riding straight through the former mining town of Bonnyrigg, turn left at a set of traffic lights on to the A768. The road drops down into Lasswade to cross the pretty River North Esk before an immediate incline. Continue straight ahead at a set of traffic lights towards *Edinburgh*.

LASSWADE TO THE ROYAL MILE

Passing under the City of Edinburgh Bypass (A720), continue straight ahead on Lasswade Road, which turns to Kirk Brae, to reach the A701. Turn right on to the A701 then immediately left on to Mayfield Road, which turns to Causewayside, continuing until you reach the wide expanse of parkland of The Meadows. Edinburgh is an amenable city that makes the most of its location amongst hills and near to the sea. It even has its own

THE ROYAL MILE AND EDINBURGH CASTLE

Unless you are riding in midwinter you will know when you have crossed the Royal Mile as street artists, selfie sticks and wheeled suitcases jostle for space. The street was traditionally used by kings and queens to travel between Edinburgh Castle (at the top of the hill) and the Palace of Holyroodhouse (at the bottom of the hill) and is Edinburgh's main tourist tramping ground today.

It is easy for the wild roving cyclist to see Edinburgh as an infuriatingly busy irritation but even for the most seasoned Edinburgh visitor it is hard not to be enchanted by the view from the Castle Esplanade – it's worth the quick detour up the Royal Mile (you may have to push rather than pedal as you weave through wandering tourists and negotiate classic cobblestones) to have a look. It is a challenge to find a premises not promoting tartan, shortbread or whisky – Scottish tourism's big three are very much on show here. The cuddly Highland cows should not be forgotten as a key souvenir item and of course all this is set to the soundtrack of busking bagpipers.

After pushing past the Scotch Whisky Experience, which shows whisky the sensory respect it deserves, a large open expanse greets you. Drink in the views: peer over the walls, appreciate the Old Town's precipitous geography clinging to the cliff sides with Arthur's Seat and the Pentland Hills providing a majestic backdrop. Be sure to abandon this advice in August when the area is given over to the Royal Edinburgh Military Tattoo.

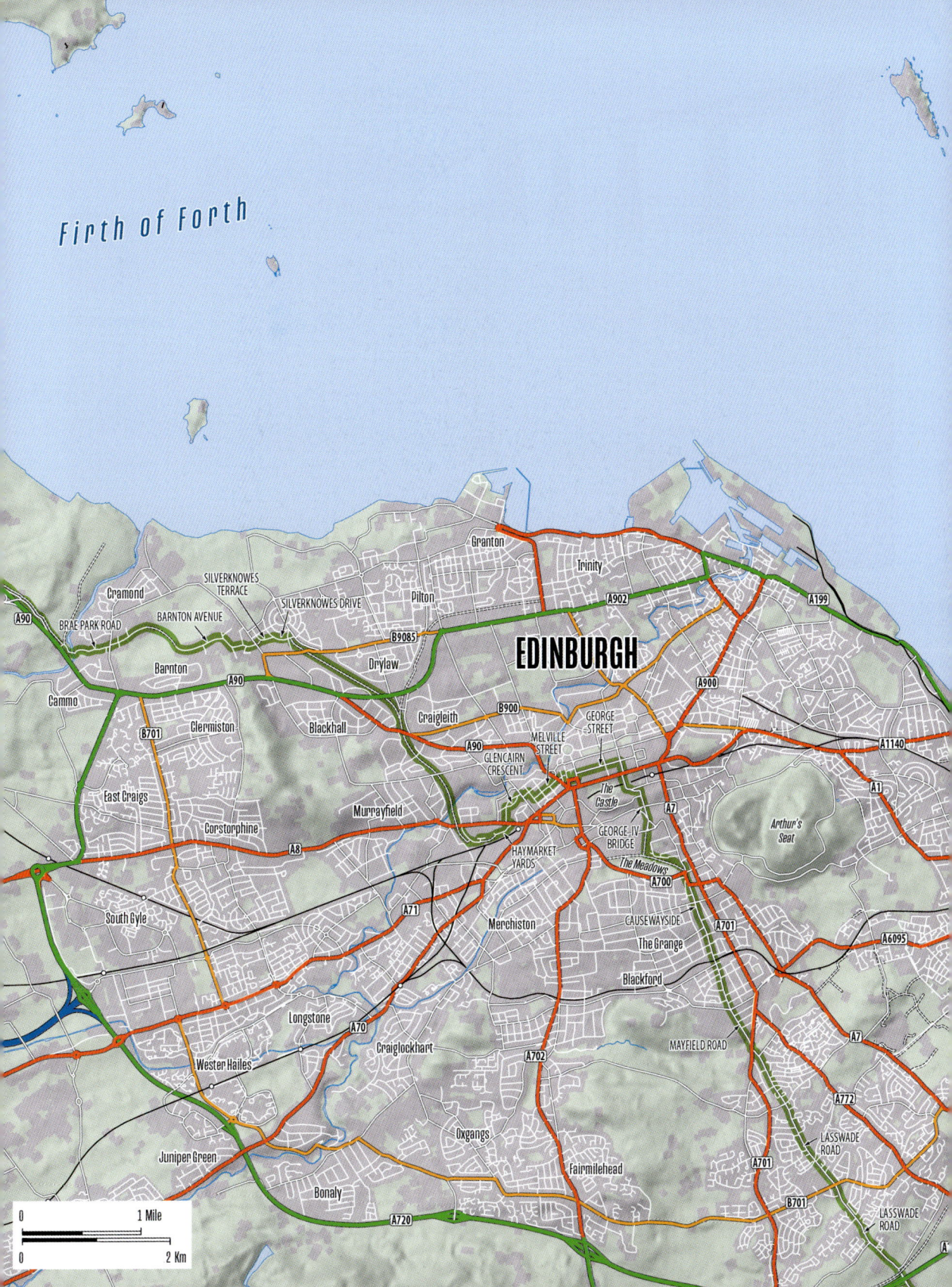

ancient volcano; you glimpse the towering crags of 251-metre Arthur's Seat as you pedal into the city. Arthur's Seat dominates Holyrood Park which also has several lochs and the remnants of four Iron Age hill forts.

A cycle path takes you along North Meadow Walk around the edge of the parkland to reach Middle Meadow Walk. The Meadows used to contain a loch which provided water for the city; it has since been drained. Today, locals come to exercise, strum guitars, play sport and lounge on those rare summer days. Turn right along Middle Meadow Walk, heading towards the Royal Mile. Continue heading north going straight ahead on to Forrest Road and Greyfriars Place, passing the National Museum of Scotland and the statue of Greyfriars Bobby. This Skye terrier maintained a vigil over the grave of his owner, who was a nineteenth-century Edinburgh police officer, for 14 years. Keep heading north along the George IV Bridge through the Old Town, until you cross the Royal Mile.

THE ROYAL MILE TO QUEENSFERRY

Until the New Town was founded in the eighteenth century, the Old Town was immensely overcrowded so the town expanded upwards with five- and six-storey tenements, the skyscrapers of their day. The merchants and lawyers lived on the middle floors above the stench of sewage in the streets but not too high up so as to minimise the number of stairs to climb.

The route dives into the New Town down Bank Street past Edinburgh Waverley railway station and straight ahead at the busy Princes Street. Turn left at George IV's statue on to George Street. Once the financial hub of the city, the grand banks are now more likely to house boutiques and fine dining restaurants. In the summer beer gardens spill out onto the street making cycling slow going. Just go with the flow and appreciate the amazing architecture.

George Street culminates at Charlotte Square, an opulent oasis of green space surrounded by grand houses including Bute House, the official residence of the First Minister of Scotland. From Charlotte Square keep an eye on your GPS device and look out for the small blue signs of Sustrans National Route 1. Stay with Sustrans National Route 1 and its blue signs for 8 miles (from Charlotte Square) as it follows a mixture of cycle paths, old railway lines, quiet residential streets and shared-use paths to keep you off or alongside busy roads, rather than riding on them. Turn left at Charlotte Square, tracing the edge of the private gardens and exiting at a dead-end road, between stately terraced buildings. Turn left on to

Randolph Lane and then right on to Randolph Place. At the traffic lights go straight ahead on to Melville Street. Where you see St Mary's Cathedral ahead, turn right. At a crossroads go left on to Chester Street, right on to Palmerston Place then immediately left on to Glencairn Crescent. At the end of the elegantly curving terrace with its private gardens turn left on to Coates Gardens, then turn left on to Haymarket Terrace. Taking the next right leads you alongside the railway line. At the end of Haymarket Yards look out for the separate cycle lane running alongside the rails. A cycle path on an old railway line leads out of the city passing close to Murrayfield, the home of Scottish rugby. Where the blue Sustrans National Route 1 signs point off to the left towards *Dalmeny*, opposite the entrance to Dalmeny House, continue straight ahead on the B924, which descends gradually and then with a sudden steepness into Queensferry.

QUEENSFERRY

The Forth Bridge is at first hidden in towering trees. A flash of resplendent red hangs above you but the best views can be seen by looking out to the Firth of Forth once you have passed underneath the bridge as the stage ends by the Hawes Pier.

CITY OF FESTIVALS
August in Edinburgh means festivals and you may wish to slip through the throngs of the Royal Mile and out of the city as quickly as possible at this time. Equally you may wish to pull up a deckchair at the impromptu bars and soak up the atmosphere with some street food or let your mind wander from mileage to be mesmerised by the street theatre on the Royal Mile. The Royal Edinburgh Military Tattoo up at the castle doesn't just have marching bands and a bounty of bagpipers but it includes acrobats and bike display teams too. The Edinburgh International Festival showcases a diverse range of music, opera, theatre and dance. The Edinburgh Festival Fringe is the biggest festival of performing art in the world and has provided the breakthrough moment for many budding comedians. As if that is not a packed enough schedule, the Edinburgh International Book Festival brings authors to a tented village on Charlotte Square. It is such a packed month that locals can experience 'firework fatigue' as early September approaches.

SLEEP

HAWES INN
Owned by a chain, it offers 14 comfy rooms and pub food right in the shadow of the iconic Forth Bridge. Author Robert Louis Stevenson penned part of his novel *Kidnapped* here.
7 Newhalls Road, South Queensferry, EH30 9TA
T 01313 311 990
www.innkeeperslodge.com/hotel/the-hawes-inn-south-queensferry-edinburgh

THE QUEENS
Nineteenth-century Gothic architecture meets personalised hospitality at this bed and breakfast. Cyclists are welcome – there is even room for a tandem!
8 The Loan, South Queensferry, EH30 9NS
T 01313 314 345
www.thequeensbandb.co.uk

EDINBURGH CLUB CAMPSITE
Close to the waterfront and the promenade of Cramond, off the route to the north of Edinburgh.
35–37 Marine Drive, Edinburgh, EH4 5EN
T 01313 126 874
www.caravanclub.co.uk/club-sites/scotland/edinburgh/edinburgh-club-campsite

EAT

SCOTTS
Fantastic views of the three bridges afforded by the huge floor-to-ceiling windows. Typical pub-style food, from fish and chips to steaks, but also worth considering for breakfast as morning light dapples on the water from the east.
Port Edgar Marina, Shore Road, South Queensferry, EH30 9SQ
T 01313 708 166
www.scotts-southqueensferry.co.uk

SUPPLIES
Stock up for lunch at the **Little Bakery** on the High Street in Queensferry. There is also a number of supermarkets in the town.

BIKE

THE BICYCLE WORKS
Scotland's capital is packed full of bike shops but this one is conveniently located near The Meadows and is open seven days a week.
29–30 Argyle Place, Edinburgh, EH9 1JJ
T 01312 288 820
www.thebicycleworks.com

GAMMA TRANSPORT DIVISION
This tucked-away store and Shimano Service Centre is a short distance off route in Stockbridge. Worth seeking out for the quality coffee to keep you focused on your ride out of the city.
15/24 Comely Bank Row, Stockbridge, Edinburgh, EH4 1EA
T 01313 321 777
www.gammatd.com

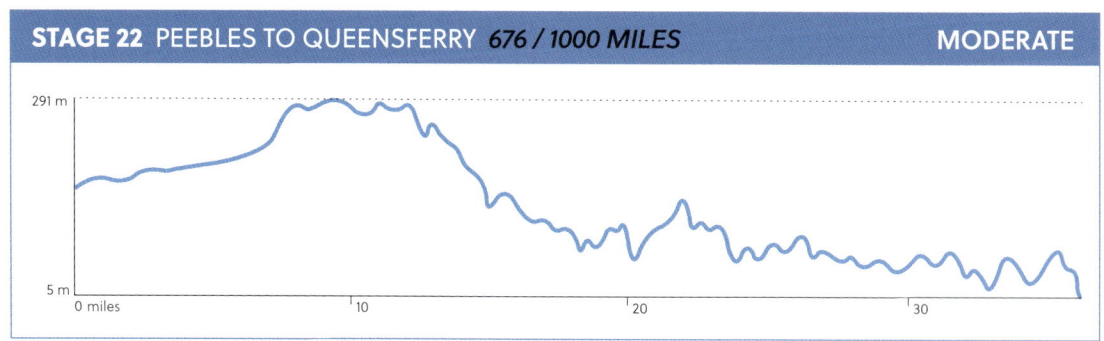

STAGE 22 PEEBLES TO QUEENSFERRY *676 / 1000 MILES*   MODERATE

291 m

5 m

0 miles   10   20   30

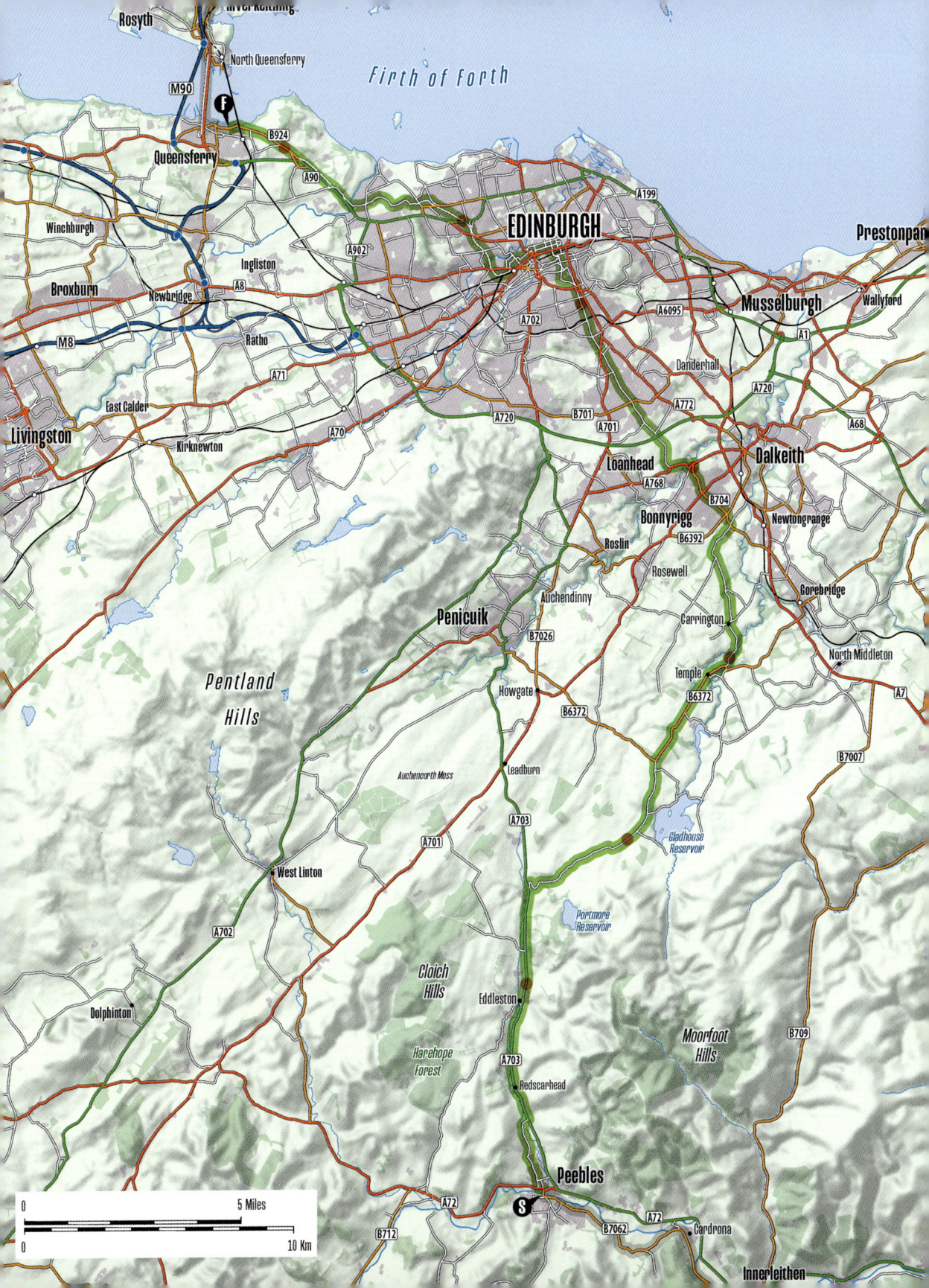

STAGE 23

23

42 miles / 68km
680 metres ascent

QUEENSFERRY TO PERTH

From the engineering ingenuity of the Forth Bridge, to the rugged beauty of the Common of Dunning and the elegant, historic city of Perth, the riding and scenery in this stage is constantly varied to make for an entertaining time on the bike.

Crossing the Forth Road Bridge is always memorable, more so if it is a windy day – it feels like a transition to a new part of Scotland. While in the early part of the stage you are aware of the nearby busy roads and towns, by the time you are climbing up through the glen of the Common of Dunning you will feel immersed in a rural area. With the sound of the river and scent of pine trees it is a highlight of this stage, and the 4-mile climb, through wooded hillsides with panoramic views opening up near the top, is rewarded with a flowing 4-mile descent. Arriving in Perth it is worth pausing on the bridge to look at the iconic image of the spire of St Matthew's Church reflected in the water of the River Tay.

QUEENSFERRY TO YETTS O' MUCKHART

From the shadows of the Forth Bridge at the end of Hawes Pier pedal slightly uphill along the B924; the surface becomes cobbled as you go through the centre of Queensferry. Turn right as the cobbles end, staying on the B924. Just before the road heads under the Forth Road Bridge, fork left on to a cycle path, which passes twice underneath the bridge before looping its way up on to the top. Cross the bridge on the cycle path. On the north side of the bridge, you will pass a viewpoint where some of the most famous sunset shots of the Forth Bridge have been taken. Follow the cycle path, keeping the road to your left, and descend alongside the A9000. A pedestrian crossing

gives you an opportunity to join the B981 heading into Inverkeithing.

Pass Inverkeithing railway station then arrive at a roundabout. Turn right here then turn left at the next roundabout (staying on the B981), leaving Inverkeithing behind. Although you can't see it, the M90 to your left sustains a low rumble, despite the farmland immediately around you. Pass through the small town of Crossgates then above the busy A92. Shortly afterwards, fork left on to the B917 (signposted *Hill of Beath*); as the name describes there is quite a kicker of a climb up to the village. The descent to the other side is interrupted by a small roundabout; turn right, staying on the B917 to reach the village of Kelty. Pass through the village then turn left at a T-junction on to the B996, entering the region of Perth and Kinross. As you ride this stretch keep an eye to your right for the distinctive lozenge shape of Benarty Hill. After 2 miles turn left on to the B9097 (following the signpost for *Crook of Devon*), which takes you over the M90.

The route passes close to the hamlet of Cleish. The presence of Cleish Castle, a sixteenth-century tower house, suggests it may not always have been so small. Stay on the B9097 for 6 miles then turn right on to a minor road into the village of Drum. After the village continue straight ahead over the A977, signposted *Yetts o' Muckhart*. After 1.5 miles turn left at a T-junction (signposted *Stirling*) on to the A91.

A short jaunt on the A91 takes you over an old

stone bridge where a sign announces your arrival in Clackmannanshire. A slightly awkward junction at Yetts o' Muckhart takes you almost back on yourself – turn right then right again on to the A823 (following the signs for *Crieff*). Yetts o' Muckhart comes from the Scots word *yett*, meaning 'gate'; it forms the natural gateway between the hills for cattle drovers and people moving between towns and villages.

YETTS O' MUCKHART TO DUNNING

After a very short distance on the A823, fork right on to the B934 (signposted *Dunning*). Entering the Common of Dunning you immediately have the sense of entering a secluded glen. Crossing the River Devon, you can hear the river rumbling over rocks; to your left you can hear, and see, a wall of water crashing over the dam that holds back the Castlehill Reservoir. A flat patch of grass at river level is a favoured spot for picnickers, fishermen and the occasional wild camper. It's a tempting spot for a very cold wild water swim.

Sensuous curves draw you upwards gradually through a glen between the fields and forests of the Ochil Hills. The more you climb, the more expansive the views become. Past Greenhill Farm the descent picks up speed. As you drop lower the turns become tighter and you naturally get faster as you rush towards the village of

Dunning. Although small, Dunning deserves a moment or two of exploration.

DUNNING TO PERTH

Dunning has a rich history: there is evidence of Bronze Age and Iron Age settlements, a Pictish stone cross dating from around AD 800 and the Roman camp at Kincladie Wood, the earthworks of which can still be found, suggesting almost continuous human habitation. St Serf's Church was largely built in the nineteenth century, but has a much older twelfth-century tower. Most of the village (excluding the church) was burned by the Jacobites in 1716. Maggie Wall's memorial is a fascinating piece of folklore to unravel. The words 'Maggie Wall burnt here 1657 as a witch' are etched on to stones at the base of a cross just outside of Dunning. For centuries someone has continued to over-paint the carving in white and lay a wreath each year. Whoever Maggie was, and why ever she was burnt, her story still has meaning to the mysterious painters. If you visit Dunning Golf Club (the cafe here is a good place to stop) then you will see a mural depicting a timeline of Dunning's fortunes.

In Dunning turn right and then turn left, following signs for *Perth*. As you leave Dunning, pause to look back at the Ochil Hills rising above the village. From

Dunning the road takes you gradually downwards, as forests are replaced with cultivated fields. Keep following the B934 as it curves to the left and crosses over a railway line, then cross the River Earn and turn right at a T-junction.

This final stretch of road climbs up through Milltown of Aberdalgie, taking you high above the tree-lined river on its lazy meandering course below. Descending under the M90, you are able to emulate the flow of the river and lazily freewheel until you reach a mini-roundabout on the outskirts of Perth. Turn right here on to the A93; pedal into the city centre and continue straight ahead on to Queen's Bridge over the River Tay where the stage ends.

PERTH

Once known as the capital of Scotland, Perth's tall spires and distinctive skyline lend a sense of grandeur while still being an accessible city to explore on foot. It has something for everyone with stunning architecture, galleries, vibrant cafes, bars and restaurants. It also has a fascinating history and has been the scene of royal power struggles, battles and political machinations. To learn more about its history follow the public arts trail alongside the river with sculptures from local artists themed around some of the most notable achievements of the city and its people.

BRIDGES OF QUEENSFERRY

You can't help but be impressed by the size and grandeur of this series of three bridges. The Forth Road Bridge, which was completed in 1964 and the chosen crossing for LEJOG1000, is sandwiched between the new road bridge, the Queensferry Crossing, which was completed in 2013, and the Forth Bridge, the older railway crossing which was completed in 1890. These three bridges represent the pinnacle of engineering from each of these three different centuries.

A regular ferry operated across the Firth of Forth between North and South Queensferry as far back as the twelfth century. By the eighteenth century it was thought to be the busiest ferry in Scotland. Ideas for an all-weather crossing began as early as 1806, with everything from tunnels to floating platforms proposed; it was not until 1882 that a plan for a suspension bridge was approved.

The original Forth Bridge is now a UNESCO World Heritage Site, as befits the world's first major steel edifice. Nevertheless, it remains a working estuary crossing. The distinctive red bridge carries around 200 trains across the Firth of Forth every day and forms a vital part of the East Coast Main Line.

SLEEP

THE SALUTATION
City centre hotel with a historical angle. Reputed to be the oldest established hotel in Scotland, The Salutation has been welcoming guests through its doors since the late seventeenth century. Bonnie Prince Charlie visited the hotel in 1745.
34 South Street, Perth, PH2 8PH
T 01738 630 066
www.strathmorehotels-thesalutation.com

THE LODGE
Situated a short distance into the next stage, The Lodge caters for cyclists with secure bike storage, basic workshop tools and a drying room.
Perth Racecourse, Scone Palace Park, Perth, PH2 6BB
T 01738 252 466
www.perthlodge.co.uk

ROSEBANK GUEST HOUSE
Cyclist-friendly accommodation with a great breakfast and secure bike parking, all within walking distance of the centre of Perth.
53 Dunkeld Road, Perth, PH1 5RP
T 01738 301 707
rosebankguesthouseperth.co.uk

EAT

BROTH3RS RESTAURANT
Right in the heart of town with a relaxed, friendly atmosphere and traditional Italian menu.
24 George Street, Perth, PH1 5JR
T 01738 445 544
www.broth3rsrestaurant.co.uk

DRINK

CULLACH BREWING
Enjoy a drink and a pizza at the taproom, a good range of craft beers, local beers and a fun, friendly atmosphere.
50 Princes Street, Perth, PH2 8LJ
www.cullachbrewing.co.uk

SUPPLIES
You can get everything you need in Perth with plenty of good-sized supermarkets and corner shops to choose from. However, if you want to make your picnic lunch a little fancy head to George Street to visit **Provender Brown**, Perth's premier independent deli and cheesemonger.

BIKE

RYAN'S BIKE SURGERY
Small but personal service shortly after crossing the Firth of Forth. Might be just the surgery your bike needs if Edinburgh's busy bike shops couldn't fit you in.
8 Hope Street, Inverkeithing, KY11 1LW
T 01383 420 777
www.ryansbikesurgery.com

J.M. RICHARDS
This shop has been in the same family for over 60 years and the site has housed a bike shop since 1906, so there is plenty of local experience to keep your wheels turning.
44 George Street, Perth, PH1 5JL
T 01738 626 860
www.jmrichardscycles.com

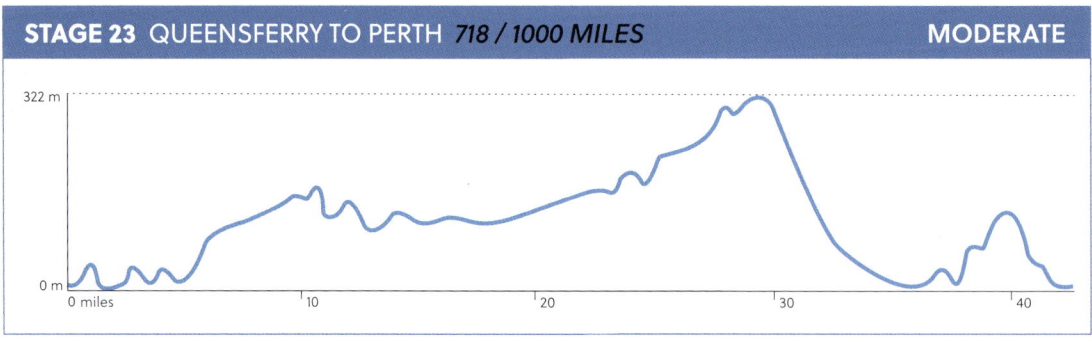

STAGE 23 QUEENSFERRY TO PERTH *718 / 1000 MILES*   **MODERATE**

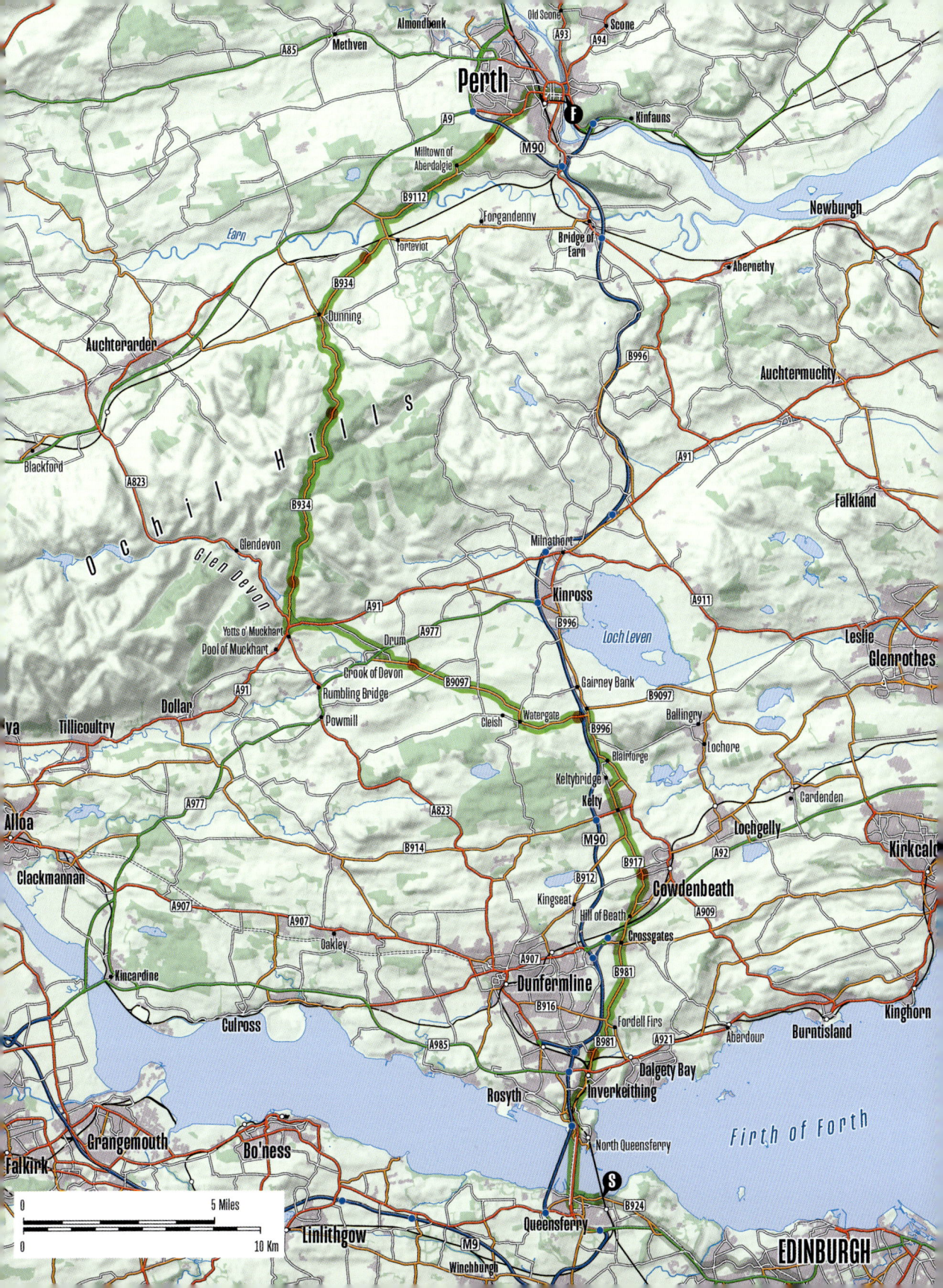

SCOTTISH HIGHLANDS

STAGE 24

50 miles / 80km
970 metres ascent

PERTH TO BRAEMAR

Sunshine and strawberries to snow resorts and skiing. Glenshee, the Glen of the Fairies, connects some of Scotland's most fertile farmland to the soaring summits of the high mountains. Despite signs of habitation, the landscape in the second half of the stage feels primaeval, empty and wild, like the ice has only recently receded.

From near sea level on the languid banks of the River Tay to the highest main road mountain pass in Britain this stage is epic, and that is not a word used lightly. It begins near Scone Palace and concludes with a descent down a grandiose glen to Braemar, famous for the Braemar Gathering. Where exactly the Highlands start geographically is often contentious, but in the psyche of this journey it begins in Glenshee, where the heather-clad mountains are simply majestic. It is a lung-busting, leg-burning climb, where at the final turn the road disappears up into the horizon as if it will never end. The vast mountain tops pricking the horizon give a feeling of insignificance in the landscape more pronounced after the comfort of the Lowlands.

PERTH TO SCONE PALACE

Pedal across Queen's Bridge – the middle bridge of three on this strategic crossing point of the River Tay. Turn left after the bridge to stay on the A93 (following the signpost for *Blairgowrie*), then after around 800 metres fork left, again staying on the A93 and following the signpost for *Blairgowrie*. Under 2 miles into the stage you pass the long driveway leading to Scone Palace. Pronounced 'skoon', the original palace, built on this site in 1580, was where Scottish kings were crowned, although what you can see now is considerably more modern. You can admire the castle from the grounds without paying the entry fee for the palace and gardens.

SCONE PALACE TO BLAIRGOWRIE

Shortly after Scone Palace and the village of Old Scone, fork left off the A93 (signposted to *Stormontfield*). This minor road keeps you off the fairly busy A93 for 5 miles. Woodlands interspersed with fields give way to a short avenue of beech trees. The route crosses a little bridge then arrives in the small hamlet of Stormontfield, passing St David's Chapel to your left.

The road straightens between fields of crops and strawberries. If you have ever bought Scottish strawberries, they were most likely from this area of Tayside. The river is just out of sight, providing moisture to the fertile soil to complement some of the driest and sunniest conditions for ripening in Scotland. This area sits in the rain shadow of the mountains of central Perthshire but in late spring a dusting of snow may linger on the tops away to your left.

Turn left at a T-junction to rejoin the A93. Just after crossing a single-track traffic-light-controlled bridge over the River Isla, the road is lined to your left by an impressive beech hedge. Part of the Meikleour Estate and laid out in 1745 by Jean Mercer and her husband Robert Murray, this is believed to be the world's tallest hedge. Robert would later be killed at Culloden fighting the English.

Arriving in Blairgowrie, the last town you will pass through for nearly 90 miles, stay on the A93 and follow the one-way system through the town, turning left over the River Ericht.

BLAIRGOWRIE TO GLENSHEE

After crossing the river, climb uphill for 200 metres then turn left on to Balmoral Road (staying on the A93 and signposted *Braemar*). We keep following the dramatic A93 all the way to the end of the stage. Passing through the suburban edge of town, the houses get less frequent and, as the road starts to climb, traffic dwindles to an intermittent trickle. Dubbed the Snow Road, it takes you higher and deeper into the mountains. The village of Bridge of Cally, which lies 5 miles after Blairgowrie, sits at a strategic meeting point of three glens. The Bridge of Cally Hotel has previously been a temperance inn and a petrol station; its village shop (which is the last store for nearly 30 remote miles) is one of the oldest in Scotland.

From Bridge of Cally it is 18 miles to the top of the Cairnwell Pass: Britain's highest main road reaches an altitude of 665 metres and has the ski resort of Glenshee at the top. The climbing is kind and gradual initially, with a long stretch in the valley keeping Shee Water to your right. There are no settlements on this stretch, just a few farmsteads and ski rental huts. Around 8 miles after Bridge of Cally lies the Cockstane, at the site of the gathering place of the Clan MacThomas. It is dedicated to the seventh Chief of Clan MacThomas; a board near the stone explains the full, chilling story.

The glen narrows after crossing Shee Water at the Spittal of Glenshee. As you try to read the topography of the landscape and work out how you will emerge from this great glen, the landscape looks blankly back. The answer becomes clearer around 3 miles further on. The snowpole-lined road drifts to the left, hugging the mountainside, ominously changing its trajectory towards the imposing Munro peak of Glas Maol, which dominates the skyline and guards the glen.

The challenging part of the climb comes at the end, with 250 metres of height gained in the last 2 miles. The last section has a gradient of 12 per cent. The roof

BRITAIN'S HIGHEST ROAD PASSES

Two tarmacked roads in the UK climb higher than the Cairnwell Pass – Lowther Hill in Southern Scotland (725 metres) and Great Dunn Fell (835 metres) in Cumbria – but they are roads to nowhere, or more specifically to radar stations, but only passes provide a true journey.

1   **Cairnwell Pass, Glenshee, Scotland, 665 metres**
    The highest mountain pass in Britain with a dramatic descent down to Braemar to boot.

2   **The Lecht, Aviemore, Scotland, 644 metres**
    A challenge for the next stage of the journey with an incredibly steep start and, like Cairnwell, a ski station at the top.

3   **Harthope Moss, North Pennines, England, 627 metres**
    This climb on the wild moors of Northern England just keeps the more famous Bealach Na Bà in fourth place.

4   **Bealach Na Bà, Applecross, Scotland, 626 metres**
    The 'Pass of the Cattle' is often misquoted as the highest road pass. The 'Belach' offers the longest continuous ascent of any mountain pass in Britain as it rises up from sea level at Applecross.

5   **Killhope Cross, North Pennines, England, 623 metres**
    A pass used by miners which divides Weardale and Cumbria.

of LEJOG1000 is at Glenshee Ski Centre. The car park is wide enough to host a Tour de France summit finish, but a few hardy tourists and the odd bird of prey are likely to be the only spectators. Glenshee is home to the largest ski and snowboard area in Scotland and one of its most challenging black runs.

GLENSHEE TO BRAEMAR

An epic 9-mile descent to Braemar awaits. Starting steep, fast and swooping, and only levelling out after crossing the river, it is a contender for the best descent of the journey. The route passes an old stone croft, perched on its own plateau above the river with mountains towering above. Watch out for white hares and black grouse darting across the road.

Braemar huddles together on the edge of a broad river plain in the Dee Valley and is ringed by imposing mountains, with many hikers coming to walk the adventurous Lairg Ghru pass to Aviemore in the west of the Cairngorms. In winter, Braemar regularly sets records for the coldest place in the United Kingdom, reaching -23 °C in February 2021; in harsh winters it is not uncommon to see deer mooching round the town looking for food. The stage ends where the A93 meets Invercauld Road in the centre of the village.

SLEEP

BRAEMAR YOUTH HOSTEL
Housed in a shooting lodge with cosy communal areas and a pool table, this is certainly not your average hostel. Set in leafy grounds on the edge of the village.
Corrie Feragie, 21 Glenshee Road, Braemar, AB35 5YQ
T 01339 741 659
www.hostellingscotland.org.uk/hostels/braemar

FIFE ARMS
For a bit of indulgence check into one of the 46 individually styled rooms at this historic listed building. If your budget doesn't stretch to staying at least check out The Flying Stag, the public bar at the hotel which serves great food and good beers.
Mar Road, Braemar, AB35 5YN
T 01339 720 200
www.thefifearms.com

EAT

THE CAIRN
Fresh Scottish produce cooked on their chargrill. All meat comes from just two local suppliers and fresh fish comes from the North Sea at Peterhead.7–9 Invercauld Road, Braemar, AB35 5YP
T 01339 741 234
www.thecairngrill.co.uk

SUPPLIES

If you want a reward for the tops of the climbs to come, stick a treat in your pocket from **Braemar Chocolate Shop**. For some savouries, there is a small **Co-op Food** in the town.

BIKE

CRIGHTONS CYCLES
Traditional bike shop without fancy spares but plenty of knowledge and skills. Useful before some of the biggest climbs of your journey.
87 Perth Street, Blairgowrie, PH10 6DT
T 01250 874 447
https://crightons-cycles.business.site/

BRAEMAR MOUNTAIN SPORTS
An outdoor equipment specialist that may be able to help with a few spares, wet weather gear, sunscreen and midge repellent.
5 Invercauld Road, Braemar, AB35 5YP
T 01339 741 242
www.braemarmountainsports.com

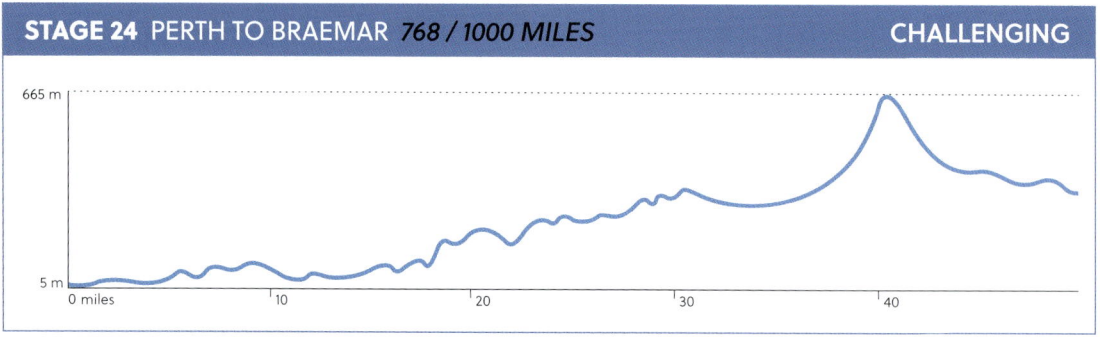

STAGE 24 PERTH TO BRAEMAR *768 / 1000 MILES* CHALLENGING

665 m

5 m

0 miles 10 20 30 40

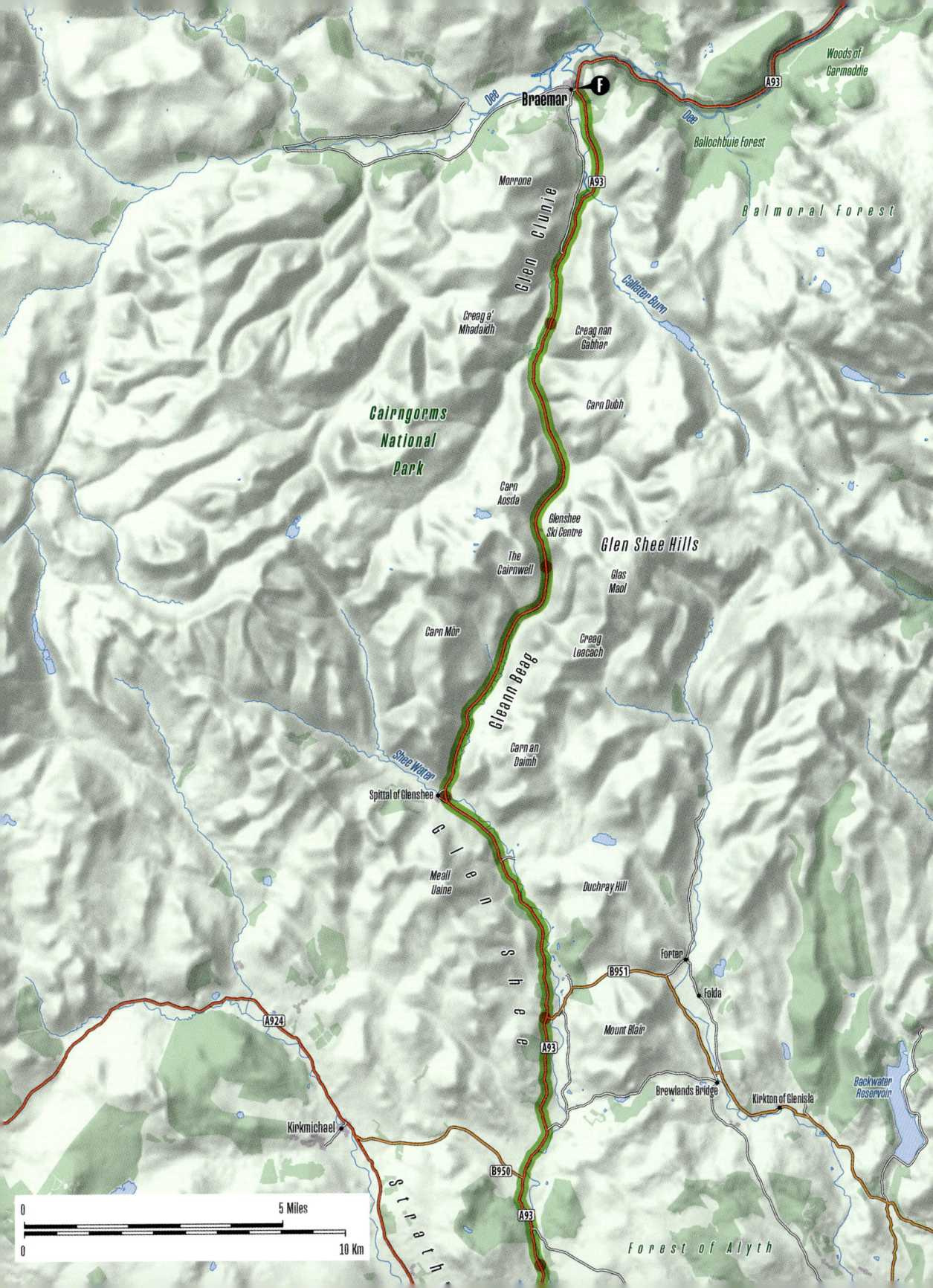

STAGE 25

46 miles / 73km
1,110 metres ascent

BRAEMAR TO GRANTOWN-ON-SPEY

The grandeur of the Grampian Mountains provides the setting for the wildest stage of the journey. Mighty granite peaks blanketed with heather are spliced with deep forest-lined glens and slashed with tumbling rivers. It is not a stage to take lightly in either its difficulty or remoteness.

A gentle cruise alongside the River Dee and quick hello to the royals at Balmoral Castle is a gentle introduction to the generous sprinkling of steepness that lies ahead. A spiky cross-profile with plenty of challenging climbing and exhilarating descents awaits. The majestic mountains, limitless landscape and open-sided roads all give you a sense of freedom, but also one of vulnerability in what can be the most uplifting but also one of the most inhospitable environments of the whole trip. The route is at its most unwelcoming at Cock Bridge, Scotland's most frequently snowbound road and arguably the most challenging climb of the trip which tops out at The Lecht ski resort. A long, almost straight road in its final stage, it stretches dauntingly ahead of you with no respite before plummeting down to the Highlands' highest village, Tomintoul, and beyond to the more genteel Speyside settlement of Grantown-on-Spey, gateway to whisky country.

BRAEMAR TO GAIRNSHIEL BRIDGE

Head north, following the A93 out of Braemar. The stage starts with a calming, sheltered stretch of road running alongside the River Dee with Braemar Castle standing watchfully on a sweeping bend. The castle is under restoration by the local community and was a strategic site for both sides in the Jacobite uprisings. Almost 3 miles into the stage the A93 crosses the torrent of the River Dee to its northern bank. Following the river for a

further 6 miles, the air is filled with the sweet succulent scent of Scots pines which crowd into the glen, complete with a carpet of heather and moss covering the ground below. On the southern side of the river lies Balmoral Castle, part of the sprawling 50,000-acre royal estate. The best view across the river to Balmoral Castle is marked by a *Police don't stop* sign!

Just before Crathie turn left on to the B976, signposted *Tomintoul*. A gradual climb starts through a wooded glen before you arrive on open heather moorland. Just under 3 miles after leaving the riverside the road tops out against a backdrop of heather which can flourish into a radiant purple carpet between July and September. In season you may spot a deer stalker here.

The road drops to Gairnshiel Bridge; turn left on to the A939 to cross the bridge. This handsome, steeply humped bridge with a fierce gradient has lasted since the mid-eighteenth century; at the time of writing a new bridge is under construction. It won't be as easy to pull a wheelie on when riding up, but it will be infinitely more friendly to long-wheelbase campervans.

GAIRNSHIEL BRIDGE TO THE LECHT

The route stays on the A939 almost all the way to Grantown-on-Spey. Leaving the bridge behind, the route rises for over 3 miles before dropping down to the River Don; turn left immediately after crossing the river to stay on the A939. After crossing the River Don twice more, the first time at The Luib and the second time at

Cock Bridge, with the fortified tower of Corgarff Castle in view, you are greeted by a vertical wall of asphalt in front of you. This is The Lecht, the start of which is a leading contender for the most challenging mile of cycling you will find between Land's End and John o' Groats. Gradients of up to 17 per cent in the first few hundred metres ensure that the legs burn as the struggle to keep heading upwards ensues.

The Lecht remains a daunting climb as it looms large above you even after the exertions of the first section. It takes the direct path up the mountainside – no hidden surprises here, it is bare and brutal, all laid out in front of you. The road tops out at of 644 metres, which is slightly lower than the Cairnwell at Glenshee, just before the ski resort emerges on the left. The hardy souls who believe in Scottish skiing persevere through bleak, wet, dreary and rain-soaked winters hoping that occasionally a winter season like 2010–2011 will emerge where the mountain drowns in snow and skiers shred the piste under piercing blue skies late into April. Fingers crossed that a freak snowstorm isn't blowing for the cyclists

riding through – it is not out of the question for late May or early October. The chatty folk at the ski resort should be able to sort you out with a hot chocolate.

THE LECHT TO TOMINTOUL

Downhill rewards are waiting for you after the ski centre with a blissful 6-mile descent to Tomintoul. Yes, you have to turn your pedals as the road flattens out in the valley, but there are not many places in Britain you can descend uninterrupted for so long. As the gradient becomes more gentle in the valley, you pass the Well of the Lecht picnic area close to the Lecht Mine, an old iron and manganese mine dating back to 1730. Nearby is the derelict Toplis Bothy named after Percy Toplis, a renowned criminal who was found hiding out in the bothy in the 1920s – an outlaw searching for solace in this inhospitable landscape.

TOMINTOUL TO GRANTOWN-ON-SPEY

Tomintoul has an air of the Wild West about it as you turn square right on to its main street (still following

the A939). Wide and often windswept with little traffic, you could imagine hardy souls riding down the street on horseback after days in the wilderness. It's the kind of place where you may well be informed if you sit in the wrong seat in the pub, but it seems everyone here has a story to tell and many people from far and wide have made their home in Tomintoul. With its central square of imposing Georgian and Victorian buildings, it is a classic example of an eighteenth-century planned Highland village. Sitting at the southern end of the Glenlivet Estate, the hardy community relies on farming, forestry and sporting activities to earn a living.

Keep following the main road out of Tomintoul; the old bridge over the River Avon shortly after the village, just downstream from the present-day road crossing, provides an attractive picnic site. The original bridge was built as part of a military road in 1754. A brief climb and steep descent leads to the Bridge of Brown and the last tough climb of this stage with a rude start next to the Bridge of Brown Tearoom.

THE WHISKY CASTLE

Tomintoul was once notorious for whisky smugglers, as well as being a stopping place for travellers over the generations. In the early nineteenth century, there were at least 200 illegal stills in the area. The inhospitable nature of the Livet Glen and surrounding area meant that local smugglers could stay one step ahead of the excise officers. When whisky from this area got into the hands of people in Edinburgh and beyond, locals say it became more popular than the legal but more fiery Lowland whiskys.

Whisky production still plays a very important role in the area with the Glenlivet and Tomintoul distilleries nearby. You can learn a lot more about the history of whisky in the area at the Discovery Centre in Tomintoul. With museum displays and artefacts, it provides fascinating insights into the history of whisky. Few visitors pass through the village without visiting the Whisky Castle shop, which has been on Main Street for over 100 years. Over 30,000 people visit the shop every year – it brings people from all over the world to this small Highland village to learn about and sample some of the 600 single malt whiskies on offer. Free tastings are available from the deeply knowledgeable staff who are keen to share their passion for whisky.

During the gradual descent which follows, heather moorland and grouse give way to green fields, sheep and cattle. Turn left on to the A95 (signposted *Grantown-on-Spey*) and pedal for 1 mile before crossing the River Spey. Go straight ahead on to the A939 through woodland to reach Grantown-on-Spey. Turn right on to the High Street; the stage finishes in a tree-lined square in the centre of the town.

GRANTOWN-ON-SPEY

If you have some free time in Grantown-on-Spey head to the banks of the Spey via Anagach Wood. Scots pine trees grow here, and it is even home to the elusive capercaillie, a large and distinctive woodland grouse, but sightings are rare. Grantown-on-Spey marks the end of the SnowRoads, a 90-mile route which begins in Blairgowrie. Grantown-on-Spey is a pleasant town for strolling around with plenty of independent shops – perhaps a welcoming sight after a few stages in the wilds.

SLEEP

THE GRANT ARMS HOTEL
A traditional Scottish building in the heart of the town which hosted Queen Victoria in 1860. Plenty of sensitive refurbishment has taken place since then.
25 The Square, Grantown-on-Spey, PH26 3HF
T 01479 872 526
www.grantarmshotel.com

THE SPEYSIDE HOTEL
Another lovely traditional Scottish hotel.
43 Grant Road, Grantown-on-Spey, PH26 3LD
T 01479 873 909
www.thespeysidehotel.co.uk

CRAGGAN OUTDOORS
An outdoor activity specialist which also manages a bunkhouse and a bothy which are situated a short distance to the south-west of Grantown-on-Spey – perfect if you are on a budget.
Craggan Golf Course, Grantown-on-Spey, PH26 3NT
T 01479 873 283
www.cragganoutdoors.co.uk

GRANTOWN-ON-SPEY CARAVAN PARK
Accepts tents despite the name. Also has camping pods and wigwams.
Seafield Avenue, Grantown-on-Spey, PH26 3JQ
T 01479 872 474
www.caravansscotland.com

EAT

CRAIG BAR
A no-fuss menu of connoisseurs' pies and chips. Perfect after one of the most challenging climbing days of the tour. Vegetarians are not excluded with several different options to choose from. Real ales, whisky selection and a pool table.
Woodside Avenue, Grantown-on-Spey, PH26 3JN
T 01479 872 669
www.thecraigbar.co.uk

SUPPLIES

The well-stocked **Highland Bakery** and a **Co-op Food** can both be found in the centre of Grantown-on-Spey.

BIKE

BASECAMP BIKES
You'll find experienced mechanics in this rider-owned specialist mountain bike shop (they repair road bikes too) in the centre of Grantown-on-Spey.
5 The Square, Grantown-on-Spey, PH26 EHG
T 01479 870 050
www.basecampbikes.co.uk

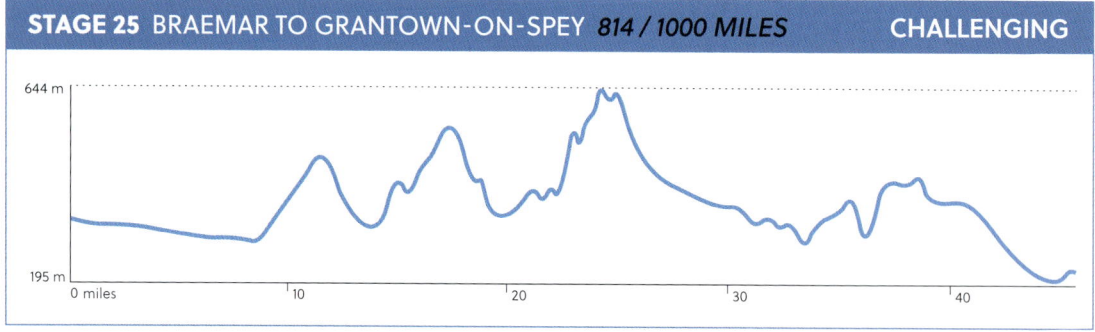

STAGE 25 BRAEMAR TO GRANTOWN-ON-SPEY *814 / 1000 MILES*   **CHALLENGING**

26

36 miles / 59km
440 metres ascent

GRANTOWN-ON-SPEY TO INVERNESS

An atmospheric stage that crosses wild expanses of moorland, traces old military roads and passes the site of the great Culloden Battlefield before arriving at Inverness, the capital of the Highlands and Scotland's most northerly city.

A gentle stage, despite being in the Highlands, which offers respite from the mountains, it even has slightly more descending than climbing. However, the exposed moorland start can be challenging in wet and windy weather, its atmosphere bleak and suggestive, as fog curls across the road and wind buffets you along. The slightly more wooded areas around Dulsie Bridge are picturesque and on a warm day the welcoming deep plunge pools in the River Findhorn may even encourage an impromptu dip. The network of old military roads leads to Culloden Battlefield, another place to not linger for long if you have a suggestive imagination and night is falling or mist obscures the moor. With so many lives lost, something of the scenes of brutality and bloodshed must linger on in its atmosphere, as it does in the mind of many Scots.

GRANTOWN-ON-SPEY TO DULSIE BRIDGE

From the square in Grantown-on-Spey continue along the High Street (A939), heading north-east. As you leave the town you have a final chance to appreciate the straight, symmetrical layout of its main street and to make sure you have enough food to last until Inverness. The town and its buildings end rather abruptly – you are quickly surrounded by trees that in turn give way to open moorland.

This is an old military road, part of a network known as General Wade's Military Roads which were constructed across the Highlands in the mid-eighteenth

century to bring order to areas that had risen up as part of the Jacobite rebellion of 1715. This section and the crossing of Dulsie Bridge was created by Wade's successor, Major William Caulfeild.

Caulfeild was credited with the lines: 'Had you seen these roads before they were made, you would lift up your hands and bless General Wade.' Maybe as cyclists we should also be thankful as while some of the roads have been absorbed into the modern road network, some like this stage's route through Dulsie Bridge now make for particularly pleasant riding.

In the moorland to your right peat bogs have concealed ancient skeletons; one such 'bog burial' was discovered at Dava Moor in 1927, but who knows what else the bog has hidden. On your left you will see a distinctly painted rock – it will most likely say 'Jesus Saves' and it is known as the Jesus Stone. The first painter of the rock was said to be a retired missionary from Africa who painted it at the turn of the twentieth century as an expression of her faith. Who paints the stone, and continues to paint over any other slogans or graffiti on it now, is unknown.

Fork left next to a *Welcome to Nairnshire* sign and an old black and gold AA call box, staying on the A939. Just over 2 miles later turn left following the signpost to *Dunearn*. Continue along this road to reach Dulsie Bridge, one of the most spectacular eighteenth-century bridges in all of Scotland. Built by Caulfeild and three companies of soldiers to cross the steep and treacherous

gorge carved by the River Findhorn, it now makes for a scenic picnic stop and a picturesque place to swim. You might also see more adventurous visitors 'tombstoning' off the side of the bridge into the deep pools below.

DULSIE BRIDGE TO CULLODEN

Continue on the military road, keeping right shortly after the bridge towards *Cawdor*. Just under 7 miles after Dulsie Bridge you reach an unremarkable and unmarked four-way junction; turn left here. (Cawdor Castle is a short detour from here – continue straight ahead to reach it. However, you won't find three witches or Macbeth's ghost, as Shakespeare took rather a large amount of poetic licence in rewriting Scottish history: he described a castle that was not even built at the time of the real King Macbeth.)

Follow the blue Sustrans signs along the lanes through Cawdor Wood and on into more open farmland. The slight elevation allows views over the surrounding farmland; a hazy lightness on the horizon and slight sparkle of blue suggests the presence of the Moray Firth to your right.

Continue to follow the blue Sustrans signs, turning

right in the direction of *Culloden* and *Inverness*. Shortly after this you will pass under the impressive Nairn Viaduct, the longest masonry viaduct in Scotland which was opened in 1898 as part of the Inverness and Aviemore Direct Railway. After crossing over the River Nairn, on a much more diminutive bridge, you will arrive at a crossroads – continue straight ahead, following the blue Sustrans sign for National Route 1. Shortly after this turn left at the Culloden Moor Inn. You are now cycling alongside the site of the Culloden Battlefield on your left-hand side; there is now a memorial and visitor centre.

CULLODEN TO INVERNESS

From Culloden Moor onwards the road becomes busier, as you would expect approaching the largest city in the Highlands. Fields give way to suburban housing estates and, before long, the road carries you over the busy A9 and deposits you at a roundabout next to a retail park. Continue straight ahead at this first large roundabout, and go straight ahead again at a second smaller roundabout. Turn right at a set of traffic lights on to Kingsmills Road between two parks. At a large traffic-light-controlled junction fork left along the one-way

Crown Street and turn left at the T-junction at the end. From here turn right, then left then right again in quick succession, going almost back on yourself each time, zigzagging your way downwards, past the castle, until you reach river level. The stage ends at the crossroads by Ness Bridge.

INVERNESS

Arriving in Inverness can feel a little fraught and busy in comparison with the vast empty moors and virtually empty military road you have followed for most of the stage. Although it is one of the fastest growing cities in Europe, it is still modest by city standards; the central pedestrian area and riverside walks allow for pockets of calm. Sometimes called the Gateway to the Highlands, Inverness is surrounded by natural beauty, which may account for why it consistently does well in surveys of happiest places to live. If you crave bright lights, lively bars and exciting restaurants, then eat, drink and dance in Inverness before going deeper into the Highlands and the final four stages of your journey.

CULLODEN

Culloden Battlefield is the location of the last major battle fought on British soil. On 16 April 1746, the Jacobite army of Charles Edward Stuart was decisively defeated by a British government force under Prince William Augustus, Duke of Cumberland. The Battle of Culloden lasted for under an hour. In that time, approximately 1,250 Jacobites were dead; almost as many were wounded and 376 were taken prisoner. The government troops lost 50 men while around 250 were wounded. The orders were given to the duke's men that 'no quarter shall be given'; by the end there was a 5-mile stretch of blood and bodies.

It's not just the battle that has left a lasting imprint on Scottish culture and politics but the aftermath; it led to the dismantling of the Scottish clans and later to the infamous chapter of the Highland Clearances. The British government banned tartan and bagpipes and the speaking of Gaelic. If you were Scottish, no matter which side you fought on, punishment followed. The visitor centre at the battlefield is well worth a visit to understand this complex and far-reaching moment in history.

SLEEP

PALACE HOTEL AND SPA
On the banks of the River Ness and opposite Inverness Castle, this lovely hotel is in a brilliant location, offering great views within walking distance of the city centre.
8 Ness Walk, Inverness, IV3 5NG
T 01463 223 243
www.invernesspalacehotel.co.uk

PITFARANNE GUEST HOUSE
Cyclists are made very welcome at this lovely guest house, close to the river, castle and city centre. A delicious traditional Highland breakfast will set you up for your day of pedalling.
57 Crown Street, Inverness, IV2 3AY
T 01463 239 338
www.pitfaranne.com

INVERNESS YOUTH HOSTEL
This hostel is within easy walking distance of the city centre yet in a quiet neighbourhood. Dorm beds and private rooms as well as plenty of communal space to meet fellow travellers.
Victoria Drive, Inverness, IV2 3QB
T 01463 231 771
www.hostellingscotland.org.uk/hostels/inverness

EAT

THE MUSTARD SEED
In a converted church on the banks of the River Ness, this restaurant is a firm favourite with guests and visitors alike. Simple cooking is done well and presented in a warm friendly atmosphere with great views of the river.
16 Fraser Street, Inverness, IV1 1DW
T 01463 220 220
www.mustardseedrestaurant.co.uk

CAFÉ 1
Locally sourced Highland food imaginatively cooked and presented. Offers intimate dining, a great cocktails and drinks menu and very friendly, helpful staff.
75 Castle Street, Inverness, IV2 3EA
T 01463 226 200
www.cafe1.net

DRINK

HOOTANANNY
Multi-award-winning pub and live music venue, this is one of Inverness' best-loved spots. Pop in for one drink or stay for the whole evening. Live music every night with a varied line-up of solo artists, bands and a healthy dose of Scottish folk music.
67 Church Street, Inverness, IV1 1ES
T 01463 233 651
www.hootanannyinverness.co.uk

THE BOTANIC HOUSE
If you want to enjoy some city nightlife before disappearing into the far north then head here for cocktails, music and street-food-style eats. Expect anything from a traditional ceilidh to a stand-up comedian or DJ club night. It's busy, lively and fun.
9–11 Castle Street, Inverness, IV2 3DX
T 01463 215 200
www.thebotanic.co.uk

SUPPLIES
Inverness has all the household grocery stores you'd expect in a city and a few interesting little independent delis as well. The Victorian Market on Academy Street has a wide range of shops set in a covered Victorian arcade.

BIKE

HIGHLAND BIKES
Conveniently located just north of the centre of Inverness on stage 27. One of many options in the capital of the Highlands.
29–31 Shore Street, Inverness, IV1 1NG
T 01463 234 789
www.highlandbikes.com

VELOCITY
The hangout of Inverness cyclists. Vegetarian cafe, bike workshop and social enterprise promoting health and well-being. Perfect for a morning coffee before heading for the far north of Scotland.
1 Crown Avenue, Inverness, IV2 3NF
www.velocitylove.co.uk

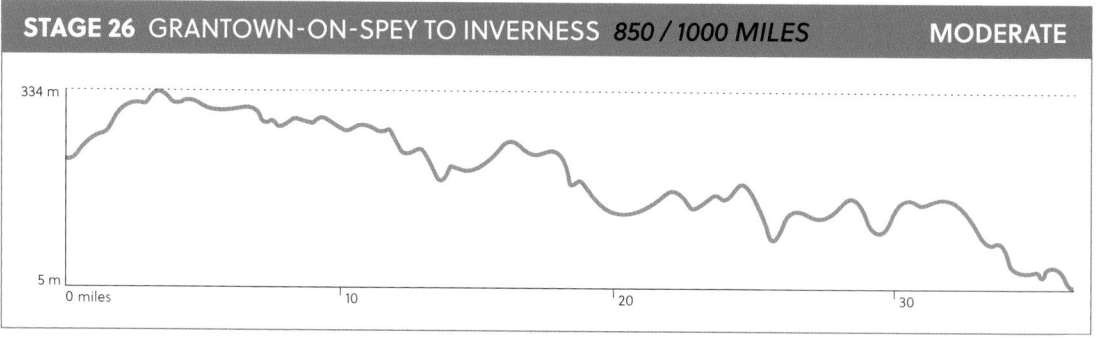

STAGE 26 GRANTOWN-ON-SPEY TO INVERNESS *850 / 1000 MILES* **MODERATE**

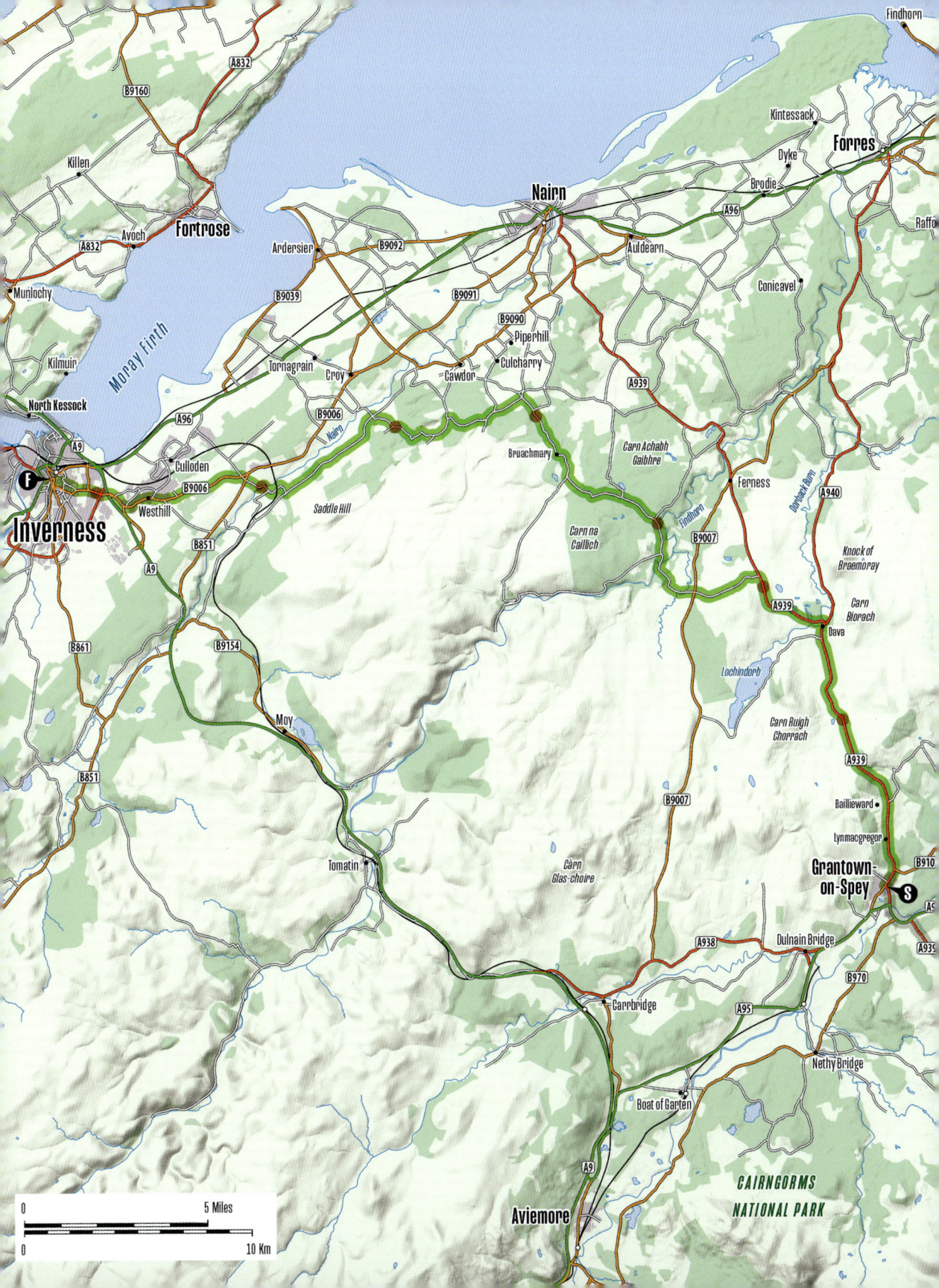

STAGE 27

45 miles / 73km
570 metres ascent

INVERNESS TO BONAR BRIDGE

Described as the Gateway to the Highlands, leaving Inverness is in many ways the beginning of the end, but some of the best riding is still to come. Following the River Ness, crossing the Kessock Bridge and tracing the edges of the Beauly Firth is the start of your journey into this beautiful and remote part of Scotland.

Every moment of these last few stages deserves to be savoured. While you may long for the satisfaction of completion, you are now completely immersed in the rhythm of cycle touring and there is a whisper of sadness that the end approaching means the trip will soon be over. Never more has the journey been more important than the destination – take your time to relish the beauty and wildness of these final stages, don't rush towards the finish. From the tranquillity of the Beauly Firth, just across the water from Inverness, this stage almost continuously gains height until, following the old drove road, you reach the Struie. Surrounded by the bold but muted tones of purple heather and golden gorse, you will see the unmistakable misty Highland light rippling across the Kyle of Sutherland, and it will paint pictures in your mind you will never forget.

INVERNESS TO MUIR OF ORD

Beginning alongside the River Ness, hug the right bank of the river by following the shared-use cycleway along Bank Street and Douglas Row and go straight on at the end of Douglas Row. Rejoin the road on Riverside Street; turn left at a T-junction and then turn right on to Portland Place (a dead-end road; cyclists can get through). Turn left on to Shore Street; continue straight ahead as Shore Street becomes Cromwell Road and then Longman Drive. Turn right, and almost immediately left, to remain on Longman Drive. Turn right at a

T-junction and turn left on to the cycle path that leads to Kessock Bridge. Turn left to cross Kessock Bridge on the cycle path next to the A9; the bridge crosses the narrow channel between the Moray Firth and Beauly Firth to reach North Kessock on the Black Isle.

While the bridge crossing is busy, as soon as you exit at the other end and get down to the shoreline, peace and tranquillity takes over – the noise and rush of Inverness is now just a scenic view across the water. In North Kessock, at the end of the bridge, turn left on to another cycle path signposted to *Muir of Ord*. Continue straight ahead as the cycle path merges with a road; turn right on to Main Street when you reach the shoreline. The shoreline of the Beauly Firth is a diverse habitat ranging from the tidal mudflats, through the salt marshes to arable farmland. This provides for a wide range of birds including oyster catchers, sandpipers, greenshanks, curlews and arctic terns. You may even be lucky enough to see an osprey or seals loitering on the shoreline.

Where the firth begins to narrow at the river mouth, the road moves inland. Turn left on to the A832, following the signpost towards *Muir of Ord*. Follow the A832 into Muir of Ord, rising over the railway bridge. To the west of Muir of Ord lies the Singleton of Glen Ord Distillery. The distillery was founded by Thomas Mackenzie in 1838. The Black Isle, as the area is known, is a peninsula of rich, dark loam, which is perfect for growing barley. In the nearby village of Munlochy you can find the Black Isle Brewery.

MUIR OF ORD TO MOUNTGERALD

Keep right after the railway bridge to join the A862 to reach the village of Conon Bridge, where you cross a bridge. Shortly after the bridge go straight ahead at a busy roundabout then immediately turn left on to a cycle path that takes you on to the old road running parallel to the A862. It is tricky to spot when on the roundabout as it is just a gap in the fence, but worth joining to avoid the traffic.

Continue to follow the cycle path next to the A862 where it is available, then continue on the A862 to reach Dingwall. Dingwall is a fairly busy town; it has been a central point for cattle and farm sales for over a century; before that Muir of Ord, at the centre of a complex gathering of drove roads, was the location of the 'tryst' for such sales. To leave Dingwall continue on the A862 then turn left on to the innocuous-looking residential Tulloch Avenue which belies the sudden steepness and

difficulty of the climb. Turn right at a T-junction on to Old Evanton Road then continue to rise up on to the ridge overlooking the Cromarty Firth.

As you gain the full height of the ridge at Mountgerald, two things will catch your eye: the long, thin bridge across the Cromarty Firth and the well-placed Highland Farm Cafe. Its coffee and cake never fail to hit the spot after the efforts of the climb.

MOUNTGERALD TO THE STRUIE VIEWPOINT

From Mountgerald enjoy a lovely run of 4 miles predominantly downhill. In the village of Evanton turn left at a T-junction on to the B817. Evanton is a relatively recent settlement, originating in the early nineteenth century and named after the son of the developer who laid out the township – 'Evan-town'. After the village turn left on to the B9176.

Follow the B9176 for the next 14 miles; without

navigation to think about you can relax and enjoy the scenery as it changes from agricultural farmland to the heather, gorse and pine moorlands either side of the Struie. This former drove road meanders, taking the path of least resistance as the cattle would have done.

As you crest the hill there's a moment when the view over the Kyle of Sutherland suddenly appears. As the descent begins and you pick up speed, watch out for the Struie Viewpoint on your right – this gives you an opportunity to observe a watery blue slash in the otherwise green, purple and gold Highland scenery. The Kyle of Sutherland empties four main rivers into the North Sea: the Carron, the Shin, the Oykel and the Cassley.

STRUIE VIEWPOINT TO BONAR BRIDGE

A long descent awaits, the first part is fast and, while the road is mainly wide, it shrinks rapidly to a single lane

REWILDING THE HIGHLANDS

While undeniably beautiful, the Highlands have changed; only around 1 per cent of what the Romans called the Great Forest of Caledon remains today. The wild open hillsides which create the far-reaching dramatic views we enjoy used to be home to lush pine forests. Even former inhabitants of just 100 years ago would notice deep change. Much of the flora and fauna that once thrived here has disappeared and the landscape has altered dramatically.

Today rich landowners are using their land and wealth to rewild the spaces that man has changed. In some places this means no more than leaving the land to naturally regenerate; in other places more active management has led to large planting programmes, culls of some animals and the reintroduction of other species, controversially including the missing large predators.

However, nothing relating to land use in this area is without conflict. With long folk memories of the Highland Clearances and the roles of hunting and fishing in providing local incomes, nothing, even something that seems as ecologically beneficial as rewilding, is as simple as it might seem.

where it crosses the frequent rivers. Some of the steep turns can feel uncomfortably tight at speed. Make sure that you slow down for the junction at the bottom next to the old AA call box; the road to the right is difficult to see unless you stop. Turn left here on to the A836.

You may spot an AA box in its black and gold livery, a private telephone box for members needing to summon assistance and one of only a handful in its original location. The final miles of the stage go quickly, with only a bit of pedalling needed. With a view of the Dornoch Firth to your right they pass enjoyably speedily. The road sweeps to the right in Ardgay village and the stage ends at a junction after crossing Bonar Bridge.

BONAR BRIDGE

The first bridge here across the Kyle of Sutherland was designed by Thomas Telford and completed in 1812; before then the village was known simply as Bonar. In 1892, some 80 years later, the bridge was destroyed by flood. A new bridge opened in 1893, also surviving 80 years, until it was replaced with the current bridge in 1973. Until the 1980s the village was an important stopover between Inverness and Caithness, but the building of the Dornoch Firth Bridge on the A9, cutting 20 miles off the route, means that Bonar Bridge is now much more off the beaten track.

SLEEP

KYLE HOUSE
Many riders prefer to press on to the Crask Inn or Altnaharra after leaving Inverness, but if you need somewhere earlier this cosy bed and breakfast will do the job.
Dornoch Road, Bonar Bridge, IV24 3EB
T 01863 766 360
www.kylehouse.co.uk

INVERSHIN HOTEL
A few miles into the next stage you'll find this classic roadside Highland hotel. Hotel rooms and a basic bunkhouse.
Invershin, IV27 4ET
T 01549 421 202
www.invershin.com

ARDGAY GLAMPING PODS
Situated in the village of Ardgay a short distance before the end of the stage you'll find two glamping pods. Single-night stays are available out of peak season.
Aspen House, Ardgay, IV24 3BG
T 07900 635 781
www.ardgayglamping.co.uk

EAT

CRANNAG BISTRO
Ross-shire ribeye and local venison burger are among the specialities. Takeaway only.
Dornoch Road, Bonar Bridge, IV24 3EB
T 01863 766 111
www.crannag.com

SUPPLIES

Bonar Bridge has a small **Spar** supermarket for basic supplies.

BIKE

ORANGEFOX BIKES
It's not often that a bike shop owner is also a nutritionist with a PhD in nutritional biochemistry, but Mark Goodwill will be able to help you out with your choice of ride snack – and your bike!
44 Muir of Ord Industrial Estate, Muir of Ord, IV6 7UA
T 01463 870 346
www.orangefoxbikes.co.uk

DRYBURGH CYCLES
Head into the centre of Dingwall for spares and repairs
9 Tulloch Street, Dingwall, IV15 9JY
T 01349 862 163
www.dryburghcycles.co.uk

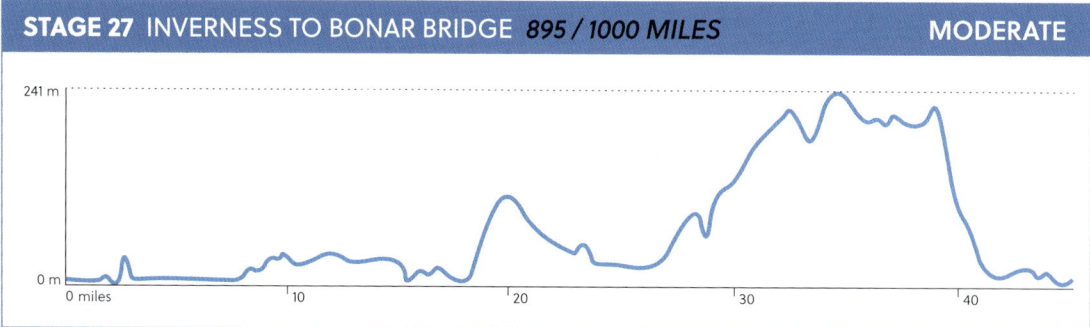

STAGE 27 INVERNESS TO BONAR BRIDGE *895 / 1000 MILES*   **MODERATE**

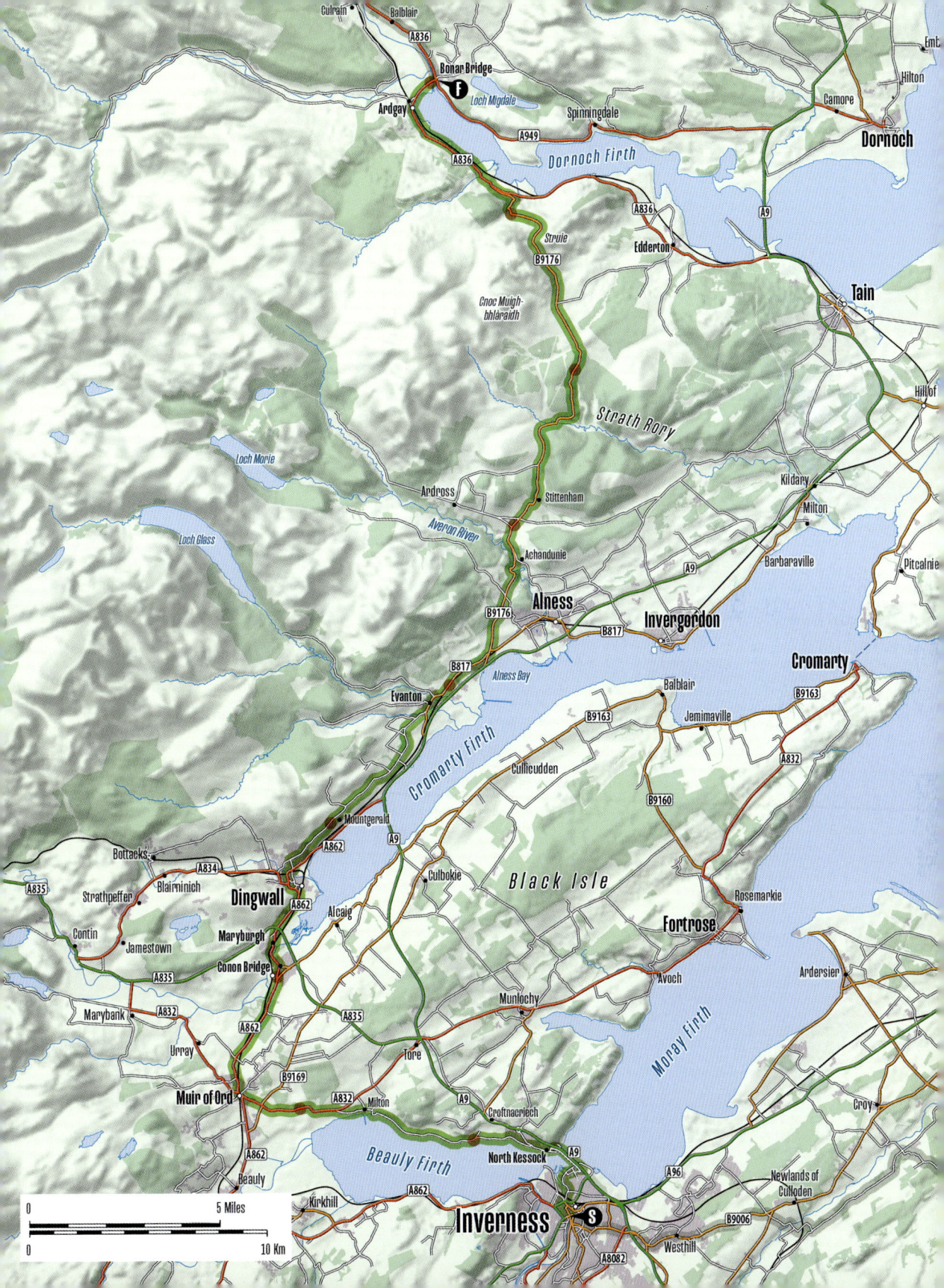

STAGE 28

31 miles / 51km
360 metres ascent

BONAR BRIDGE TO ALTNAHARRA

There is a breathtaking emptiness to the interior of the far north. Riding in the landscape you feel insignificant, yet alive, and uplifted by its vastness and wild beauty. This is in fact one of the most sparsely populated areas of Europe, in complete contrast to the crowded, highly urbanised environment which is many people's daily experience of Britain.

Follow the trail of the Arctic salmon along the Kyle of Sutherland and up the valley of the River Shin to Lairg, as the fish look to return to the place of their birth. Make use of the civilisation at Lairg, as it is your last chance to get some supplies before a land of peat bogs, passing places and birds of prey soaring overhead awaits. On the final 20-mile stretch of this stage the lonely welcome of the Crask Inn is the only solitary cluster of buildings you will see before descending to Altnaharra, which may well be the last staging post on your journey north. The remote landscape allows time for reflection and contemplation, but also the possibility of complete absorption in the moment and the wish for the journey not to end so you can continue to pedal into the vastness around you and to explore more deeply.

BONAR BRIDGE TO INVERSHIN

Turn left (staying on the A836) after crossing the bridge, signposted *Lairg*. The route follows a wide and straight road for 4 miles with the Kyle of Sutherland shimmering or looking a steely grey colour off to your left, as the weather dictates. Around 3 miles after Bonar Bridge the route passes underneath a railway viaduct at Invershin. If you glance up through the trees to your left, you may catch a glimpse of Carbisdale Castle perched high on the opposite bank of the Kyle of Sutherland.

Carbisdale Castle has had a colourful history and could probably lay claim to once being one of the world's most opulent youth hostels up until its closure in 2011. Built for Mary Caroline, Duchess of Sutherland, in the early twentieth century, the castle was recently on the market – a snip at £1.5 million – getting you over 40 bedrooms and 20 acres of land complete with a private loch stuffed with brown trout. Sutherland is world renowned for its trout fishing, with the region said to have more lochs filled with wild brown trout than it has permanent human inhabitants.

The duchess, the second wife of the 3rd Duke of Sutherland, wasn't too popular with her husband's family. When he died a spectacular family row of inheritance erupted and the 4th Duke took her to court to contest the will. The duchess was thrown into prison for six weeks, found guilty of having destroyed documents to secure her inheritance. A compromise was found whereby the Sutherland family had to build her a castle outside of their estate.

The duchess found a piece of hillside just next to the edge of the estate to ensure the family were reminded of her on a daily basis. Clocks were installed on all faces of the new castle's tower at the duchess's behest except the one that faced towards the Sutherland Estate. The location may have been picked out of spite, but the views are sublime over the Kyle of Sutherland and beyond to the Dornoch Firth.

INVERSHIN TO LAIRG

Just under 1 mile after Invershin, turn left on to the A837 (signposted *Lochinver*), then shortly afterwards turn right on to the B864. This very pleasant single-track road gradually rises through woodland taking you to the Falls of Shin. It's a short walk to see the falls themselves which are beautiful at any time of year but at their best between May and September as the Atlantic salmon attempt to return to their birthplace by jumping the falls. The Falls of Shin are the final challenge for the fish, who have previously braved deep sea fishing nets, seabirds and otters (which can occasionally be spotted at the falls too) on their long journeys from waters close to Greenland.

The salmon have a unique set of anaerobic muscles which contract quickly and when released generate intense power for a few seconds propelling them forwards and at great speed – a routine yet spellbinding sight. If a leap fails it can take a fish days to recover before taking another attempt. Rather like a hill-shy cyclist searching for a tour with the least amount of climbing, salmon listen to the water to see how much is gushing over the falls to find the path of least resistance before attempting a leap. Though the falls are geared for tourists it is not uncommon to see locals popping down to the river fishing if not for their supper at least to unwind after work.

A further 4 miles after the falls turn right on to the A839 (signposted *Ferrycroft Visitor Centre*) – this inconspicuous-looking A road feels more like a minor road in this tranquil hinterland. Cycle into Lairg, 'the crossroads of the Highlands'. Just before crossing the river there is a small but interesting visitor centre – Ferrycroft – which is dedicated to the water, land and the people of Lairg. Cross the river then turn left on to the A836 which edges round the small loch keeping your eye out for the 'wee hoose' on its own island. Lairg may not seem like the epicentre of the Highlands and rush hours may be a sedate affair, but it is an important place, home to a community market and a train station. For the journeying cyclist it is also home to the last shop for nearly 50 miles, so make sure you stock up on snacks as you leave the village.

LAIRG TO THE CRASK INN

Shortly after leaving Lairg on your left is the Lairg Dam and Scotland's most northerly hydroelectric power station, holding back the 17-mile-long Loch Shin which stretches into the horizon in the north-west. Just over 2 miles after Lairg the wide double-track section of the A836 ends abruptly at a junction. To the left lie the wilds of the north-west and Loch Shin and to the right, where you are heading, lies a beautiful single-track road with only the postman, cycle tourists and the odd logging wagon for company. This is the longest stretch of single-track road riding of the entire trip. If you come across a logging wagon, be sure to stop and pull into the heather at the edge of the road.

Just over 10 miles on the single-track road takes you to the Crask Inn, an understated, unassuming building in a vast peat bog in front of the towering expanse of the steep slopes of Ben Klibreck in the east. The interplay of light on the heather-clad slopes can be beguiling, adding to the drama of the landscape as you cycle. At 962 metres, Ben Klibreck is the second most northerly

THE CRASK INN

A small unassuming sign squeaks in the gentle breeze at one of Scotland's most isolated inns. You would be forgiven for thinking it was a homestead as you're riding past and it's true in some ways as you are made to feel just like you are at home with a warm welcome and often a comforting peat fire. The Crask Inn is a national treasure to anyone who has passed it on their way from Land's End to John o' Groats. There is no light pollution and no mains electricity here.

Originally built as part of the Sutherland Estate around 1815, draught Black Isle beer, venison stew and home-made scones are the order of the day. If the chickens need locking up, you wait for your pint to be poured. Priorities and perspectives are sorted here.

Unusually, the inn is in the care of the Scottish Episcopal Church. The warmth and character of this pub is sadly increasingly rare on a crowded, hurried island.

Munro after Ben Hope. Munro baggers (those climbing all mountains over 914 metres in Scotland) often choose this pair of geographical outliers as their final peaks.

THE CRASK INN TO ALTNAHARRA

A few hundred metres after the Crask Inn is a gradual 7-mile descent of gentle bends and passing places to one of the remotest villages in Scotland, Altnaharra. In this lonely region you might actually find more cyclists for company as those journeying from Land's End face less choice in the far north with either a trudge up the coastal A9, devoid of inspiration and with plenty of passing supermarket delivery lorries, or this exhilarating journey embedded in the soul of the handsome Highlands. The stage ends at the Altnaharra Hotel – from here you can see the entire village.

SLEEP
ALTNAHARRA HOTEL
There are 14 individually styled rooms here, with a quint-essential Scottish country house vibe. This is definitely a 'whisky by the fire after a day's fishing' kind of place. Adapting to growing demand, there is now a LEJOG Cabin for those on a budget comprising three single rooms and a shared bathroom.
Altnaharra, IV27 4UF
T 01549 411 222
www.altnaharra.com

ALTNAHARRA BED AND BREAKFAST
There is a warm and relaxed welcome from Mandy and Lindsay at their homely bed and breakfast. They also provide evening meals.
1 Macleod Crescent, Altnaharra, IV27 4UG
T 01549 411 258
www.altnaharra.net

THE CRASK INN
A unique place with 4 bedrooms and an area for camping. Be sure to book ahead for accommodation and home-cooked evening meals. It is situated around 7 miles before the end of the stage, but rest up and relax and don't worry too much about the extra riding in the morning as its nearly all downhill to Altnaharra.
The Crask Inn, By Lairg, IV27 4AB
T 01549 411 241
www.thecraskinn.com

EAT
The **Crask Inn** and the **Altnaharra Hotel** are your options depending on where you are staying.

SUPPLIES
The most remote part of the ride in every sense – after the small **Spar** supermarket in Lairg there are no more shops until you reach Bettyhill on the north coast at the end of stage 29.

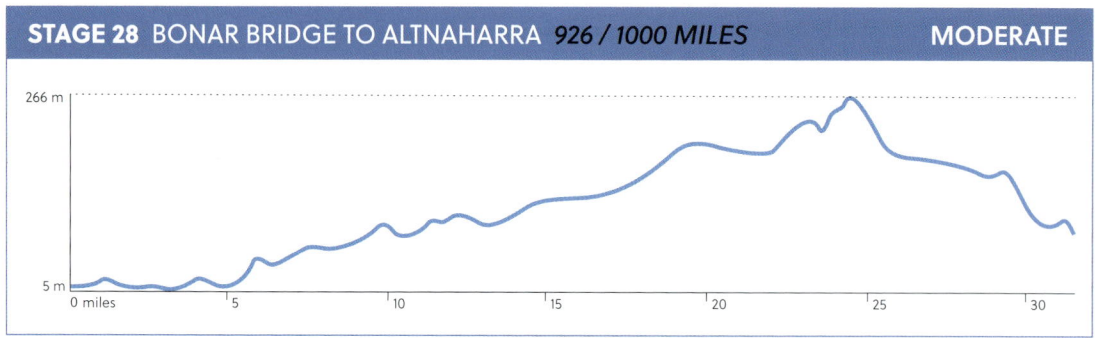

STAGE 28 BONAR BRIDGE TO ALTNAHARRA *926 / 1000 MILES*   MODERATE

29

STAGE

24 miles / 39km
170 metres ascent

ALTNAHARRA
TO BETTYHILL

On the surface, Strath Naver seems wild and remote, but it offers shelter, salmon fishing and an interesting history as it has been a trade route for thousands of years. Neolithic tombs, battles with Norseman and the brutal removal of crofters during the Highland Clearances means the empty landscape still contains the echoes of human history.

With only a few turnings between Altnaharra and Bettyhill, turn your GPS off and immerse yourself in the impressive scenery. Starting alongside Loch Naver, this predominantly downhill stage gives you the time and ease to reflect on the landscape and its stories, of which there are many. 'Remote' and 'wild' are often overused hyperbolic descriptions, but here they are apt and permissible. In this section there are no shops, no cafes and barely any habitation until you reach Bettyhill, an experience almost unique to this area for a road cyclist in the UK. When the stage ends it takes a while to shrug off the sometimes eerie desolation of Strath Naver, especially if you spent the miles considering the cruelties of the Highland Clearances. By comparison, Bettyhill, with its sandy beaches, campervans and welcoming hotel, feels lively and hospitable. The first sight of the sea along the northern coast of Scotland may set you heart racing with the realisation that you have now reached the end of the country and you are entering into the final stage.

ALTNAHARRA TO SYRE

Leaving the Altnaharra Hotel behind, continue through the small hamlet of Altnaharra, crossing the bridge over the River Mudale and then turning right (signposted *Syre* and *Bettyhill*). You can now more or less forget about navigation for a while, as we follow the road to Bettyhill. To your right is Loch Naver, beyond which Ben

Klibreck casts its shadow on the water. The loch is 6 miles long and feeds the River Naver, one of the best private salmon fishing rivers in Scotland. It is not unusual to see Land Rovers with impressive rod displays mounted on their bonnets.

Where the road traces the edges of the loch there are many small bays allowing easy access to the water – how tempting this is very much depends on the weather! A loch swim will definitely be an 'invigorating' experience. The one thing that might drive you to try the water is the midges. Scotland's 'wee beastie', its most prolific and irritating wildlife, can feel like it is at its worst along the banks of Loch Naver.

Midges can't fly very fast and are put off by even light winds – they won't bother you as long as you keep your speed up! However, stopping even for a moment can mean your eyes, ears, nose and any available skin is covered. It has literally driven people mad. Make sure you stock up on midge repellent before you get here.

Most of the sites of interest along this section require a little bit of walking. The Grumbeg burial ground lies to the north of Loch Naver, where you can see the remains of a chambered tomb which is between 4,400 and 6,000 years old among some later nineteenth-century ruins. At the eastern end of the loch there is the Clach An Righ Stone Circle and the Dalharrald Battlefield, where the Norse Earls of Orkney were beaten in battle by the Kings of Scotland.

Closer to the road at the eastern end of the loch

you can easily see the 'Gloomy Memories' Memorial. Donald Macleod was born in Rosal, a now deserted nearby township, and personally witnessed the Highland Clearances. Later he wrote 'widely and passionately' about what he had seen and the 'Gloomy Memories' are a collection of his writings, examples of which are on the memorial.

SYRE TO BETTYHILL

The white walls and red roof of the 'tin church' at Syre stands out from the landscape as one of the first complete buildings you will have seen since leaving Altnaharra. Syre Church, sometimes referred to as Strathnaver Parish Church or Strathnaver Mission Church, was built in 1891. Tin churches were common across the Highlands at the time as a way of quickly constructing buildings in difficult and inaccessible areas. Syre Church was reputedly created from a kit of parts produced by the Glasgow works of Frederick Braby & Co. Ltd., a London-based company. Details of the church align with drawings printed in their catalogue at the time. Go straight ahead in Syre, signposted *Bettyhill*.

A nearby church at Achness, 2 miles south of Syre, was abandoned between 1811 and 1821 when the Countess of Sutherland and her husband, the

Marquess of Stafford (later to become the Duke and Duchess of Sutherland), began their estate clearances. It took around 70 years for the population to regrow sufficiently to justify the new church at Syre being built; it then provided a place of worship for the local population of shepherds, gamekeepers and ghillies employed by the Sutherland Estate.

The road continues to follow the edge of the river, its narrow strip cutting its way through damp heather. Another monument might catch your eye, this time to the raising of a well-known regiment, the 93rd Sutherland Highlanders. In the Crimean War soldiers from the 93rd were the only infantry unit to win their battle at Balaklava (25 October 1854), holding off repeated Russian cavalry charges. It was here that war correspondent William Russell, writing in *The Times*, coined the phrase 'the thin red line', referring to the 93rd Sutherland Highlanders.

Turn right at a T-junction on to the A836 (signposted *Bettyhill*). It can feel strange to share the roads again – this section is popular as it is part of the North Coast 500. The road crosses a bridge over the River Naver, placing you on the opposite bank for the first time. (The road coming in from your right here takes you to the Neolithic-era Coille Na Borgie Horned Chambered

Cairns; slightly further along is the Achanlochy settlement, the remains of a clearance village. There is not a lot to be seen, but there are information boards with the full story and layout.) Continue on the A836 into Bettyhill; the stage finishes outside the Bettyhill Hotel.

BETTYHILL

The original village on this section of coast was Farr, now a crofting settlement, lying a short distance north-east of Bettyhill beyond the sands of Farr Bay. As part of the Highland Clearances the Countess of Sutherland had a resettlement village built near the coast on the eastern side of the mouth of the River Naver. In a move that smacks of colonialism and arrogance, she named it after herself: Bettyhill.

Forgetting for a moment its origins, Bettyhill is picturesquely located above the north-facing Torrisdale Bay with its glorious expanse of sand. Spreading east in a sheltered bowl are the older areas of settlement, including the Parish Church of Farr, now the Strathnaver Museum. The Bettyhill Hotel is found on the main road as it climbs to the east above the River Naver and is a good place to break the journey for a final mission to John o' Groats the following day.

NORTH COAST 500
The North Coast 500 – NC500 – is a specific circular route created by the North Highland Initiative in 2015 to foster wider awareness of this remote part of Scotland as a tourist destination and to help boost and diversify the local economy. The roads always existed but by creating an itinerary, giving it a name (and a social media identity), it has grown rapidly in popularity. LEJOG1000 meets the NC500 at Bettyhill.

It is undeniably a stunning route along the coastal edges of the North Highlands of Scotland and understandably popular with cyclists, as well as people in campervans, cars and on motorbikes. However, its rapid growth, and particularly the number of motor vehicles on the route, have brought pressures as well as benefits to the communities it passes through. New restaurants, pop-up cafes and accommodation have been developed along the route bringing welcome new revenue as intended, but some communities have suffered from the increase in traffic and even litter. Not every resident sees it as a benefit. It is the double-edged sword of tourism in places described as 'wild' and 'remote' – how do you retain the very essence of what attracts people in the first place against a backdrop of burgeoning popularity?

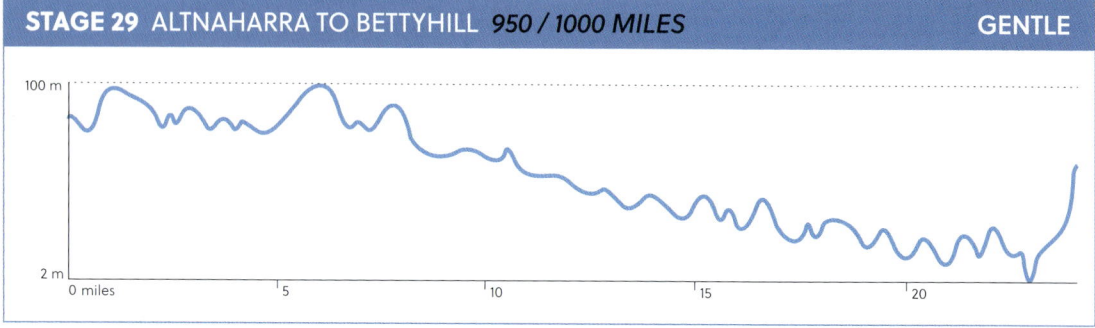

SLEEP

BETTYHILL HOTEL
This 200-year-old, family-owned hotel started life as a coaching inn. It has fantastic views of the bay from its dining room window and is a cosy place to stay.
Bettyhill, KW14 7SP
T 01641 521 202
www.bettyhillhotel.com

FARR BAY INN
Formerly the home of the local minister for the Church of Saint Columba of the Parish of Farr, this listed building was established as an inn in 1983. Warm and welcoming.
Bettyhill, KW14 7SZ
T 01641 521 230
www.farrbayinn.co.uk

CRAIGDHU CARAVAN CAMPING SITE
Great views out to Farr Beach and basic facilities.
Dunveaden House, Bettyhill, KW14 7SP
T 01641 521 273
https://craigdhu-caravan-camping-site.business.site
....

EAT

THE STORE CAFE
The hotels both serve evening meals, but The Store Cafe is open until 8.00 p.m. at weekends.
Bettyhill, KW14 7SS
T 07944 978 332
www.storecafe.co.uk
....

SUPPLIES
Head to **The Store Cafe** or **Bettyhill General Merchants** for snacks for the final stage of your journey.

STAGE 29 ALTNAHARRA TO BETTYHILL *950 / 1000 MILES* **GENTLE**

[Elevation profile chart: vertical axis marked 100 m and 2 m; horizontal axis marked 0 miles, 5, 10, 15, 20]

30

BETTYHILL TO JOHN O' GROATS

50 miles / 80km
710 metres ascent

It is tempting to see this final stage as nothing more than a procession to the finish, but it is a beautiful, yet challenging, ride in its own right. Distant mountain views, hidden sandy bays and the almost constant presence of the sea gives the final 50 miles a completely different texture and a sense of reaching the end of the land.

A stage of contrasts: the first part is full of plunging descents that lead to stunning sandy bays but necessitate slow climbs back up. Highland peaks remain visible behind you and the sea glitters close by, with narrow tracks tempting you down towards secluded coves. The second part is flat expanses of farmland with occasional sea views until you reach Thurso, before passing Dunnet Head, the most northerly point of mainland Britain. The final half of the final stage can feel like a drag, both physically and mentally. As the anticipation of the end builds as each mile ticks past, don't let your focus drop – it's not over, until it's over. Drink in the last few hours of life on the road because soon all the experiences, both difficult and inspiring, will be behind you.

BETTYHILL TO REAY

Arriving at Bettyhill is a significant moment as it is the first time you have seen the wide, open sea since coastal Cornwall and it will feature throughout this final stage. Continuing on the A836 through Bettyhill, the road descends rapidly, passing the road down to Farr Bay and the Strathnaver Museum before climbing steeply up to the Bettyhill Viewpoint. This is a pattern you need to acclimatise to as it repeats throughout the stage!

Although not long into the stage the viewpoint is worth a quick stop to appreciate the mountainous landscape you are leaving behind. Here the road threads through a wild, open space, bordered by mountains and sea.

A fast descent towards Armadale Bay briefly reveals a pocket of water, enclosed by two rocky headlands. When the wind comes from the south you may spot a hardy surfer making the most of this quiet beach. A track leads to the beach from the bridge over the burn and the vast sandy beach is tempting as a place to break the ride but there are more secluded bays to come.

Lochan Ealach on your left marks the top of the next ascent. Another sandy beach attracts the eye as you sweep down to cross the River Strathy. With views across the Pentland Firth, sea caves and stacks to explore, and a wander through wild-flower-strewn grass to reach the beach, this may be a temptation worth giving in to.

While pristine and beautiful to the eye, before swimming in the sea consider the nearby nuclear plant of Dounreay. Now decommissioned, Dounreay was the centre of the UK's fast reactor research and development for around 40 years; however, despite its technological advancement for its day, it still allowed radioactive particles to leak into the sea between 1963 and 1984. Particles have been found along some beaches of the North Coast. Part of the decommissioning and clean-up programme is to recover the particles and restore the seabed.

REAY TO THURSO

Once again, the road climbs, hiding the sea from view, until you reach the *Welcome to Caithness* sign – your final county sign of the journey – marking the top of

the climb. You'll notice you have arrived in Reay, at the bottom of the next descent, when you see the long, low white building of Reay Parish Church. Built in 1739, it is unusual in that it is a T-shaped church. Despite its diminutive size, it is a distinctive landmark – its white walls reflecting any available light, picking it out from its surroundings.

Keep an eye out for the lines of broken and jagged-edged flagstones which are placed vertically to form field boundaries, sometimes alongside hedges. Caithness Flagstone has been exported far and wide – it can be found on the streets of Boston and decorating King's Cross St Pancras railway station in London. The

rock was formed around 370 million years ago and is a result of layers of sediment forming in the bottom of a lake. It can be split into very precise and thin layers.

Just after leaving Reay, after 20 miles spent on the A836, turn right on to a minor road, signposted *Shebster*. This road takes you slightly inland for a while – it is quieter than the coastal road which gets busy between Dounreay, still one of the region's largest employers, and Thurso. Here, with the sea out of sight, it is farmland that fills the horizon.

Caithness is thought to have an impressive 4,000 different prehistoric sites. A recent archaeological survey of Shebster revealed a cluster of burial cairns

DUNNET HEAD

Dunnet Head is the most northern part of mainland Britain. It has none of the tourist trappings of John o' Groats, instead its dramatic cliffs and spectacular views into the Pentland Firth and the Orkney Islands are reward enough for your efforts. These far-reaching views meant that Dunnet Head was used as an observation post during World War II to protect the naval base at Scapa Flow in the Orkney Islands. The lighthouse at Dunnet Head, perched on the sheer edge of the cliffs above the sea, was built in 1831 by Robert Stevenson,

the grandfather of writer Robert Louis Stevenson.

Dunnet Parish Church was presided over by the Reverend Timothy Pont from 1601 until 1614 – he was the first person to produce a complete and detailed map of Scotland. As a cartographer he undertook all surveying and drawing himself, showing great care and attention to detail. When his maps were published posthumously in 1654 in the Dutch *Blaeu Atlas Maior*, a collection of cartographers' work from around the world, Scotland was one of the most comprehensively mapped countries in Europe.

and a hut circle. Although some sites in the area have been robbed and damaged, their presence still offers something mystical, yet human, to the landscape.

Turn left on to the B874 to reach Thurso, the most northerly town in the mainland of Great Britain. After what could have been several days of cycling the quiet rural roads of the Highlands, this really quite modestly sized town can come as a bit of a shock. Thurso began life as a Norse port, allowing trading between the mainland, Orkney and Scandinavia.

Arriving in Thurso, look up at the wall of the Pentland Hotel to spot the distinctive three-winged Cyclists' Touring Club badge; this iconic cycling logo was released by the CTC (now known as Cycling UK) in 1886. It appeared on hotels as a sign of recommendation and to show that cyclists were welcome. Take the next available right-hand turn after the Pentland Hotel then a staggered straight ahead at a set of traffic lights, joining the A9. (To detour to the beach, turn left before crossing the river. Out in the bay surfers and sea kayakers ride the waves of the wild Pentland Firth. One of the most famous cold water surf spots in the world, it has hosted international competitions.)

THURSO TO JOHN O' GROATS

To leave Thurso, cross the river and turn left on to the A836, signposted *John o' Groats*. There is often a sense among riders of 'right, let's get this done' – finishing becomes the goal, rather than enjoying the ride. The long, incredibly straight and fairly boring 5 miles between Thurso and Castletown does little to ease this feeling.

Thankfully, there is the redeeming feature just after Castletown: Dunnet Bay. The beauty of its sandy beach and wild-flower-covered sand dunes instils some fresh energy. As you trace the end of the bay, in the village of Dunnet you will see a turning for Dunnet Head, the most northerly point of mainland Britain. Dunnet is also home to Dunnet Bay Distillery which produces the fine Rock Rose gin.

Continuing on the A836 from Dunnet, riding through an avenue of high hedges you might get a brief sight of the Castle of Mey, bought by the Queen Mother in 1952. Square edged with elaborate and often improbable-looking turrets, it looks very much like a child's drawing of an imaginary castle. From here, the road drags up towards Mey Hill, the very last climb of the trip.

At the T-junction in John o' Groats the Seaview Hotel reminds you that there will be a pint waiting for you, but first turn left on to the A99 for your moment at the long-awaited signpost. Whether you race towards it full of exhilaration or freewheel down the long drive towards the sea spent and exhausted, it is over. With 1,000 miles beneath your wheels, you have completed LEJOG1000 – welcome to John o' Groats.

SLEEP
SEAVIEW HOTEL
The Seaview Hotel has been welcoming cyclists and other travellers for decades. A range of different styles of accommodation are available. The food is plentiful, and they serve beer from the John o' Groats Brewery.
John o' Groats, KW1 4YR
T 01955 611 220
www.seaviewjohnogroats.co.uk

JOHN O' GROATS BY TOGETHER TRAVEL
Right at the very end of the road these luxury cabins and apartments are a fantastic way to unwind and recover from the physical challenges of your journey.
John o' Groats, KW1 4YR
T 01625 416 430
www.togethertravel.co.uk

JOHN O' GROATS CARAVAN AND CAMPING SITE
Pitch your tent within a stone's throw of the iconic sign and wake up to views of the sea and island of Stroma. Booking for cyclists with tents is not required but places are limited, so make sure you arrive early.
John o' Groats, KW1 4YR
T 01955 611 329
www.johnogroatscampsite.co.uk

EAT
THE NORTHERN POINT
Right next to the iconic John o' Groats sign, this cafe is a welcome sight for refuelling and celebrating at the end of your ride.
John o' Groats, KW1 4YR
T 07478 553 334
www.thelunchboxboys.com/the-northern-point
....

DRINK
With an artisan tasting room and seating options with views over the Pentland Firth, the welcoming bar at the **John o' Groats Brewery** makes the finish a much more desirable place to linger and celebrate. In the evening, the bar at the **Seaview Hotel** has been a meeting point for many a LEJOG celebration and is a proper locals' bar as well.
....

BIKE
THE BIKE SHOP
If you haven't got a spare tube head here so your sprint into John o' Groats is not disrupted.
35 High Street, Thurso, KW14 8AZ
T 01847 895 385
www.facebook.com/thebikeshopthurso

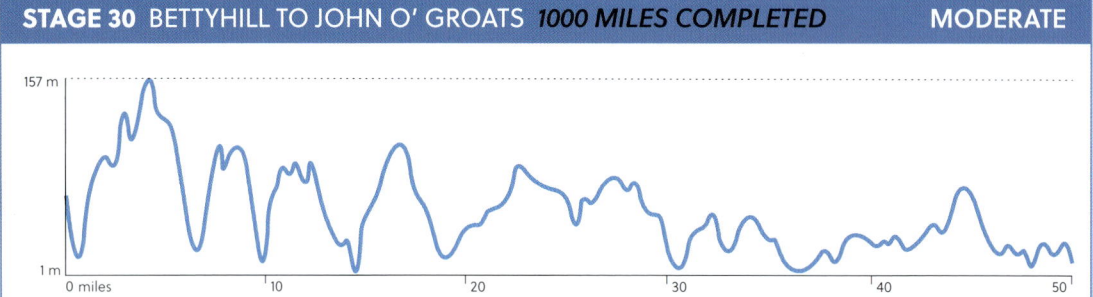

157 m

1 m

0 miles
10
20
30
40
50

Atlantic

Ocean

Strathy
Point

Totegan

Strathy
Bay

Armadale
Bay

Strathy

Portskerra

Melvich
Bay

Sandside
Bay

A836

Lednagullin

Armadale

Melvich

A836

Reay

Farr
Bay

Kirtomy

Torrisdale
Bay

Swordly

Crask

A836

kerray

Bettyhill

S

Loch Meadie

Achiemore

A836

Strath Naver

Cnoc
Dalveghouse

Dalhalvaig

Loch
Shurr

Borgie
Forest

Cnoc
Carnachadh

A897

Cnoc
Chealamy

B871

och Syre

Syre

THE END | JOHN O' GROATS

Reaching the end of the road can bring all kinds of emotions to the fore: pride in completing the distance, exhilaration, or even for some a feeling of loss or anticlimax that the journey is over. Having ridden all the way here, take the time to celebrate the moment.

John o' Groats developed not as the end of the mainland but as the access point to the islands beyond. It was reputedly named after Jan de Groot, who ran the ferry between Caithness and the Orkney Islands. It is a place where journeys start and end, goals are achieved and long-held dreams are realised. John o' Groats draws thousands of visitors each year; it is often surprising how few cyclists you see on the journey but how constant the procession of arrivals at the finish is. You only need to be a few minutes ahead or behind someone for the full 1,000 miles to never see them at all.

The final yards of what is, for many, the culmination of not just 1,000 miles of cycling but also months of planning and preparation, is hardly momentous. Currently your final few hundred metres is comprised of a utilitarian service road to a campsite with views to an uninspiring shopping complex and a small ferry; however, plans are afoot for changes that will create a more celebratory arrival.

From the iconic fingerpost sign ahead lies only the Pentland Firth. Depending on the weather, you might be able to make out the island of Stroma. The Pentland Firth has been a major shipping route for centuries, but navigating this short but treacherous seaway between the North Sea and the Atlantic Ocean is fraught with hazards. Stormy weather and violent sea conditions have led to many shipwrecks.

But those who arrive spend little time looking out to sea; instead their focus is on the much-photographed, windswept, white fingerpost sign, not on the ferry or the trawler with lobster pots behind it. Record breakers, leisure cyclists and tourists alike take their turns amidst popping champagne corks and camera flashes to have their moment with the sign.

Stood, quite likely, in the rain and buffeted by the wind, finishers usually behave in one of three ways. There are those that feel the goal has been achieved, the tick box ticked and once the celebratory photo has been taken immediately rush off to the next thing; there are those who arrive euphoric and ready to celebrate; and there are those who feel almost a loss and sadness at the journey being completed.

John o' Groats is changing: luxury lodges, a glass-fronted cafe overlooking the sign and the John o' Groats Brewery. If you have the time to spare it's becoming the perfect base to relax, recover from your efforts and explore further afield with a visit to Orkney or a walk to Duncansby Head, right on the north-eastern tip of Scotland.

Close to the sign you will see the original John o' Groats Hotel, now with the addition of colourful tofts providing self-catering accommodation, against the backdrop of the spectacular Pentland Firth. A uniquely designed octagonal building, its architecture harks back to the story of Jan de Groot. A successful merchant who ran the ferry to Orkney, he found that as he aged the other seven members of his family were jostling

for power. He pledged to settle the question of precedence in time for the family's next annual meeting. He commissioned an octagonal table so each person could claim to be the 'head of the table'.

Many finishers spend their final evening in the bar at the Seaview Hotel. You are guaranteed a warm welcome, hearty meal and a decent pint. It's a fascinating mix of LEJOG finishers and those who live and work here. The bar will be lined with locals and honestly not one of them will give a damn about how long it took you, which route you chose, your punctures or your saddle sores. They have seen it all before. To them John o' Groats isn't a destination, it's home.

ONWARD JOURNEY

Very few people reach John o' Groats and decide to turn around and cycle back, however that is of course an option! Independent travel from John o' Groats means retracing your steps to Thurso to connect with the rail network; alternatively it is possible to fly from Inverness Airport. Bike transport to Inverness can be arranged with local taxi firms or you can opt to pack your bike and have it shipped directly to your home address.

TRAIN

Thurso is slightly further to cycle than Wick but it shortens your train journey slightly so there is no real time saving in going to Wick. Thurso connects to Inverness from where trains can be caught to Aberdeen, Glasgow and Edinburgh for connections further south. You can take your bike for free on Scotrail but you need to reserve a place in advance on some services.
www.scotrail.co.uk

PLANE

Served by British Airways, easyJet, KLM and Loganair you can fly direct from Inverness to a number of destinations across the UK. Check with individual airlines for their rules on bike transportation and packaging.
www.hial.co.uk/inverness-airport

BIKE TRANSPORT

JOHN O' GROATS BIKE TRANSPORT

Bike taxi or courier service to take you and your bike to Inverness or arrange for your bike to meet you at your home address.
T 01463 419 160
www.johnogroatsbiketransport.co.uk

SHERPR BIKE BOXES

Order one of Sherpr's custom boxes to arrive at your accommodation in John o' Groats, pack your bike and arrange for collection. Your bike makes its own way home leaving you to travel with ease.
www.sherprbikebox.com

PACKING AND PREPARATION

Before embarking on this epic journey, it's worth taking time to think about how you will get yourself ready for your trip.

A monumental journey like LEJOG1000 may seem daunting but, broken down into sections, it is well within the reach of even the most casual cyclist. A little bit of preparation before you go can make all the difference to your enjoyment.

It is not necessary to be at the peak of physical fitness to undertake the journey, it is more important to be comfortable in the saddle for several hours every day – without feeling tired – so you can fully enjoy the experience of the ride. Your posture on the bike plays a huge part in feeling comfortable. A bike that doesn't fit you can lead to all sorts of problems, from backache to saddle sores. Many bike shops offer a bike-fitting service so consider doing this before you go, allowing yourself plenty of time to get used to any changes in your position.

If you aren't a regular cyclist, build up to your trip by gradually increasing the lengths of your rides and try riding back-to-back days, so your body gets used to riding for multiple days in a row. One of the joys of a long trip is it often gets easier as the trip progresses, with many riders flying by the time they get to Scotland as fitness increases. Some aches and niggles are inevitable, particularly in the early part of the trip, but taking some breaks during your ride to stretch and walk around will help.

Whether you are going for a few days or a few weeks, whether you are camping or staying in hotels, whether

you're going to be self-sufficient or fully supported, there are some essentials every cyclist needs, starting with a good pair of padded cycling shorts. You might want to go for brightly coloured Lycra or cover them with baggy shorts for a casual look; it's entirely up to you. It's easy to take too much casual wear for a long tour – remember a large part of your day will be spent on your bike. When you are cycle touring it helps if your clothes can do double duty, and there are plenty of brands making clothes that look as good in a pub as they do on a bike.

Scottish company Endura (*www.endurasport.com*) make a wide range of quality cycling clothing and gear suitable for the ever-changing British weather.

There are bike shops along the route, but they are infrequent in rural areas, so be prepared to deal with basic problems yourself. Carry spares with you and if you are travelling unsupported make sure you have a few simple skills, such as how to change an inner tube, to keep yourself on the road.

Packing for cycle touring needs careful consideration and even a practice trip to make sure you have got it right. In addition to our essentials kit list, if opting for camping rather than credit card cycling you will need a lightweight tent, a sleeping mat, sleeping bag, bike light or torch. There is a simple equation to consider for every item you wish to pack – how much do you want it versus how much it weighs. Bikepacking kit can be bought from several brands, but we like the quality and affordability offered by both Ortleib (*www.ortleib.com*) and Alpkit (*www.alpkit.com*).

ESSENTIALS

Planning is part of the pleasure and anticipation of a trip; here you will find some helpful tips on how to get the most out of using this book as you begin your journey.

REGIONS AND STAGES

The route is divided into eight regions outlined on pages x–xi. Many reflect the official names for the dominant counties where many miles are spent, although for the purposes of this journey the regions have been classified based on their landscape, style of riding and sense of identity. Some counties where the cyclists pop in for a few miles as a taster do not make it into the regional headlines. For example, High Bentham (at the start of stage 17) is indeed in North Yorkshire, but a much greater proportion of that particular stage is in Cumbria. Ardent geographers need not be offended as, particularly in Scotland, regions are often referred to with little respect for their official boundaries, such as the 'Scottish Highlands'. Locals often prefer to take into account a sense of place, identity and landscape, rather than a line on a map.

The 30 stages (page vii) which make up the route are the building blocks of your journey. They vary in distance and have been chosen where possible, to end in an interesting place, usually with a range of facilities. The Classic, Explorer and Challenge itineraries (pages xx–xxv) are suggestions depending on the time you have available, your fitness and importantly the style of journey you are after, but the stages can equally be constructed to make your own bespoke itinerary.

METRES OF ASCENT PER STAGE

Each stage includes a figure for the number of metres climbed during that stage. These figures are approximate. It is entirely possible for two riders to complete the same ride using the same model of GPS device and stand next to each other at the end of their ride with different totals. The figures are useful for managing your expectations of how hard a day might be relative to another day, but they won't paint the full picture. Embrace the experience, not the statistics.

MAPS AND THE ROUTE

The maps provided for each stage show an overview of the riding. Note that they are not all the same scale; however, we have used red dots every 5 miles to

make the scales easier to visualise. In urban areas the route tries, where possible, to avoid main roads and intersections but on a sometimes-crowded little island it is not always attainable. The route strives to get you out on to hidden lanes and country roads.

The GPX files provided (page v) can be easily uploaded on to a GPS device or smartphone to aid with navigation.

As Britain's landscape varies, so does the level of attention needed to navigate the route. In the old industrial heartland of Lancashire there can be a turn every mile as we seek out the most pleasant way through a populated area, whereas on the penultimate stage simply turn off your GPS device and pedal, revelling in the lack of roads and the remoteness of the Highlands.

EAT, SLEEP, SUPPLIES

Most stages include a variety of accommodation options for a range of budgets including hotels, pubs and bed and breakfasts. Lists are not exhaustive in most cases, although in some remote places options are limited. Where they are available, campsites and youth hostels are included. An evening meal option is listed and places for a drink are included where there are good watering holes.

Wherever there is a bike shop along the route it is listed in the relevant stage. Most places have direct websites listed, but not all. Bike shops are often closed on Sunday and Monday and there is a growing trend for them to be located on the edge of towns.

GUIDED RIDES

With limited holiday time and busy lives, not everyone has time to painstakingly plan their route or book multiple nights' accommodation. Travelling with Saddle Skedaddle (*www.skedaddle.com*) from Land's End to John o' Groats (although not the LEJOG1000 route) makes preparation for your holiday effortless and your guides will help ensure everything runs smoothly, giving you more time to enjoy riding your bike, exploring and relaxing.

A FINAL THOUGHT

LEJOG1000 has been designed for both the wanderer and those seeking a thousand-mile challenge across the length of Britain, and for everyone in between.

For the wanderer, the information is by no means comprehensive, you will discover your own special places. An impromptu cafe stop, or wild swimming opportunity, can form memorable moments of a journey. Follow your whims, make this journey your own, duck down interesting-looking roads and climb up hills to see what the view is like. It is from such a sense of curiosity and the occasional 'wrong' turn and an eye for an interesting road that this route was born. Wherever you sit on the challenge-versus-wanderer spectrum, ride with an appreciation of the sights, smells and sounds of Britain.

Connect with the LEJOG community at

www.lejog1000.cc
#LEJOG1000
hello@lejog1000.cc

ACKNOWLEDGEMENTS

With grateful thanks to everyone who has been part of the journey. Thank you to our friends who rode with us and appeared in our pictures: Emily and Kris Baldock, Jo and Ash Alexander, Adam Perry, Isobel Riley, Radu Mann and Rowan Walsh. Thanks to Endura for kit and cycle clothing. Our beautiful cover and eye-catching illustrations are thanks to Neil Stevens (*www.crayonfire.co.uk*). Thanks to Daniel Start who gave us the opportunity to begin this series with *France en Velo*.

Thank you to the team at Vertebrate Publishing who have taken so much care and attention over detail, for their patience and understanding with our vision of how the book should look and for helping bring that to life. To commissioning editor Kirsty Reade who approached us about one book and ended up with two – thank you for believing in this one.

A big thank you to Sylvia and Chris Walsh for everything they do for us, so we have the time for writing.

PHOTOGRAPHY

All photographs © Hannah Reynolds and John Walsh except: page 116, with permission of *www.visitlakedistrict.com*; pages 152, 158–159, 206, © Andy Jones.

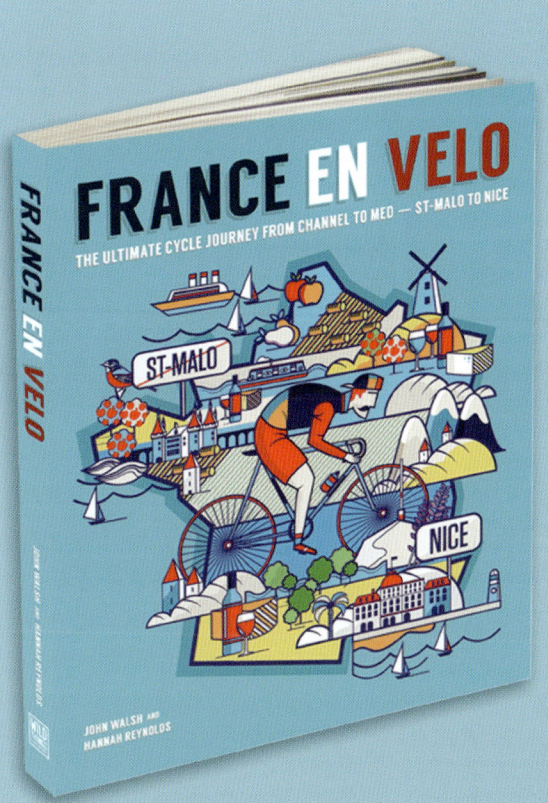

WHAT'S NEXT?

If LEJOG1000 has given you a taste for long-distance cycle touring, then it is time to plan your next adventure.

For another iconic thousand-mile journey, check out *France en Velo*, the ultimate cycle journey through France from Saint-Malo to Nice, from Wild Things Publishing.

Discover hidden lanes, stunning gorges, amazing places to eat and stay, plus the best of French cycling culture. The journey takes you through 19 of France's regional *départements* and into some of the country's most striking and dramatic landscapes, helping you to discover the true heart of rural France.

For a **10 PER CENT DISCOUNT** unique to readers of *Britain's Best Bike Ride* enter code **LEJOG1000** at *www.franceenvelo.cc*

If possible, buying direct rather than through multinational web giants really does help support independent guidebook writing and small publishers.

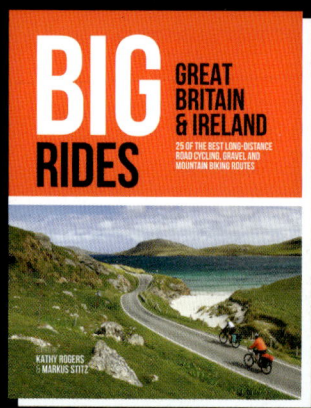
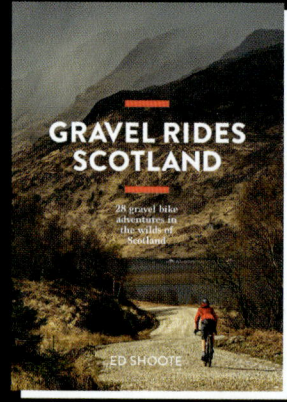

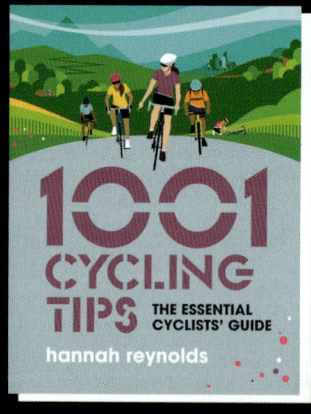

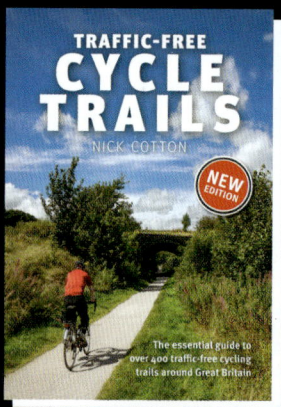